The
White
Welfare
State

The White Welfare State

The Racialization of U.S. Welfare Policy

Deborah E. Ward

The University of Michigan Press   Ann Arbor

To Ivan

A CIP catalog record for this book is available from the British Library.

Library of Congress Cataloging-in-Publication Data

Ward, Deborah E., 1967–
    The White welfare state : the racialization of U.S. welfare policy / Deborah E. Ward.
      p.   cm.
    Includes bibliographical references and index.
    ISBN 0-472-11455-7 (cloth : alk. paper) — ISBN 0-472-03095-7 (pbk. : alk. paper)
      1. Public welfare—United States.   2. Welfare recipients—Government policy—United States.   3. Social service and race relations—United States.   4. Racism—United States.   5. United States—Race relations.   I. Title.

HV95.W335   2005
361.6'089'00973—dc22   2005004223

57682213

Acknowledgments

I BEGIN MY ACKNOWLEDGMENTS with my academic advisors from Columbia University's political science department. Although this book has evolved significantly from its original form as a dissertation, I am indebted to the inspiration that these colleagues have provided and continue to provide. So, I extend my deepest gratitude to Ira Katznelson, Robert Shapiro, Ester Fuchs, and Robert Lieberman. I also owe special thanks to Nancy Degnan, who helped guide me down the road toward a Ph.D. in the first place. Thank you all for your guidance and friendship. I also want to recognize the grants and fellowships that I received from various departments at Columbia University, especially the Public Policy Consortium Fellowship and the Center for Urban Research and Policy, which facilitated the timely completion of my doctoral studies.

My gratitude extends to Seton Hall University, specifically the political science department and its chair, Joseph Marbach, for the time and support given to finish this project. Transcending the axiom "the best dissertation is a done dissertation," Joe reminded me that the best dissertation is a published book. Obviously none of this would have happened without an editor. I feel very fortunate that the University of Michigan Press made this an enjoyable experience. Specifically, I thank Jim Reische for believing in my work and for patiently directing me through this publication process.

The assistance of many individuals in libraries and archives across the country was critical to the data collection for this manuscript, and a few deserve special mention. I am grateful to Gus Stamatopoulos of the Lehman Library at Columbia University for facilitating access to the state agency collection and, thereby, expediting the completion of my research. I also want to thank Timothy Slaughter, Reference Librarian at Harvard University's Littauer Library, for his assistance in locating critical state and national government documents, and the Widener Library Circulation Services at Harvard College Library for granting me access to these collections. I also want to acknowledge assistance from the staff at the National Archives in Bethesda, Maryland, as I combed through boxes and volumes of Department of Labor records.

I next turn to my family. It seems a lifetime ago since I started this project. In fact, it has been many lifetimes. Since I started down this road in 1994, I have experienced both heartbreak and heartfelt joy, balancing the deaths of some of the most significant people in my life and the births of the two most important people in my life. Throughout, I have been fortunate to have a family that has consistently and selflessly given me their love, support, and encouragement. To my grandparents, who each in their own way were critical to my education, as well as my rearing, Lucy Ainilian Kaprelian, Edward Karnig Kaprelian, Esther Price Ward, and Stuart E. Ward Sr.: I miss you, but I know that you are smiling and sharing this with me, wherever you are. To my mother, Helen Kaprelian Ward: thank you for being my most honest critic, my most dedicated fan, and my best friend. To my father, Stuart E. Ward Jr.: thank you for introducing me to the path of political inquiry and for opening my eyes that the left is right. To my brother, Stuart Edward Ward: thank you for being you and for encouraging me, in your own special way, to always strive to be a better person. To my son, my heart, Jairo Karnig Stuart Gonzalez Ward: your birth both challenged and inspired me, and in the end, you made me a better scholar in addition to making me a mother. To my daughter, my soul, Ani Helen Elizabeth Esther Gonzalez Ward: thank you for reminding me every day that we must not forget our spirit and our passion, because that is what makes everything in life worthwhile. I thank my children for being patient, for sharing me with my work, and for bringing a smile to my heart. To my family: thank you all for giving me the courage and strength to pursue my dreams. I love you very much.

Finally, to my husband, Ivan D. Gonzalez: I am indebted to you for editing numerous drafts with a mighty pen and for the countless conversations and debates about my research, resulting in a better organized and better argued book. In many ways this has been a joint venture and a joint achievement. Most of all, thank you for being there for me all these years, encouraging me to forge ahead while finding a balance in my life . . . by being that balance in my life. It is a small but heartfelt acknowledgment: I dedicate this book to you.

Contents

Tables & Figures

Tables

Figures

1

Introduction

History, Race, & Building the
American Welfare State

The Congress shall have Power To lay and collect
Taxes, Duties, Imposts and Excises, to pay the Debts
and provide for the common Defence and general
Welfare of the United States
—U.S. Constitution, art. 1, sec. 8, cl. 1

In September 1996, the U.S. government terminated Aid to Families with Dependent Children (AFDC), the oldest social welfare program in the history of our nation. AFDC's institutional and ideological roots date back to 1911, the year the first state mothers' pension law was enacted. Mothers' pensions represented social reformers' pioneering response to calls for change in public policy toward indigent children. Prevailing policy called for the removal of indigent dependent children from their homes and their placement in orphanages, penal institutions, or workhouses. Early welfare reformers, championing the values of motherhood and the importance of child nurturing, wanted a policy that would give poor women "pensions"[1] so that they could provide for their children in their homes. What evolved were state programs across the nation that aided poor children, primarily in families where the mother was widowed.

In 1931, twenty years after the adoption of the first state mothers' pension law, approximately $34 million was expended for mothers' pension grants in forty-four states and the District of Columbia,[2] and 93,620 families including 253,298 children were receiving assistance.[3] By 1935, every state except South Carolina and Georgia had passed a mothers' pension law, and mothers' aid programs operated in 1,490 administrative units across the nation. Under Title IV of the Social Security Act, the national government assumed the responsibility for partially funding these state programs. In 1936, no longer state-based, mothers' pensions became Aid to Dependent Children (ADC), and in 1962 the program became AFDC.

This program's eighty-five-year evolution holds a unique place in U.S. state-building history. Although the New Deal ushered in catholic social welfare developments and the solidification of a new state-society relationship, the social legislation of the Progressive Era—specifically, mothers' pensions—defined the ideological and institutional development of the U.S. welfare state. Whereas social programs such as old-age pensions and insurance, health insurance, and unemployment insurance formed the bedrock of European social welfare systems, the United States failed to adopt such programs as social welfare policy until the New Deal era or later. At the same time that these other social welfare initiatives stalled, mothers' pensions were politically and philosophically successful. Mothers' pensions challenged prevailing assumptions about the state's role in providing economic assistance to the poor. For the first time, long-standing policies that relegated the care of the poor to private, voluntary institutions was questioned. Furthermore, the principles that emanated from the mothers' pension movement not only defined the development of state mothers' pension programs but became a seminal declaration of American social welfare policy that continues to influence the contours of the U.S. welfare state through the upheavals of 1996 and the present.

For the purposes of this analysis, what matters most in this story of U.S. welfare state development, or U.S. state-building more broadly, is race. These nascent social welfare programs aided many poor children. However, certain categories of poor children, especially African-American children, were excluded from both mothers' pensions and their progeny, ADC. This exclusion occurred systematically from the initial movement and advocacy period through the legislative period and into administration and implementation. After race, through its institutionalization, had defined the contours of this state-based program, it influenced welfare state development at the national level.

Narrowly, this book shows how the embeddedneess of race in the incipient institutional structures has framed subsequent welfare policy development. More broadly, the arguments have larger implications about the role of race in American society and how the national government and the states have institutionalized the role of race. Many scholars agree that race constituted a critical factor in U.S. state-building and that race's role was itself influenced by the development of the national state.[4] However, this state-building relationship has played out in a more nuanced and a more complex way at the state and local levels. Just as racial distinctions informed and were informed by national institutional development, racial disctinctions informed and were informed by institutional developments at the state and local levels. Furthermore, race has differed in every local environment. So whether involving African-Americans in Mississippi, Mexicans in Texas, American Indians in Utah, or Czechoslovakians in Massachusetts, racism was a systematic feature of these early programs. Herein lies the complexity: racialization at the state and local levels influenced race's role in nation-building. The study of state mothers' pensions programs and their path to nationalization under Social Security through the present enables us to see both the impact of and ramifications of this racialized state-building.

Why Race?

Scholarship from a variety of disciplines has documented the significance of the nascent mothers' pension programs in the evolution of U.S. welfare history.[5] More recently, historians Kathryn Kish Sklar, Alice Kessler-Harris, and Sonya Michel have offered insightful analyses of social welfare during this early period. Ann Shola Orloff and Theda Skocpol have bridged the sociological and political perspectives, creating even more nuanced studies of the development of the social welfare state. The most provocative work on the origins of mothers' pensions, Theda Skocpol's *Protecting Soldiers and Mothers*, provides an insightful reperiodization of U.S. welfare origins and policy feedback mechanisms. Finally, scholarship focusing on the significance of gender in this state-building story have enriched the study of welfare state development during the Progressive Era.[6] This body of scholarship explains the significance of maternalist social policy, women's political participation, education and assimilation, industrial homework, and the racialized gender state.

This literature provides a rich and valuable contribution to the study of U.S. development during the Progressive Era, and a review of this scholarship amply proves that certain perspectives have been sufficiently explicated. More important, however, this review reveals the absence of race—or an appropriate exposition of the primacy of race—in this critical state-building story. The existing body of scholarship does not sufficiently explain the uneven racial distribution of social welfare benefits during this pivotal state-building era or consider this bias's impact on subsequent policy developments at both the state and national levels. Even Skocpol's seminal book only alludes to the role of race, acknowledging that "there may have been cultural discrimination against widows from subordinate racial and ethnic groups."[7] This book will shatter this deafening silence precisely by focusing on race. By considering the development of these policies from the perspective of race, I elucidate how race and its embeddedness in and intersection with politics and society informed subsequent administrative structures and policy developments.

The Institutionalization of Race

Although most social welfare scholars do not focus on the role of race in Progressive Era policy-making, a growing body of scholarship considers the politics of race in policy development more broadly. On one extreme, a vein of scholarship acknowledges the existence of racism at some point in U.S. history but denies that it has been institutionalized and proposes other reasons for racial imbalances in our society. In his influential *Declining Significance of Race*, sociologist William Julius Wilson argues that although racism existed, our national government began solving the problem of racism through different policies beginning with the civil rights era. Wilson's argument that race had declining significance gave fodder to social scientists and policymakers advocating the elimination of social programs targeted at African-Americans and other racial minorities. Historians Abigail and Stephen Thernstrom have taken this a step further and have argued recently for eliminating any policy that is "race-conscious." For these scholars, the disadvantages that racial minorities face are directly attributable to issues that are beyond the state's control, such as the structure of the minority family, educational attainment, or crime rates.[8]

Two major trajectories exist within the scholarship that recognizes the significance of race. Some scholars consider race and its attendant imbalances as relative to the weak fiscal capacity of the state or as epiphenomenal to the policy development at hand. Instead of being an active contributor to state-building, racial outcomes constitute a by-product of existing social and economic inequalities or are the fault of administrative inequities and so forth. Exemplified by the work of Gareth Davies and Martha Derthick,[9] this scholarship acknowledges the existence of an uneven distribution of social welfare benefits but attributes the root cause to factors independent from the administration of these specific programs. New scholarship that challenges traditional explanations for the exclusion of African-Americans from social welfare provision, such as the work by

Mary Poole, still reduces this exclusion and discrimination to an economic argument. She contends that the Social Security Act represented the reproduction of an economic hierarchy that placed African-Americans at the bottom rung; racist intent did not radicalize the Act.[10] For these scholars, racially based exclusion or, more important, the institutionalization of race, was not intentional.

On the other side of the debate is the argument, most cogently put forward by Robert Lieberman in his landmark book, *Shifting the Color Line*, that racially based exclusion was deliberate and, furthermore, that proving racist intent is not necessary to prove this racially based exclusion. Lieberman and scholars including Kenneth Neubeck, Noel Cazenave, Michael Brown, Linda Gordon, Jill Quadagno, Gwendolyn Mink, and Mimi Abramovitz have considered the way in the social welfare policy in the United States has been informed by race and racial politics. Brown and his coauthors of *Whitewashing Race: The Myth of a Color-Blind Society* have demonstrated the persistence of racism in institutions across the nation and the resulting systematic disadvantages that African-Americans experience as a result of this institutionalized racism. For Gordon[11] and Quadagno,[12] racially based exclusion during the New Deal era was deliberate and represented a necessary political response to the racist interests of southern congressmen. Mink[13] and Abramovitz,[14] whose scholarship primarily considers the intersection of gender and race, have argued that policymakers have accommodated racism through compromise. Neubeck and Cazenave have contended that through a racialized social system, racism has shaped U.S. public assistance policies and practice.[15] This scholarship has made considerable headway in helping us properly understand the role of race in American political development.

This book takes up and expands on the debate on the role of race in the development of social welfare in the United States. First, this book takes the argument from the level of national welfare policy-making down to the states, reflecting the decentralized nature of policy-making at that critical point in U.S. political history. An understanding of the administration of these state-based welfare programs is critical to an understanding of subsequent state- and national-level welfare policy. Second, this book argues that not only does race matter in this state-building story but that the key administrative linkages between two early welfare programs, mothers' pensions and ADC, were most significant because of race. Certain administrative tenets of mothers' pensions that permitted racially based exclusion—most notably local, decentralized administration and nonstandard definitions of eligibility—were carefully and intentionally carried over to

ADC. Following the path from mothers' pensions through ADC through the enactment of the Personal Responsibility Act in 1996 enables one to see how race became the central factor in this policy-making process.

Consequently, two questions emerge. What are the linkages between the early mothers' pension programs and ADC? What is the role of race in this state-building story?

Local Government as a Unit of Analysis

The United States has two interdependent dynamics that are very important for understanding the development of institutions. The first is the process through which institutions evolve, and the second is the capacity of these institutions in a political system whose organizing principle is the fragmentation of power.

Institutions are unique to the environment within which they develop. Ira Katznelson writes, "as bundles of intersubjective, connected and persistent norms and as formal rules and organizations, institutions shape human interaction, limit and define the scope of choice, and confer social and political identities out of the welter of possibilities through language, incentives and sanctions."[16] The process of institution-building is the synthesis of the political and social environment and new forces that are acting on it. The resulting institutions reflect and reinforce existing societal structure and political configurations, and policies are generated that attend to the issues at hand.

In the United States, federalism has often constrained the central bureaucracy, with the result that the autonomy and capacity of national institutions are limited.[17] Thus, fragmentation occurs in authority and capacity in most policy areas. Policy-making is often an amalgam of different institutions, local and national, whose respective evolutions reflect unique, often competing, and parochial interests. The effects of fragmentation and parochialism can be seen in social and political development across the United States. "The commitment to parochial administration," Lieberman writes, "has itself become a powerful force in the politics of American social policy."[18] Decentralization of institutional development has permitted local norms and values to determine policy formation and implementation at the local level and, through the codependence between national and local institutions, the national level. Consequently, policy developments at the local level are very important for understanding policy developments at the national level.

This national-local state-building dynamic is very important to U.S. policy developments. While state-building efforts at the national level involve endowing one agency or a few institutions with policy-making responsibilities, state-building at the local level requires intergovernmental relations and joint action by agencies at different levels of government. As a result, local state-building "enterprises" can be substantially more complicated and more political than national state-building ones. Russell L. Hanson makes an important observation about the impact of these different state-building processes on actual policy development and implementation: the "weakest" partner determines the joint capacity required in state-building. In particular, whether a population is served depends not solely on the existence of an effective central agency but also on how well the weakest partner, in this case the local government, performs its job.[19] Furthermore, joint capacity will be uneven across states, reflecting the varying capacities of state and local partners.

My study of state-based mothers' pension programs and their evolution into the nationally based AFDC exemplifies this state-building dynamic. The policy-making apparatus that created and sustained mothers' pensions was decentralized and virtually beyond the reach of national controls. Beginning with mothers' pensions, I follow the path whereby local and state institutional structures and administrative capacities eventually influenced national policy-making and politics. Influence in the case of mothers' pensions came from the bottom and worked its way up: advocacy initially was localized and then penetrated state and national decision-making institutions. Consequently, the political capacity and coherence of the federal government comes into focus through this analysis. During the Progressive Era, federal capacity to formulate and implement public policies directed toward dependent children and their mothers was weak. The evolution of mothers' pensions into the national program ADC illustrates the fragmentation in policy-making and the national government's inability to produce consistent and objective policy determinations across the nation. In fact, a study of New Deal welfare politics reveals how this fragmentation in the mothers' pension era affected the scope of national policy-making during the 1930s. Both the content and administration of early welfare policies left an imprint on the U.S. welfare state in terms of benefit scope and delivery.[20] The diffuse and decentralized administration of mothers' pension programs affected the capacity of national social welfare institutions because the national welfare program had to rely on the existing local state structures. As a result, the variations in state mothers' pension programs carried over to the national ADC program. The Social Security Act was influenced by both

the political considerations of a national system of government and the
weight of existing state-based welfare programs.[21]

Racialized State-Building at the Local
& National Level

This book demonstrates that mothers' pension programs have a twofold
legacy. Mothers' pensions represented the beginning of a new relationship
between the state and society. This early welfare program institutionalized
the idea that the government, whether local, state, or federal, should assume responsibility for the care of its poor. Mothers' pensions also provided a model for the development of subsequent noncontributory welfare
policy, particularly ADC, Title IV of the Social Security Act. The principles
embodied in mothers' pension legislation and administration, such as decentralized administration and the imposition of "suitable home" and "fitness" criteria, carried over to ADC, resulting in the disproportionate and
deliberate exclusion of African-Americans and other nonwhites from this
benefit stream for almost fifty years. These inherited principles also ultimately provided the basis for the abolition of AFDC in 1996.

The development of this early social welfare program was premised on
separate spheres for women of different races and ethnicities. The value
of motherhood was not universally upheld; it was selectively championed
for poor women who were considered superior or more worthy than their
counterparts along racial dimensions. Race, as a critical state-building
feature, enables us to more completely understand the institutional development of social welfare policy in the United States. In current debates
on welfare state development in the United States, the New Deal continues to be perceived as the pivotal period in establishing the institutional
and policy framework from which the American welfare state evolved. A
reperiodization and reorientation of welfare state development that places
the mothers' pension period at the root of the development of the modern
welfare state, enables us to see how the racialization of society during the
Progressive and New Deal eras limited social welfare reformers' opportunities. The evolution of the modern welfare state in the United States is
inextricably tied to the racial policies and institutions that developed at
this critical juncture.

On August 22, 1996, the Personal Responsibility and Work Opportunity
Reconciliation Act was signed into law, effectively eliminating a U.S. welfare policy tradition that had begun eighty-five years earlier. Devolving re-

sponsibility to state and local jurisdictions, this legislation regressed certain U.S. social welfare policy principles to the mothers' pension era. The lessons of mothers' pensions, however, are far more nuanced and far more discouraging than those of local administrative ineptitude—they are the lessons race, or, more specifically, the lessons of policies of inclusion and exclusion based on race. As policy initiatives, neither mothers' pensions nor ADC were ever intended for African-Americans. In fact, the data in this book show conclusively that the programs functioned in a way that systematically excluded African-Americans and were only provisionally available to those immigrants willing or able to Americanize. Just as race and ethnicity became important factors in the design, implementation, and administration of these social welfare programs, they became equally important in their demise.

The distinction between "deserving" and "undeserving poor," a distinction that was emblematic of nascent welfare state developments and was legally discarded during the 1960s, found a new avenue and returned with a vengeance by the 1970s. The number of minorities on welfare rolls had steadily increased since the 1960s, and a policy backlash was inevitable. In that environment, propaganda and political ideology trumped the real statistics. Although the door was opened to more minorities during the 1960s and consequently more minorities received welfare benefits, African-Americans have never represented a majority of those receiving welfare. Even concerns over the "disproportionate" number of minorities on welfare rolls are obviated when considered in relation to minority poverty rates. It is not that a disproportionate number of minorities found their way onto the welfare rolls but that there were and continue to be a disproportionate number of poor minorities. Nevertheless, the raw numbers were enough for policymakers to jump on the "end welfare as we know it" bandwagon. Instead of defending the rights of these mothers, the racial rhetoric reemerged, and being an AFDC recipient became synonymous with the stereotypical "welfare queen"—a black, single mother of five children who had been on welfare for ten years. Despite attempts to dispel these myths,[22] they have prevailed, and the distinction between worthy and unworthy has once again become inextricably tied to race.

Ultimately, the legacy of mothers' pensions is the legacy of racial institutionalization. Race and racial distinctions had become so embedded in our welfare state that changes in recipient demographics—perceived or real, justified or not—led to the dismantling of a long-standing system, and this dismantling both reflected and reaffirmed the racial division between the worthy and unworthy poor.

Methodology

The data I collected for this manuscript come from both primary and secondary sources. I use data from several reports generated by the Children's Bureau[23] from the early 1900s until the 1930s. I use archival documents collected by the Children's Bureau and/or the Department of Labor from the early 1910s until the 1930s, including correspondence between the bureau and various parties, such as mothers inquiring about aid programs, administrators of local and state mothers' pension programs, and other parties and policymakers interested in mothers' pensions. I also use documents and correspondence that the Children's Bureau received from state and local welfare agencies in response to survey questionnaires. For the New Deal period, I use archival documents collected by the Federal Emergency Relief Administration and the Social Security Board.[24]

I supplement this data with other government records and information, including census data, congressional testimony, and committee reports as well as documents written by contemporary welfare reformers, advocates, and policymakers. For state and local analyses, I collected data published by state social welfare agencies or their equivalent in annual reports or other official documents. I collected articles from national and local media sources and magazines published by women's federations and consumer groups. Finally, I draw on the work of other social welfare scholars. Using this data, I generated several databases with which I examined the correlation among a variety of factors in the administration of these programs. All of the multivariate analyses presented in this text were generated from these databases.

Book Organization

Chapter 2 considers the historical and political context within which mothers' pensions evolved. This history frames the racialized environment within which the modern U.S. state and, more specifically, the U.S. welfare state evolved. The Progressive Era represented a critical juncture in U.S. state-building. The social and political arrangements of that period determined the boundaries of inclusion and exclusion in public policy-making, and the policies institutionalized during the Progressive Era set a path for future state-building.

Chapter 3 examines the history of mothers' pensions, focusing particularly on whose behalf mothers' pension programs evolved and who supported this very successful movement. Social policy for dependent children is examined from the nineteenth century through the 1909 White House Conference on the Care of Dependent Children, where the modern guiding principles for the care of dependent children were established. The chapter provides a sketch of these reformers' ideological and political motivations and tactics in procuring mothers' pension legislation.

Chapter 4 examines state mothers' pension legislation, focusing on the state statutes that mandated program components, including administrative structures, benefit eligibility, program financing, and aid amounts. The enactment of mothers' pension legislation was primarily correlated with race, not, as alternate hypotheses contend, with a state's wealth or with urbanization. Eligibility requirements statutorily excluded African-Americans and immigrants because of residency, marital status, and other requirements. Furthermore, state legislation did not require that each administrative unit adhere to uniform administration of the programs, standardized budgets, or standardized conditions. This lack of standardization intentionally gave great latitude to local administrators to implement the programs to reflect parochial, often prejudicial, norms. The latent consequence of these laws was the exclusion of African-Americans from mothers' pension benefits.

Chapter 5 provides a detailed analysis of the implementation of the mothers' pension laws, examining program administration, fiscal operation, extent of program coverage, mothers' employment, and the racial composition of recipients. The chapter demonstrates that the administration of the mothers' pension programs resulted in nonstandardized budget and aid awards. One consequence was that native white families received higher grants than did immigrant white and African-American families. Furthermore, the degree of implementation of programs varied within the states depending on the racial composition of each county's population. Counties that had high percentages of African-Americans did not operate mothers' pension programs. The application of the "suitable home" provision resulted in the disproportionate distribution of benefits. African-American and immigrant white applicants were disproportionately considered "unsuitable," and white recipients were disproportionately considered "suitable."

Chapters 4 and 5 also look at regional differentiation with regard to mothers' pension laws and administration. In particular, these chapters examine differences in laws and administration that would have a disproportionately negative effect on the African-American population. I take this regional approach for two reasons: first, during the first two decades

of the twentieth century, African-Americans constituted a greater proportion of the population in southern states than in other regions, and the majority of African-Americans lived in the South; second, more overt discrimination against African-Americans occurred in the South—for
example, in the form of Jim Crow laws, lynching campaigns, and voting
restrictions—than in the North. The existing social and political climate
made race a more important variable in the development of the mothers'
pension programs in the southern states than in other regions. The analysis in this book is the first to show systematically that southern states implemented mothers' pension programs later than the northern and western states, that southern states' aid amounts were lower, that the number
of people aided was lower in the South, and that a lower percentage of
African-American recipients existed in the South than in the other regions.

Chapter 6 examines the institutional linkages between mothers' pensions and ADC, examining Title IV's provisions as well as eligibility conditions of the ADC plans, program administration, the number of families aided, and the demographics of beneficiaries. This chapter reveals
that the legislative framing of ADC mirrored the mothers' pension legislation in two important ways: (1) decentralized administration to local
agencies; and (2) ambiguous eligibility requirements and conditions for
receiving aid. The chapter explicates the administrative and legislative
continuity between the two programs. In some states, ADC programs
were institutionally the same, administered by the same organizations
and with the same "institutional logic"[25] as the prior mothers' pension
programs. The same suitability and fitness requirements that granted
such latitude to local administrators in the mothers' pension programs
continued under ADC. Furthermore, the discriminatory outcomes that
existed in mothers' pensions were mirrored in ADC. In particular,
African-Americans continued to be disproportionately excluded from the
ADC rolls. County-level analysis of nine southern states demonstrates in
greater detail how ADC inherited a structural legacy of racial discrimination directly from mothers' pensions.

The concluding chapter considers the legacy of mothers' pensions with
respect to ADC and the American welfare state and how the sixty-year institutional history of excluding certain classes of otherwise eligible poor
helped define our current welfare state. In particular, the chapter examines how this early welfare policy birthed a welfare system that continued
to distinguish between deserving and undeserving, worthy and unworthy
poor. Mothers' pensions provided an institutional legacy on which subsequent welfare policy for dependent children was built, and the ideology

of differentiation embedded in mothers' pensions came to define welfare provision more broadly. Mothers' pensions became a vehicle through which race permeated U.S. welfare state-building, following a course that continues to this day.

To fully understand the origins of the U.S. welfare state, it is necessary to examine the first social welfare benefit program and the environment within which that program was conceived and implemented. Prior to the New Deal legislation, no social welfare policy, including soldiers' pensions, was as effective and politically successful as mothers' pensions. Only through an examination of the philosophical and institutional history of mothers' pensions can the development of the U.S. social welfare state be fully understood. Because of their institutional success, mothers' pensions created a framework for the care of dependent children on which subsequent national policies were built. Mothers' pensions were also philosophically successful. The mothers' pension philosophy of distinguishing between deserving and undeserving poor became embedded in, and a distinctive part of, our national welfare state. I hope that this book will better specify the institutional history and development of U.S. national welfare policy and how race became a central element of this history.

2

The Political & Social Context
of Mothers' Pensions

An Era of Racial & Ethnic Discrimination

> The Americans have this great advantage, that they
> attained democracy without the sufferings of a
> democratic revolution and that they were born equal
> instead of becoming so.
> —Alexis de Tocqueville[1]

> Come all you foreigners and jump into this magic
> kettle. You are colored and discolored with things that
> do not fit in well with affairs in America. In fact, to
> speak frankly, there is a certain taint about you, a stain
> brought from the old world. Your clothes are ugly and
> ill-fitting. Your language is barbaric . . . Immediately
> you will become like us, your slacks will be exchanged
> for the latest Fifth Avenue clothes. The magic process
> is certain. Your money back if we fail.[2]

A BRIEF OVERVIEW OF POLITICS and society during the early 1900s captures the moment within which these social welfare programs evolved. The Progressive Era retains a distinctive place in the state-building story of the United States. This era ushered in a new relationship between the U.S. state and its citizens. National and state governments instituted an unparalleled number of legislative and administrative actions aimed at protecting the social and economic rights of women, children, and workers. However, at the same time, this "progressive" period was wrought with regressive civil rights policies that reflected and reinforced the subordinated status of African-Americans and non–northern European immigrants. An unprecedented number of legislative, executive, and legal actions aimed at limiting or eliminating the political, social, economic, and civil rights of African-Americans and certain immigrant populations were reinforced or instituted.

At such a critical moment in our institutional history, our political traditions of egalitarianism and individualism reached the peak of their expression. However, the progressivism that sprung from these traditions was far from Tocqueville's ideal, veiling an undercurrent that was profoundly unprogressive and illiberal. The institutional development of the American state in the Progressive Era was compromised and overlaid by other traditions, those of inegalitarianism and racial differentiation. The balance between these opposing traditions not only influenced the institutions growing out of the Progressive Era but set the tone and tempo for subsequent institutional developments premised on hierarchically ascribed norms and social categories. These institutions, coupled with non-egalitarian ideologies, further depressed the status of certain racial and ethnic groups.[3] American public policy continued to be defined by and institutionalized according to certain racial and ethnic hierarchies. The outcome was a hybrid—a progressive but nonetheless racially divided state.

Understanding early-nineteenth-century society and politics illustrates the impact of this period on American political development. A great deal of scholarship on state-building during the Progressive and New Deal eras places welfare policies at the center of analysis. However, those welfare policies must be considered within the context of regressive civil rights policies, race relations, and other state-building efforts. This juxtaposition of progressive welfare policies and regressive civil-rights policies has been referred to as the "policy paradox" of the Progressive Era.[4] It is difficult to separate the two policy agendas in any analysis of state-building because the discrimination prevalent in society became embedded in welfare policies just as these policies had been embedded in other state-building processes.[5] To fully understand the availability and accessibility of social welfare programs at that time, it is important to understand the political, economic, and social status of potential social welfare beneficiaries. This story of Progressive Era society and politics will delineate the boundaries of exclusion and inclusion in mainstream social, economic, and political life that were established during that period. Prevailing social values and norms precluded the inclusion of certain racial and ethnic groups in the emergent U.S. state. Within the social and political landscape of the Progressive Era, the modern U.S. welfare state evolved.

Race & Race Relations during the
Progressive Era

One of the defining characteristics of this era was the doctrine of racial inferiority that permeated U.S. politics and society. Prejudice toward African-Americans and certain groups of non–northern European immigrants became institutionalized through national and state policies aimed at limiting these groups' access to mainstream society. This period saw an increase in legal and locally sanctioned racial separation and prejudice. Rulings such as the U.S. Supreme Court's 1896 *Plessy v. Ferguson* decision and the congressional failure to pass antilynching legislation and to protect the constitutional rights of African-Americans and immigrants demonstrated the judicial and legislative systems' profound unresponsiveness to the idea of protecting African-Americans and immigrants from civil rights violations. Although for several years after *Plessy* the courts dealt no further blows to African-American civil rights, the judicial system stood idly and complicitly by as the newly won electoral rights of African-Americans were eroded through poll taxes, literacy tests, registration requirements, and grandfather clauses. The Fourteenth and Fifteenth Amendments were eviscerated, and neither the courts nor any legislative body responded.

This retrogressive current in civil rights is also evidenced in the behavior of the highest elected officials at that time. Prior to Woodrow Wilson's administration (1913–21), a fifty-year period had witnessed a trend toward the racial integration of the civil service. Yet Wilson's administration ushered in one of the most regressive periods in African-American civil, political, and social rights. In 1913, he ordered that all executive departments be segregated. Furthermore, his administration instituted the segregation of toilets, lunchrooms, and working areas in the departments of the treasury and the post office as well as other administrative branches, such as the armed forces and penitentiaries. The consequence was the relegation of African-American federal workers into custodial, menial, and clerical positions—if they were hired at all. Wilson claimed that the segregation of federal employees was in the best interests of African-Americans because it would protect them from the friction that could arise from working with whites and because it would advance their independence.[6] During Wilson's first four years in office, Congress considered twenty-four antiblack laws, including legislation to segregate public transportation, the armed forces, and the civil service; to repeal the Fifteenth Amendment; and to prohibit miscegenation.

In 1913 the Democratic Fair Play Association was formed to advance the interests of southern Democrats in Washington, with Wilson an honorary member. Senator James Vardaman of Mississippi, an active member of the association, lauded the benevolence with which white southerners had treated African-Americans in the South. However, he declared, "the white people have assisted [blacks] in every possible way, except to make citizens or voters of them, and, of course, that ought not to be done and, indeed, will never be done."[7] Even the judiciary was not immune to these racist sentiments. The chief justice of the Supreme Court, Edward White, had ridden with the Klan and had arranged for *Birth of a Nation* to be shown for an audience of sympathetic justices, congressmen, and senators.[8]

By adopting segregation and emphasizing the second-class status of African-Americans, the federal government was implicitly sending a message to southern legislators that Jim Crow and the southern racial system would not be interfered with. Through its actions and omissions, the government was justifying the discrimination, segregation, and continued oppression of African-Americans in both the South and the North. In essence, the federal government under Wilson became a defender of segregation and a promoter of the idea of African-American and immigrant inferiority. Prejudice became institutionalized through legislation and customs that excluded or sharply limited African-American political, economic, and social participation and opportunity.

The Politics of Lynching

The expression of this prejudice was not limited to civil and political life. White men also used violence to institutionalize the subordinate status of African-American men and women. The Ku Klux Klan was founded in 1866, a time when white racial hegemony in the South was successfully being challenged. Journalist Ida B. Wells wrote that lynching was a response more to the African-American community's advances than to any alleged crime. The more Wells "studied the situation the more I was convinced that the Southerner had never gotten over his resentment that the Negro was no longer his plaything, his servant, and his source of income."[9] A 1904 article in *Harper's Weekly* sums up this prevailing resentment. The magazine referred to the "New Negro Crime" attributed primarily to middle-class African-American men. Many in the white establishment feared that the middle-class African-American man was "most likely to aim at social equality and to lose the awe with which in slavery times, Black men had learned to respect the woman of the superior race."[10] Senator Benjamin Tillman of South Carolina publicly claimed that southerners would lynch a "thousand niggers" to remind African-Americans of their place.[11]

Lynching had a powerful effect on the African-American population's psyche, helping maintain the group's oppressed status. An estimated 3,220 African-Americans were lynched in the South between 1880 and 1930.[12] Nine-tenths of the people lynched from 1900 to 1932 were African-American. Twenty-one lynchings took place in 1930, nineteen in southern states and two in Indiana.[13] Ballads often recalled these barbarisms, with some even composed for executions. Went one ballad for a North Carolina lynching:

> They hung Alec Whitley to a red oak limb,
> Just to show the world what they'd do for him.
> It was about the tenth of June,
> When they hung that cunning old coon.[14]

Another ballad, "The Death of Emma Hartsell," grimly commemorated other North Carolina events.

> In eighteen hundred and ninety eight, sweet Emma met with an
>   awful fate.
> Just as the wind did cease to blow, they caught the men, 'twas Tom
>   and Joe.
> They got to town by half past seven, their necks were broken
>   before eleven.
> The people there were a sight to see, they hung them to a dogwood
>   tree . . .
> And one thing more my song does lack, I forgot to say the men
>   were black.[15]

Whether written as a justification for the violence, as a warning to others, or as a means of solidifying communities' understanding of their own behavior, these narratives speak to the banality of this violence at this time in U.S. history. Furthermore, this violence occurred with sufficient regularity and with little or no response from the legal community, so that African-Americans feared challenging the system and the existing racial balance.

Economic Marginalization

Significant economic disadvantages attended this social and political isolation of African-Americans. Although census data on the income and
wages of African-Americans were not available until 1939, Progressive
Era scholars wrote about the growing poverty in America and its disproportionate effect on the African-American community. In 1915, the Commission on Industrial Relations issued a report that examined the wages
and standard of living of America's working class. The report concluded
that taking into account the labor of women and children and other income from lodgers and boarders, 50 to 60 percent of working-class families were poor, and one-third lived in "abject poverty."[16] In 1920, three
out of every four African-American farmers were sharecroppers, share
tenants, or cash tenants. Their income ranged from fifty cents to one dollar a day.[17] By the late 1920s the average African-American in the urban
North was "working class"—semiskilled at best and more typically un-
skilled. Men worked as porters, waiters, messengers, elevator operators,
and janitors, while women were employed predominantly as domestics. In
1925, for example, 60 percent of New York's African-American female
population worked as laundresses or servants.[18]

The occupations dominated by African-Americans paid substantially
less than the occupations dominated by whites. Table 1 indicates annual
earnings by occupation from 1910 to 1930. During this period, African-
Americans were primarily involved in agriculture and domestic occupations, which paid roughly one-third the amount earned by workers in
other occupational categories.

One obvious indicator of social and economic independence is literacy.
During the Progressive Era, the United States had one of the highest illiteracy rates in the industrializing West. Although illiteracy remained relatively high among whites, the illiteracy rate among African-Americans is
startling and shows how illiteracy disproportionately affected the black

TABLE 1.   **Average Annual Earnings per Full-Time Employee by Industry, 1910–30,
in 1970 Dollars**

	Agriculture	Domestic	Manufacturing	Mining	Construction	Transportation	Trade	Government
30	388	676	1,488	1,424	1,526	1,610	1,569	1,553
25	382	741	1,450	1,580	1,655	1,539	1,359	1,425
20	528	665	1,532	1,684	1,710	1,645	1,270	1,245
15	236	342	661	716	827	711	720	753
10	223	337	651	668	804	607	666	725

Source: Data from U.S. Department of Commerce, Bureau of the Census, *Historical Statistics*, ser. D 739–764, 166.

population: almost a third of the African-American population was unable to read or write an application for public assistance.

Southern Politics & Society

Southern politics has a unique relationship and place within the United States and its history, especially racial history. In the words of one scholar, the South

> has been the part of America closest to Old World Europe, but it has never really been Europe. It has been an alien child in a liberal family, tortured and confused, driven to a fantasy life which, instead of disproving the power of Locke in America, portrays more poignantly than anything else the tyranny he has had.[19]

Alien child or not, Democratic hegemony in the South sounded the death knell for national civil rights legislation and other Reconstruction-era efforts to alter the region's racial balance. Furthermore, Democratic hegemony in the South eliminated the possibility of interparty competition in regional elections. African-American suffrage and the consequent return of the two-party system would threaten the existing southern political order, so white southerners began to move to disenfranchise African-American males in the 1890s, and effectively accomplished that goal by 1908. This disenfranchisement was implemented through a variety of formal procedures within the limits of the Fifteenth Amendment including literacy tests, poll taxes, and most importantly, the white primary.

Although the Fifteenth Amendment prohibited states from denying someone the right to vote on the basis of his race or color, it did not prohibit private organizations from denying enfranchisement. To exploit this legal loophole, southern states designated the Democratic Party a club from which African-Americans could legally be excluded. The lack of interparty competition meant that voters in the Democratic primaries effectively decided elections,[20] and African-Americans did not participate. Race is thus inextricably woven into the history of the southern primary process.

The one-party system enabled the South to prevent northern intervention in the region's existing racial balance. The south was unified in national politics, thereby eliminating the possibility that divisive issues being raised in national campaigns would be raised in the South. Since there was no forum for these divisive issues, especially race issues, in state and local politics, Republicans were denied the opportunity to effectively challenge the Democratic incumbents. As V. O. Key writes, "two-party competition would have been fatal to the status of black-belt whites . . . and it would have meant the destruction of southern solidarity in national politics."[21] States in the South started to institute the primary system in the first two decades of the twentieth century, and by 1920 all southern states were selecting their senatorial and gubernatorial nominees through the primary system. Ten years later, all southern states except Florida, North Carolina, and Tennessee excluded African-Americans from the primaries by state party rule.[22]

Not until 1944 did the U.S. Supreme Court hold the white primary unconstitutional. In *Smith v. Allwright*, the Court declared that the primary was an integral part of the election process for selecting federal and state government leaders. Nevertheless, many southern states rallied to preserve the white primary. For example, Governor Olin DeWitt Talmadge Johnston of South Carolina convened the state legislature to discuss the course of action in the wake of the Supreme Court ruling, stating, "we South Carolinians will use the necessary methods to retain white supremacy in our primaries and to safeguard the homes and happiness of our people. White Supremacy will be maintained in our primaries."[23] Informal illegal and extralegal pressures also worked to limit African-American political participation, with the result that white supremacy was reestablished in southern politics during the Progressive Era, especially in areas where whites constituted the minority of the population.

This portrait of the social, economic, and political status of African-Americans during the Progressive Era provides a lens through which to view Progressive Era policy and political developments. In assessing state-building processes during this period, the subordinated and oppressed status of African-Americans in mainstream civil, political, and economic life must be considered. While the Progressive Era represented the expansion of social and economic rights for some citizens, for others, most notably African-Americans, it represented not only continued or increased exclusion but the repeal of certain newly won civil and political rights.

Nativism

Not only African-Americans experienced alienation and exclusion in the United States during the Progressive period. The immigrants who arrived at America's shores during this time were welcomed, at best, with attempts at cultural rehabilitation; more likely, they felt the barbs of nativist resentment. Immigrants from southern and eastern Europe and Asia were placed in the same ascriptive hierarchy that defined the political status of African-Americans. During the Progressive Era, immigration and citizenship laws made the majority of the world's population ineligible for American citizenship solely because of their nationality or race.[24] Millions of immigrants trying to escape social, political, and economic misfortunes confronted beliefs and practices that set boundaries for their incorporation in the polity.

Between 1900 and 1915, 14.5 million people immigrated to the United States.[25] In 1910 alone, more than 1 million immigrants arrived, approximately 25 percent of them from central Europe,[26] 21 percent from Italy, 20 percent from eastern Europe,[27] and 4 percent from other southern European countries.[28] Immigrants from northwestern European countries[29] comprised only 16 percent of this total. In 1914, the 1,218,480 immigrants to the United States represented an all-time high, with the majority of these new arrivals coming from central Europe (22.8 percent), eastern Europe (22.7 percent), and southern Europe (27.8 percent).[30]

A sudden drop in immigration in the late 1910s corresponded with the end of the "open-door" policy that had existed from the beginning of colonial settlement in 1607. The closing of the door coincided with a change in the immigrants' nationalities. At the end of the nineteenth century, immigration shifted from western and northern Europe to eastern and southern Europe. U.S. popular opinion reacted strongly to this change in immigrant populations. Many Americans with northern and western European ancestry considered people from eastern and southern Europe to be inferior. The assault on the U.S. open-door immigration policy became ardent in the 1890s. The superintendent of the census, Francis Walker, complained that the new immigrants were drawn from "great stagnant pools of population which no current of intellectual or moral activity has stirred for ages."[31] Walker, a former president of the Massachusetts Institute of Technology, believed that immigrants from Austria, Italy, Hungary, and Russia were "vast masses of peasantry, degraded below our utmost conceptions . . . beaten men from beaten races, representing the worst failures in the struggle for existence."[32] He claimed that immigrants crowded native-born Americans out of job opportunities, specifically manual labor. Because of limited job opportunities, Walker concluded, native-born Americans had fewer children. Others followed Walker in proclaiming the racial inferiority of non-Anglo-Saxons and the potential danger of inferior Slavic and Latin immigrants. Walker's theory of the declining native birthrate fueled the argument that immigration was threatening the American nation by threatening to overwhelm the "superior" stock with "inferiors."

Even social workers and scholars responsible for the welfare of these immigrant groups looked down on the immigrants' culture, religion, dress, cuisine, and social interaction. Charles Loring Brace, a profoundly nativist reformer who supported the Americanization of immigrants via Protestantism, observed of tenement houses filled with indigent Italian immigrants,

> In the same room I would find monkeys, children, men and women, with organs and plaster-casts, all huddled together; but the women contriving still, in the crowded rooms, to roll their dirty macaroni, and all talking excitedly; a bedlam of sounds, and a combination of odors from garlic, monkeys, and most dirty human persons. They were, without exception, the dirtiest population I had met with. . . . So degraded was their type.[33]

Social welfare scholar and practitioner Grace Abbott, a leader of the mothers' pension movement, offered clear insights into the minds of many American reformers during that period, writing in 1917,

> the immigrant is so inadequately protected against fraud and exploitation and because he so frequently suffers from racial discrimination, it is perhaps necessary to get him into a room and to tell him how different our beliefs with regard to social and political equality are from our practices. But until we live these beliefs we cannot honestly represent them to the immigrants as American. . . .
>
> These Americans are led by their prejudices to accept sweeping condemnations to the effect that our political corruption is due to the immigrant's ignorance and inexperience; that crime and poverty can be traced to him; that the declining birth-rate among the native Americans is the result of his coming; that he is responsible for our backwardness in giving political recognition to women; and other evil results are predicted for the future. . . . Indeed, there is scarcely a national defect that has not been charged by some one at some time due to the influence of the immigrant.[34]

Abbott's sweeping criticism of her contemporaries and their efforts to inculcate immigrants with "American" values was lost in an environment bent on protecting the "American way of life" from the perceived threat from certain immigrant populations.

Anti-Immigration Legislation

Legislation to formally limit immigration first appeared in 1896 when the House passed by a vote of 195-26 an immigration bill with a literacy requirement. The Senate approved the bill that year with a 52-10 vote. However, President Grover Cleveland vetoed the bill, claiming that it represented a departure from traditional American policy and was not in harmony with the spirit of U.S. institutions.[35] In 1912 Abbott testified before a congressional committee against a literary restriction on immigration. Although the bill passed Congress, President William Howard Taft vetoed the measure, persuaded, he claimed, by Abbott's statement before Congress.[36]

Several federal commissions in the 1910s recommended that the U.S. restrict its immigration policy and include certain qualifications for admission.[37] A 1911 report by the Dillingham Commission claimed that certain ethnic groups did not assimilate as well as others and were consequently less desirable immigrants. Eugenicist Harry Laughlin prepared a report for the House Committee on Immigration and Naturalization in which he claimed that scientific evidence showed that while all foreigners were inferior, those from southern and eastern Europe were especially inferior. He advised that "the surest biological principles to direct the future of America along safe and sound racial channels is to control the hereditary quality of the immigration stream."[38]

William Dillingham served as one of the leaders of the movement toward restricted U.S. immigration policy. A U.S. senator from 1900 to 1923, Dillingham also served as chairman of the U.S. Immigration Commission from 1907 to 1911.[39] The Dillingham Commission recommended that immigrants should be literate and that no immigrants be admitted from China, Japan, and Korea. In 1917, based on the recommendations, Congress passed a law requiring a literacy test for immigrants and passed the Asiatic Barred Zone Act excluding immigrants from South or Southeast Asia.

Dillingham was also the architect of the Quota Immigration Act of 1921, the first such measure ever passed by the U.S. Congress. This temporary act limited the number of aliens coming to the United States as permanent residents to 3 percent of the number of foreign-born persons of that national origin enumerated in the 1910 census, which was chosen because of the great number of northern and western European immigrants who had arrived before that date.[40] The act sought to limit immigration from eastern and southern Europe.

However, the Immigration Act of 1924 marked the zenith of the crusade to limit Asian and southern and eastern European immigration, creating a system of quotas based on national origin and on citizenship eligibility. This measure made the national quota permanent and limited the yearly immigration of the people of any nation to 2 percent of their U.S. population listed in the 1890 census. It also completely barred native Asian immigrants. Northern and western European immigrants, who dominated the 1890 census, received the largest quotas. Importantly, the act did not apply to Latin America, Mexico, or Canada. Even though various nativist organizations wanted to exclude Mexicans and other Latin Americans on the basis that they were racially ineligible for citizenship, congressmen from the southwest wanted to maintain a cheap labor supply, and diplomats and businessmen wanted to preserve their relations with Canada[41] and Latin America. In her analysis of the act, Mae M. Ngai states that "immigration law and policy were deeply implicated in a broader racial and ethnic remapping of the nation during the 1920s."[42]

The 1924 law required immigrants to be literate, to have good health and character, to be free of association with communist or other radical political organizations, and to be of certain racial or ethnic origin.[43] Discrepancies between legislated ceilings or quotas and actual immigration in part result from policymakers' decisions to exempt certain countries or categories of immigrants from these quotas and to retain some flexibility in responding to special circumstances.[44] When immigration totals increased again from 1920 to 1924, the nationalities of the immigrants were very different than had been the case from 1910 to 1920. The immigrant groups that fared the best under the new statutes came predominantly from northwestern Europe, while immigration from south, central, and eastern Europe dropped off precipitously.

Immigration statistics from 1925 reflected U.S. officials' intention to change the immigrant pool: 48 percent of the new arrivals came from the Americas[45] (73 percent of those immigrants came from Canada), 26.9 percent from northwestern Europe, 3.4 percent from central Europe, 2.6 percent from southern Europe, 1.6 percent from eastern Europe, and 1.2 percent from Asia.[46] Although the Department of Commerce categorized Germany as a central European country, it did not experience the same immigration trends as the rest of the region and thus appears separately in table 2.

Immigrants experienced prejudice and discrimination, just like African-Americans, albeit with different historical precedents, roots and, ramifications. Immigrant access to social service resources, although not as limited as for African-Americans, was restricted and carried with it a heavy cross

TABLE 2. Immigration to the United States, 1910, 1914, 1922, and 1925

	1910 (%)	1914 (%)	1922 (%)	1925 (%)
Northwestern Europe	16.4	10.5	19.8	26.9
Central Europe	24.8	22.8	18.7	3.4
Germany	3	2.9	5.8	15.6
Eastern Europe	20.4	22.7	10.4	1.6
Southern Europe	24.3	27.8	15.1	2.6
Asia	2.3	2.8	4.6	1.2
Americas	8.6	10	25	48
Total	99.8	99.5	99.4	99.3

Source: Data from U.S. Department of Commerce, *Historical Statistics,* ser. C, 89–119, 105–9.

to bear—that of becoming Americanized and of rejecting the immigrants' native culture, religion, value systems, cuisine, and language.

Progressivism, Race, & State-Building

The attitudes and ideologies that framed the development of U.S. social welfare policy were rooted in American Progressive society. Important for the purposes of U.S. state-building, multiple strands of racial rhetoric existed during the Progressive Era. On the one hand, a discourse opposed African-Americans, while on the other hand a discourse opposed ethnic or immigrant groups. In many ways, the effective exclusion of African-Americans from mainstream social life was taken for granted; consequently, African-Americans were rarely considered in these debates. Many Progressive reformers believed that immigrant women could be Americanized, whereas African-Americans could not. The outcome was a state-building period that solidified the marginalization of African-Americans and imposed white, middle-class norms on immigrant populations deemed worthy of Americanization.

Reactive and retrogressive public policies at both the national and local levels effectively institutionalized the depressed position of African-Americans and other minority groups and immigrants. Institutions developed premised on hierarchically ascribed norms and categories. Furthermore, public policy-making during this period reinforced local autonomy and local social and political arrangements. This alternate story of the Progressive Era implicitly explains which groups were excluded from mainstream social and political life. Prevailing social values and norms precluded the inclusion of certain racial and ethnic groups not only in the growing U.S. state but more specifically in the developing U.S. welfare state. Those excluded from the benefits and rewards of citizenship in the polity at large were excluded from nascent social welfare policy developments. The exclusion of African-Americans from mainstream political and social life was mirrored in their exclusion from mothers' pension advocacy, legislation, and administration. When mothers' pensions evolved into a national program through the Social Security Act, its administration continued to reflect local political values, and African-Americans continued to be excluded. ADC only strengthened at the national level the existing institutions and existing patterns of exclusion that had become institutionalized in the state welfare programs. The isolation and exclusion of African-Americans from mainstream society during the Progressive Era prescribed a path of exclusion from mainstream social welfare policy provision—an exclusion that has continued to the present. The racialized politics and society of the early twentieth century have informed and continue to inform welfare policy developments.

3

The Mothers'
Pension Movement

Establishing Boundaries of Exclusion
& Inclusion

More women have agreed on the wisdom of mothers'
pensions than on any other single piece of social
legislation.
—Mothers' Pension advocate, 1915[1]

If producing citizens to the State be the greatest service
a woman citizen can perform, the State will ultimately
recognize the right of the woman citizen proctection
during her time of service.[2]

THE MOTHERS' PENSION MOVEMENT was part of the Progressive
Era social activism that attempted to address ills generated by modern industrial society. Representing an important break with the past, the Progressive Era movements, including child-labor laws, civil service reform,
and workers' protection laws, all contributed to a change in state-society
relations and increased the state's responsibilities to its citizens. However,
as discussed in chapter 1, these reforms arose during a period of racial, ethnic, and class divisiveness. The mothers' pension movement both reflected
and reinforced the prevailing race and class structures. Existing support
for mothers' pensions was based on gender, racial, and class distinctions.

The mothers' pension movement had its inception in the need to protect poor families from separation and institutionalization. Prevailing social policy at the turn of the twentieth century called for the dissolution
of impoverished families, particularly one-parent families headed by
mothers. In 1900, 9 percent of all children lived with just one parent; the
majority of single-parent children lived with their mothers. Being a single

mother forced poor women to carry both economic and domestic responsibilities. Because of this dual role, these women were forced to work in
low-wage occupations such as cleaning, domestic service, hand sewing,
and agriculture that enabled them also to care, albeit in an inadequate
fashion, for their children. The income that these mothers generated often
was not sufficient, forcing older children to help make ends meet. From
1900 to about 1910, single mothers earned two to four dollars per week,
while eight dollars per week was considered the living wage for a single
person. Paradoxically, some working women in certain full-time occupations could earn enough money to support their families, but doing so
often required them to leave their children at home unsupervised, a situation from which the children could be removed for neglect.

A contemporary social worker described the living conditions of one
poor single-mother family on New York City's Lower East Side in 1909:

> You live in three rooms in Essex Street. . . . There is a boarder who
> helps out with the rent. . . .You only have one bed. The boarder must
> have it. The three older children slept on a mattress on the floor after
> she brought them in from the street at eleven o'clock. The baby who
> is only eight months old, slept with you on the fire escape, and you
> stayed awake half the night for fear you might lose your hold on him
> and he might fall. Willie has a running nose and they tell you at the
> day nursery that if it is not better to-day you will have to keep him
> home. . . . That means that Nellie will have to stay away from school
> and take care of him. You are only thirty-six years old, but you look
> forty-nine.[3]

Many reformers believed that forced labor in almshouses would teach
these dependent wards behavior patterns that would enable them to become self-supporting members of the community. In particular, the incar-
ceration of dependent youth was considered important to the search for
solutions to poverty and the fight against economic dependency. Many reformers believed that poor children achieved better health and moral development in the almshouses than in their homes. Orphans and poor children were treated similarly, without regard to family bonds or the parental
rights of the poor. Table 3 exemplifies the limited rights that the poor—
even poor adults—had at the turn of the century. Just like their parents,
indigent children were punished for being impecunious and were often
housed in institutions with the insane and with convicts.

Statistics on the number of children taken from female-headed households are alarming. At the 1909 White House Conference on the Care of

Dependent Children, it was learned that of the 93,000 children in orphanages and children's homes, 50,000 children in foster homes, and 25,000 children in juvenile delinquent institutions, a "disturbing portion" were from families lacking a male head or breadwinner. A study of children's institutions in the early 1900s revealed that 80 percent of these children had at least one parent living.[4] A 1912 Massachusetts study revealed that 57 percent of children not living with their single mother had been taken from their mother only because she could not financially support them.[5] It was also discovered that half-orphans considerably outnumbered full orphans. In 1900 California had 5,399 half-orphans and 959 full orphans living in state institutions.[6] In 1913 in New York State, approximately 1,000 children had been placed in public institutions because their widowed mothers were ill, primarily because of the burdens and overwork of being both breadwinner and homemaker. Another 3,000 children in New York were in institutions because their parents could not support them.[7] A 1921 study of 9,000 mothers' pension cases by the Children's Bureau revealed that in 75 percent of them, widowhood was the predominant factor in the family's destitution.[8]

By the end of the nineteenth century, these various children's institutions were not producing the desired reformed children and thus were becoming less palatable to social reformers. Reformers were concerned that the existing children's institutions did not distinguish among homeless, criminal, and poor children but instead housed them all together. These reformers began to criticize institutional life as artificial, unnecessarily regimental, incapable of preparing youth for the real world, and unable to provide individual care. For these reformers, the "natural" home came to replace these institutions as the ideal environment for a child's development.

TABLE 3.   Selected States and the Termination of the Rights of the Poor at the Turn of the Twentieth Century

All paupers deprived right of franchise and right to hold office	Only inmates of poorhouses deprived of franchise
Delaware	Louisiana
Maine	Missouri
Massachusetts	Oklahoma
New Hampshire	Pennsylvania
New Jersey	
Rhode Island	
South Carolina	
Texas	
Virginia	

Source: Adapted from Brown, *Public Relief,* 10.

Saving Children in the Progressive Era

Contrary to Puritan child-rearing guides, which emphasized harsh discipline and the breaking of a child's spirit, the early-twentieth-century philosophy of child rearing and successful parenting prescribed prudent guidance and supervision and a great deal of love and affection. Moreover, the responsibility of child rearing passed from the father to the mother. The formation of a child's character became the primary goal of socialization within the family. Many reformers concluded that even a poor home was better than an institution. Women were seen as having the natural capacity to provide the nurturing necessary for children's appropriate upbringing. The idea that women's primary role was to raise children slowly extended from the middle and upper classes to the working classes.

The Progressive Era also ushered in an entirely different philosophy about the causes of poverty. Most Progressive reformers rejected the philosophy of nineteenth-century charity workers that the poor were socially deviant and should be uplifted. Instead, these reformers attributed the plight of the poor to industrialization. The Progressives, unlike their predecessors, also strongly believed in preserving the family. The Progressives' political agenda included stricter child-labor laws, kindergarten programs, maternal health services, and other programs aimed at securing the welfare of children. Most importantly, the reformers incorporated contemporary views of womanhood, mothering, and childhood in developing new social policies for dependent children.[9]

A corollary and significant administrative development for the movement for aid to mothers with dependent children was the establishment of boards of public welfare. The central idea behind these boards was the redefinition of government's role in the matter of social welfare. In 1908, Kansas City established the country's first board of public welfare. The city's Board of Pardons and Parole was originally established on behalf of inmates in workhouses, but its role expanded within a few years to include administering various programs aimed at the poor and the unemployed and various other social welfare programs. Within a few years of the Kansas City experiment, Chicago, Cleveland, Cincinnati, Dayton, Grand Rapids (Mich.), St. Joseph (Mo.), St. Louis, Dallas, and Omaha established similar types of boards of public welfare,[10] seeking to consolidate the administration of various municipal and in some cases philanthropic programs aimed at alleviating or ameliorating various social ills. This movement was grounded in the developing belief that poverty and social ills were as much attributable to social inequities as to individual personal failure and that the government bore responsibility for addressing these inequalities. The end result was the growing challenge to the power and prestige of private philanthropic and voluntary agencies, with the balance of power shifting to the public sector.

Early Forms of Aid to Dependent Children

To some extent, the proposed pensions for mothers evolved out of the juvenile court system, where many judges had to separate mothers from their children because of poverty. Juvenile court judges were becoming reluctant to break the mother-child relationship by institutionalizing the child for economic dependency alone. Many reformers depicted state institutions for poor children in the worst light, describing institutions where good innocent children were forced to associate with "undesirable" children and where some children died or were mentally weakened because they were deprived of their mothers and their mothers' love. Many observers concluded that children could properly develop only in their own homes.

Consequently, reformers had for several years proposed home-based public aid for dependent children as an alternative to public relief and private charity. Different arguments surfaced in favor of mothers' pensions as an alternative to existing practice. As already discussed, many pension proponents rejected institutional care for children and believed that a mother's love in her home provided the best environment for her children. Other reformers rejected private charity as an adequate or appropriate proxy for certain governmental functions, notably social welfare. Many commentators focused on the relationship between the fertility rates of native-born women and mothers' pensions. Finally, some reformers distinguished between mothers' pensions as a right and other forms of social assistance, such as public poor laws or outdoor relief.[11]

As early as 1897, the New York State legislature debated and passed a "destitute mothers' bill," but the governor and the mayor of New York City vetoed the measure in response to strong opposition to the bill on the part of private charities, who labeled the measure the "Shiftless Fathers Bill," playing on officials' anxieties that such legislation would encourage fathers to abandon their responsibility. A year later, however, New York enacted a measure that gave widowed mothers a grant equal to the cost of institutionalizing their children. Certain California juvenile courts in 1906 and the New Jersey attorney general in 1910 liberally interpreted laws to grant aid to children in their own homes. Oklahoma in 1908 and Michigan in 1911 established programs that used educational funds to aid the dependent children of widows. Although none of these laws established the state's or national government's responsibility for aiding dependent children in their own homes, these measures distinguished such programs from general poor relief.

A National Mothers' Pension Movement

The mothers' pension movement became an extension of the broader "knowledge movement" that developed during the Progressive Era as a result of a systematic and organized knowledge base that included political leaders, settlement house leaders, the legal community, and intellectuals. For the first time, public policy-making became based in universities and extended itself to central national administrative units. Mothers' pensions drew support from all the major strains of Progressivism: "Moral reformers and economic-efficiency buffs, women's clubs and labor unions, middle-class do-gooders and relief recipients, New Freedom advocates and New Nationalism partisans, all jumped onto the bandwagon."[12] The majority of these social welfare reformers, including the women, came from the country's intellectual elite. According to Lina Gordon's research, while less than 1 percent of all American women held a college degree at that time, 86 percent of these reform women were college educated, and 66 percent had attended graduate school.[13]

The push for an organized system of social support for impoverished children came to a head at the 1909 White House Conference on the Care of Dependent Children convened by President Theodore Roosevelt. The participants at the White House conference represented and reflected the diverse knowledge base from which this movement grew, but only two of the hundreds of participants were African-American, and no discussion occurred regarding the plight of African-American children, who were more likely than white children to be poor. One of the African-American participants, Booker T. Washington, president of the Tuskegee Institute, claimed that the white system was not responsible for caring for poor African-American children.[14] Reflecting the movement's broader goals, the conference focused solely on the care of dependent white children.

Roosevelt opened the White House conference by discussing the plight of poor widows with dependent children. In his words, "surely in such a case the goal toward which we should strive is to help that mother, so that she can keep her own home and keep the child in it; that is the best thing possible to be done for that child."[15] Prominent social reformers addressed the shortsighted practices then in place for dealing with poverty-stricken children. Widows' and mothers' pensions or mothers' aid offered a solution to the reformers' goal of reuniting families that had broken up because of the loss of the primary breadwinner and of preventing such breakups.

Participants at the White House conference called for upholding the value of "home life," agreeing that it represented "the highest and finest product of civilization. It is the great molding force of mind and character. Children should not be deprived of it except for urgent and compelling reasons."[16] The slogan "No child should be removed from its family for the cause of poverty alone" became the basis for the mothers' pension campaign. The overt rationale was to protect the future of the United States by providing the support within the home that would enable children to grow up to be good citizens. In this way, reformers often compared widows with civil servants providing a service for the country: "He is paid for his work; she for hers. And she should be paid by those for whom she does it—all the citizens of the state, not the subscribers to the charities."[17] These mothers' pension advocates thus distinguished between charity and the state's obligation to provide a mothers' pension, maintaining that the paternalism and obloquy associated with charity could not be transferred to mothers' pensions. Almost unanimously, these advocates considered the pension to be payment for services rendered to society, not a handout. Caring for and raising her children was the best form of employment a mother could have. Other advocates insisted that because society was responsible for the husband's death—either as a result of inadequate wages or as a result of a preventable disease or accident—society was also responsible for assuaging the widow's poverty.

The view that these women were entitled to aid was novel in the history of American welfare. Both public and private aid had previously been associated with the recipient's failure to provide for her or himself. Other than Civil War veterans, no other aid had been associated with service or an entitlement.[18] The request for mothers' aid would constitute not a sign of moral baseness or failure but payment for service. Aid to these poor families focused on two beneficiaries, one direct (the child) and one indirect (the mother). Although the benefit was intended solely for the care and support of the child(ren), the mother was the individual to whom the benefit should appropriately be given.

For many social welfare reformers, the recommendations for pension programs that emerged out of the conference embodied the most advanced child welfare ideas of the time. Three principles that emerged from the White House conference became the foundation of the mothers' pension movement and the bedrock on which the state mothers' pension programs were built: (1) the decentralization of administrative control to local agencies; (2) targeting a "select" group of families for whom this elite social service provision could be granted; and (3) establishing eligibility principles based on the maintenance of a proper home. The last principle was echoed in the unanimous resolution adopted by conference members. The conference's resolution emphasized that funds were to be provided only to "children of parents of worthy character" and that the parents must maintain "suitable homes for the rearing of children."[19]

Mothers' Pension Supporters

The mothers' pension movement garnered a great deal of support from groups and individuals inside and outside of the social service community. Judges in juvenile courts were the leaders of mothers' pension movements in many states, including the first three states to pass mothers' pension legislation. Although Progressive politicians were not central to the movement, several of them were several notable proponents of mothers' pension legislation, including Theodore Roosevelt, Robert La Follette, Louis Brandeis, Calvin Coolidge, and Alfred Smith.

Progressive Era newspapers and magazines actively advocated mothers' pensions. The most influential was the *Delineator*, a women's fashion magazine published by Butterick with a mail circulation of 1 million in 1912. In fact, some claim that the 1909 White House Conference was an outgrowth of the crusade launched by the *Delineator* and its editor, Theodore Dreiser. During his 1907–9 tenure, each monthly issue of the magazine contained case histories of dependent children up for adoption by social agencies.[20] The *Delineator* became an important voice on behalf of mothers' pensions, sending a lecturer around the country to promote the movement. The *Delineator* reached millions of women across the country, including residents of small towns and rural areas. The magazine had a history of sponsoring social reform causes and of collaborating with various women's clubs, social reformers, and settlement house workers to promote these causes. Journalist William Hard, a former settlement worker and a close friend of Jane Addams and Julia Lathrop, launched the *Delineator*'s tenacious and impassioned campaign for mothers' pensions in 1912 with an article, "Four Counties That Prefer Mothers to Orphan Asylums," in which he wrote,

> every year man puts asunder those whom God, with bonds even more sacred than those of matrimony, has joined together. Every year thousands of American children are torn from their mothers to be given to strangers. Not because those mothers are bad. Only because, through no fault of their own, they are poor.[21]

In December of that year, the magazine's first page proclaimed,

> Our Christmas Wish for Women: That Every Decent Mother in America Could Have Her Babies With Her. . . . [W]omen's clubs, clubs of loving and hopeful women, in Massachusetts and in California, and in many States in between, are working hard to get laws which will give to the mother the money which is now being given to the institutions in which her children are imprisoned. Set the children free! Let them go back to their mothers! And let the mothers earn their living from the State by doing the most useful thing they could possibly do—bring up their children![22]

The *Delineator* thus saw mothers and children as well as society in general as the victims of state and local policy that ignored the value of home life and "mother love" in raising future generations. This rhetoric sharply contrasts with that of the 1980s and 1990s, when a mother's staying at home and raising her children became synonymous with laziness and fraud.

From 1912 to 1914, a crucial period during which many state legislatures considered mothers' pension legislation, the *Delineator* continued to publish emotional appeals in support of mothers' pensions and to feature stories of women who had been forced to give up their children for reasons of poverty alone under such titles as "Motherless Children of Living Mothers"[23] and "Financing Motherhood."[24] Finally, the *Delineator* put together a pamphlet on proposed legislation throughout the nation.

The *Delineator* was not alone in its support of mothers' pensions. *Good Housekeeping*[25] and *Collier's*, two very popular women's magazines, also published articles supporting mothers' pensions. With respective circulations of 375,000 and 2 million, these magazines contributed greatly to the movement. In addition to media targeting women, other widely distributed papers and journals published articles in support of mothers' pensions, including the *New York Evening World*, *Outlook*, *Survey*, *Nation*, *Public*, and *Hearst's Magazine*. A 1913 edition of *Hearst's Magazine* contained an article, "Mothers' Pension Bills," that discussed legislation already passed in a few states:

> There has never been more sensible legislation than this. Mothers are of vastly more importance to the country than rivers and harbors, new post-offices or any other thing. Every dollar invested in supporting mothers is worth ten dollars put into penitentiaries and reformatories. The oldest institution is the family, and it is the best. . . . [W]hoever brings a child into the world has added to the wealth of the nation more than one who builds a steamboat or an iron foundry. Mothers are greater assets than millionaires to a country.[26]

Survey published numerous articles about mothers' pensions from 1913 to 1915. One 1913 article stated,

> It is a recognition by the state that the aid is rendered, not as a charity, but as a right—as justice due mothers whose work in rearing their children is a work for the state as much as that of the soldier who is paid by the state for his services on the battlefield.[27]

A 1914 article in the same journal made an even more impassioned appeal for support for mothers' pension laws:

> We cannot hope for results by way of stronger, more resolute bodies and minds which shall in the children's later years mean a larger initiative, efficiency and productiveness, unless we remove from their lives today that constant crushing anxiety that not only deadens hope and aspiration in the mother's life, but also gradually lays its withering, paralyzing hand on the lives of the children.[28]

Even in the earliest stage of national advocacy, national magazines were hinting at possible discrimination or racial disparities in benefit provision. A 1914 *Survey* article on the provision of mothers' pensions in Cincinnati commented by the author that of the first hundred mothers receiving aid, only four were "negroes," "not quite the number to which their proportion of the city's population would entitle them."[29] Another *Survey* article expressed the importance of uniformity in the provision of mothers' pensions: "it is highly important, in our opinion, that similar needs in different families should be met with some approach to consistency, that there should be a degree of uniformity as to methods and standards of treatment. Without such a controlling principle there is bound to come unfair discrimination."[30] Discussing remedies of poverty, another article pointed out the need "to segregate those who should not propagate their kind," arguing for "the segregation for life, or at least during child-bearing age, of a whole generation of the feeble-minded."[31] Although this reference apparently covers both whites and nonwhites, it clearly indicates the strong intent to differentiate.

Local newspapers and social service agencies joined the national media in publishing articles and related materials on behalf of mothers' aid laws. The *Nashville Tennessean* included in its legislative report section an announcement about "two remarkably good and progressive pieces of legislation" that would be of "great benefit to the people of this state." One was Tennessee's recently enacted mothers' pension law. The newspaper lauded the members of the Tennessee Congress of Mothers and the Parent-Teacher Association who had "labored long and earnestly for a state law providing mother's pensions" and who achieved this victory after a "hard battle." The newspaper also included a drawing with a mother holding her child in the center, surrounded by policymakers making "Appropriations for Everything and Everybody Except the Unfortunate Kiddies" and defending the value of poorhouses and orphanages. The caption states, "The opposition fails to consider that the best orphanage in the world is no fair substitute for the home. The Mother's Pension—Not Charity but for Service Rendered."[32]

Reports by state welfare agencies included iconography and slogans to encourage the passage of mothers' pension laws. Georgia's Department of Public Welfare compared the economic loss from the cotton boll weevil to the economic loss society faced by not protecting its children from neglect and abuse.[33] A caption under a photograph of a destitute child in another report read, "Help Me Now, I'll Help Georgia Later." One of the Alabama State Child Welfare Department's annual reports included a drawing of an arm extended down like a ladder for children waiting at the bottom to climb up. Several of the department's annual reports included sections encouraging the state legislature to enact mothers' aid legislation.[34] In Pennsylvania, the executive secretary of the Mothers' Assistance Fund stated, "Recognition by the State of a good mother as the best caretaker for dependent, fatherless children, and of the family unit as the environment best suited to develop the young child, has been one of the outstanding social advances of the Twentieth Century."[35] That state also boasted a very active and well organized Mothers' Pension League, which promoted the mothers' pension movement and worked to secure larger appropriations for the Mothers' Pension Fund.

In 1915, even the academic journal *American Political Science Review* printed an article on the "Administration of Mothers' Pension Laws" that reviewed the different laws and administration of those laws in several jurisdictions.[36] The mothers' pension movement also received support from unions, specifically the Executive Council of the American Federation of Labor (AFL), which during the 1920s played an important role in promoting mothers' pension legislation for the District of Columbia. The Executive Council incorporated mothers' pensions into the AFL's old-age pension legislation pending in the U.S. Congress. Although Congress never acted on the legislation, it is significant that this powerful labor organization, which had historically protected the interests of male laborers, supported mothers' pensions, at least at the local level, demonstrating the broad and diverse support for such pensions.

White Activist Women's Organizations

The primary actors in the mothers' pension movement from the early 1900s to the 1930s were women, particularly the women's organizations that had begun to flourish around the turn of the century, including the General Federation of Women's Clubs, the National Congress of Mothers and the Parent-Teacher Association. (No nationwide organizations protected the interests of fathers who lost their children because of poverty.) The various women's organizations differed in their support of mothers' pensions. The General Federation of Women's Clubs offered an endorsement in 1912 but left the responsibility of action to the discretion of the local clubs. Conversely, the National Congress of Mothers passed a mothers' pension resolution at almost every convention after 1911 and claimed that every state affiliate supported and worked for such legislation.[37] Other women's organizations active in pursuing mothers' pension legislation included the National Consumers' League, which was more militant than the other groups but whose membership was younger and more educated; the Women's Suffrage League of Virginia; the Woman's Christian Temperance Union in Tennessee; and several Mothers' Pensions Leagues. Members of these women's federations claimed that they, not the scores of doctors and sociologists affiliated with the charity institutions, were the experts on family policy. Prevailing social attitudes on gender relations lent enormous credibility to that claim, thereby granting these members an advantage in the public debate on mothers' pensions.

In advocating mothers' pensions, these organizations implicitly if not explicitly expressed their interests in maintaining the racial status quo. These organizations championed the universal values of motherhood while simultaneously promoting the preservation of white middle- and upper-class values. Their actions if not their rhetoric precluded any possibility of a universal conception of motherhood that embraced multiracial or multiethnic values, nor did they embrace mothers, advocates, or pensioners who were not white. In essence, these women's organizations focused exclusively on advancing the rights and honor of white women.

Two women's organizations significantly contributed to the mothers' pension movement: the General Federation of Women's Clubs (GFWC) and the National Congress of Mothers.[38] Launched in 1890 in New York, the GFWC served as an umbrella organization that brought together affiliated state federations of women's clubs, which in turn brought together local clubs. The GFWC hosted biennial conventions, published an official journal, maintained a national office, and held regular meetings of elected national officers and had standing committees focused on art, civil service reform, education, public health, child labor, and other issues. The state federations held annual conventions and maintained committee structures that paralleled those of the national federation. At the local level, thousands of clubs met weekly, biweekly, or monthly in towns and cities across the nation to discuss issues related to culture and society. By 1911, women's clubs met in all forty-eight states. At its 1912 biennial meeting, the national GFWC endorsed mothers' pensions, adopting a resolution that stated,

> among the continuous interests of organized women, in these times when the home is shaken by economic changes, there should be a progressive legislative policy for the greater honor and greater stability of home life. Such a policy should include laws . . . adequately protecting the widow against unnecessary impoverishment at her husband's death. We believe that the function of motherhood should bring to a woman increased security rather than increased insecurity and that the legislative policy above outlined, in safeguarding motherhood, safeguards the race.[39]

The word *race* often entered the mothers' pensions advocacy rhetoric. While *race* was not explicitly synonymous with *white* or *northern European*, the sentiments of the period leave little doubt that safeguarding the "race" meant more than simply the human race. This rhetoric clearly appeals to those with nativist interests as well as those who were more generally concerned about the welfare of children.

Because of its decentralized structure, the activities of the state federations were essential to mothers' pension advocacy. Beginning at the 1912 biennial meeting, lobbying initiatives specifically for mothers' pensions were reported by twelve state federations, and Theda Skocpol presents evidence that another eleven state federations also supported mothers' pensions.[40] Until 1916, dozens of other state federations claimed their support for mothers' pensions and boasted that their support had been integral to getting the legislation passed. The peak years in the support for mothers' pension legislation were 1913 and 1915.

Founded in 1897, the National Congress of Mothers was an elite maternalist organization comprising almost solely white middle- and upper-class women. By 1910 the congress boasted 50,000 dues-paying members in twenty-one state branches, and ten years later the group's membership had grown to 190,000.[41] Unlike the GFWC, the National Congress of Mothers was organized from the top down. In 1924 the congress changed its name to the National Congress of Parents and Teachers, also known as the PTA. The congress held an annual convention and hosted an "international" convention every three years. The activities of the National Congress were as important as those of the GFWC in getting mothers' pension legislation enacted. Although branches of the congress existed in only twenty-two states in 1911 and in only thirty-seven states in 1920, their advocacy, unlike that of the GFWC, continued until mothers' pension laws were passed in almost every state. The National Congress of Mothers formally endorsed mothers' pensions and began a campaign on their behalf in early 1911, before the pioneering Illinois law was passed. The Congress unanimously resolved that

> it is the sense of this Congress that families should, if possible, be held together. That the mother is the best caretaker for her children. That when necessary to prevent the breaking up of the home the State should provide a certain sum for the support of the children instead of taking them from her and placing them elsewhere at the expense of the State, And . . . that each branch of the Congress, located in the several states, be urged to assist in securing such legislation as will accomplish this result.[42]

The Congress's official journal, the *Child-Welfare Magazine*, regularly ran stories on mothers' pension legislation and programs, and members were active in a variety of advocacy activities, including contacting members of state legislatures and communicating with every club in the state to solicit their endorsement of proposed mothers' pension legislation. In some states, different women's organizations worked together to promote mothers' pensions.

As previously mentioned, these women's organizations comprised well-to-do white women who, although undeniably altruistic in their intent, modulated their support through a class and ethnic lens. Their interest in mothers' aid was colored by the concern about the influx of immigrants, mostly poor. Their agenda also featured a social-control element in that members feared that new immigrant groups threatened the existing social order and would raise their children to be undisciplined and unruly. Although in most cases these reformers empathized with the plight of poor immigrant single mothers, their approach was based primarily on the image of uplifting the downtrodden, ignorant mother to a level that they deemed respectable. Whereas these poor women expressed the need for financial assistance, these reformers saw education as the key to the redemption of the poor. These groups' child- and mother-saving campaigns were filled with condescension for poor women. Finally, the rhetoric of these women's organizations was sufficiently ambiguous that claims of protecting the mothers of the "race" like those of the National Congress of Mothers could have as easily meant Anglo-Saxons as the human race. Although many of these women were sincerely concerned with the welfare of poor mothers and their children, class and race prejudice created a disconnect between what these mothers and children needed and what was being provided for them.

The National Congress of Mothers and the GFWC were on the conservative end of the continuum of public welfare advocacy. Other organizations at the vanguard of the public welfare campaign, such as the National Consumers' League, the Women's Trade Union League, and the settlement houses, saw mothers' pensions as only one step in the right direction and focused more on successive steps.

Finally, thousands of poor, single mothers wrote to local, state, and national agencies, urging support for mothers' aid legislation. One New York mother wrote in 1897,

> I am a scrubwoman in City Hall where you daily come to your office and since the mothers' bill has passed the Senate and Assembly I have watched the papers to see by your inhumanity and injustice how long will the widows and orphans be deprived of the benefits of this bill? I am a widow with seven orphans and their sole support is thirty dollars per month with sixty cents a week deducted for carfare.[43]

An Illinois mother wrote in 1916,

> No food for the ones I already have, and nothing to nourish the coming. Only *abuse* and *torture* at the hands of the man who *promised to*

provide and protect woman. And *no law to enforce this promise.* . . .
[I]f possible start an association to protect mothers who are to give
birth and after that help them to help themselves, and enable them to
do for their babies. The Soldier receive[s] his pension, What do mothers'
receive? Abuse, torture, slurs, that is the best they receive. Men in long
service receive their pension. Mothers deserving receiv[e] nothing.[44]

And a Pennsylvania mother wrote in 1927,

I am writing you concerning my children support. My husband died
last fall leaving me with 3 little boys and I am not able to work to
support them as I am expecting to take my bed any day now. So I
wanted to see if I could get this mothers Pension.[45]

These letters not only reflect the great need that existed during this time
period but demonstrate the movement's impact on public discourse. Each
letter demonstrates some familiarity on the part of the author with the
mothers' pension legislation or programs and, perhaps more importantly,
used language resembling that used by other advocates to promote these
programs.

The Children's Bureau

An important institutional development for the mothers' pension movement was the establishment in 1912 of the Department of Labor's Children's
Bureau. Congress mandated the bureau "to investigate and report . . . upon
all matters pertaining to the welfare of children and child life among all
classes of our people."[46] The Children's Bureau acted as a research center
for gathering information on child health and welfare, conducting field surveys and investigations into every aspect of child welfare, including child
labor, child health and nutrition, education, and juvenile delinquency. In
that capacity, bureau staffers published numerous reports specifically on
mothers' pensions, including tabular summaries of state benefits, comparisons of state and local laws and administration, surveys of beneficiary demographics, and in-depth studies of programs in specific localities. Although the mothers' pension programs were not a federal program, the
Children's Bureau closely monitored them. Furthermore, the bureau developed close working relations with program administrators, provided assistance to states interested in establishing and administering mothers' pension programs, advised states about the development of state departments

of public welfare, and often served as a mediator and point of reference for dependent mothers interested in applying for benefits.

The Children's Bureau also acted for decades as a conduit between needy mothers in jurisdictions across the nation and the state or local agency responsible for providing aid in that jurisdiction. Mothers, unfamiliar with local laws providing aid, contacted the bureau for information on mothers' aid or other aid programs in their areas. The bureau would contact the appropriate state and/or local agencies on behalf of the mother. For example, when one mother inquired about aid in 1927, the bureau responded,

> We are in receipt of your letter of April 19. Alabama has no law such as is known in other States as the "mother's pension" or "mother's allowance" law. We are, however, forwarding your letter to Mrs. A. M. Tunstall, Director, State Child Welfare Department, Montgomery, who will, no doubt, have one of her workers communicate directly with you and advise you in regard to the care of your children and grand children.[47]

In addition to helping mothers find the appropriate social service agencies to address their problems, the Children's Bureau also assisted organizations and local policymakers interested in developing or adopting mothers' pension legislation. The bureau received thousands of letters with these types of inquiries from parties as diverse as the South Carolina Board of Public Welfare, the Oklahoma City Welfare Board, the Social Service Bureau of Missouri, the North Carolina Board of Charities, the Public Charities Association of Pennsylvania, the Oregon Child Welfare Commission, the Committee on Children's Aid in Louisiana, and the United Charities of Chicago.[48]

Controversy & Opposition to Mothers' Pensions

The movement for official public relief was not without opposition. There were a variety of arguments against adopting mothers' pension laws. One vein of opposition focused on the inappropriateness of a state system of support. Along these lines, some people argued that private charity would be more efficiently organized than a public assistance system. Others rejected the notion that a pension was a reward for service. In their view, a pension would not symbolize anything other than charity. Finally, there was concern about the increase in public expenditures: charity should originate in the private sector, not come from public coffers. Some social workers and charity organizations argued that private societies already existed had the knowledge base to appropriately manage poor relief and that public provision was superfluous at best.

A second vein of opposition focused on the negative effects, or "pauperizing tendencies,"[49] that pensions would have on society. On the one hand, the opposition believed that, public assistance would lead to fraud and deception and discourage "industrious" habits and thrift. In addition, opponents believed that families would no longer take responsibility for their unfortunate members, dumping them on the government for support. The rhetoric used for dismantling AFDC in the 1990s echoes this earlier line of argument against mothers' pensions.

A third vein of opposition related to other social welfare programs being advanced, albeit unsuccessfully, at that time. Some reformers believed that public aid would retard the development of social insurance and programs to support workers.[50] Significantly, the successful mothers' pension movement had a negative impact on more progressive social insurance plans put forward at the same time. The spread of the targeted mothers' pension programs quickly dashed the notion of an across-the-board entitlement social insurance program. This small program that distinguished between deserving and undeserving mothers did not threaten most policy stakeholders; however, it put more progressive and comprehensive social insurance plans on the defensive. Since the mothers' pension laws were mostly optional, local authorities did not have to appropriate funds or burden taxpayers. Furthermore, steadfast supporters of the mothers' pension programs who had at one time strongly advocated supporting all single mothers as a right backed down from this rhetoric. By the late 1920s, widespread support for mothers' pension as an entitlement had vanished, and policymakers in many localities came to see mothers' pension programs as more appealing than other social welfare programs that were more inclusive and rights-based.

Other reformers questioned the logic of giving the government the responsibility of providing allowances to dependent children in their own homes. During the late nineteenth century, social workers worked with private charities to defeat public outdoor relief programs and prevented their development in many localities. This became more difficult at the turn of the twentieth century, when new state legislation regulated private children's institutions, thereby asserting the government's role. Social work leaders were divided on the matter of government intervention in

outdoor relief and more specifically on mothers' pensions. Opposition to
the mother's pension movement pervaded most of the country's private charities and orphanages as well as significant associations, such as
the National Conference of Charities and Corrections and the Russell
Sage Foundation, that spoke on behalf of charities. Many of these agencies carried with them a distrust of government agencies that had accu-
mulated over the fifty years that the charity movement had existed. In
fact, many private agencies had been giving allowances to mothers of dependent, fatherless children. Many social workers feared that these children would become charges of the state or of politically appointed public
officials. Consequently, these social workers did not support government
involvement until an administrative apparatus had been established with
social case work standards comparable to approved practice in charity organization societies.

In 1915, Edward Devine, the general secretary of the New York Charity
Organization Society and one of the most vocal opponents of the mothers' pension movement, expressed many leading charity workers' concerns about the imminent attack on private philanthropy and its perceived hegemony: "who are these sudden heroes of a brand new program
of state subsidies to mothers? Who are these brash reformers who so
cheerfully impugn the motives of old-fashioned givers, of the conscien-
tious directors of charitable institutions, of pious founders of hospitals
and all manner of benefactions."[51] These reformers feared that any social
welfare program would grow unchecked as it became a pawn of party
politicians. Two lines of argument dominated the charity workers' assault
on mothers' pensions. The first was a defense of orphanages and private
charity to care for dependent children. The second was based on the emphasis on "scientific philanthropy," which provided the foundation for
the charity workers' case against government grants for dependent children in their own homes. These social workers believed that public officials were incapable of learning the lessons of scientific philanthropy and
that government relief agencies would be subject to corruption and political interference, would not recognize the importance of employing competent trained administrators, and would not provide adequate supervision of the relief beneficiaries. The concern over patronage politics was
justified at that time, especially in light of the widespread fraud connected with Civil War pensions, the only national public welfare program
to that time.[52]

Finally, the Elizabethan poor law tradition and subsequent theories
building on it rejected any notion that the poor had a "right" to any so-

cial welfare benefit. Many opponents of public relief postulated that it would lead to recipients to believe that relief was a right. Many opponents felt that the poor had only themselves to blame for their plight and therefore were not entitled to any public relief. At an annual meeting of the National Conference of Charities and Corrections, Columbia University President Seth Low expressed the view that private sources alone should provide relief to avoid creating dependency. Many opponents of mothers' pensions believed that giving recipients cash instead of providing them with basic necessities was foolish and only tempted the recipients to spend money recklessly.

New York City offers a neat illustration of the polarization within the social welfare community over mothers' pensions. Every major private charity in New York state opposed a widows' pension bill in 1913. However, the Association of Neighborhood Workers, which represented the New York City settlement houses, favored the bill. The same year, sponsors of mothers' pensions persuaded the legislature to appoint the Commission on Relief for Widowed Mothers, which reported favorably on a mothers' pension bill and was vituperative in its indictment of private social agencies. The commission reported that in 2,716 children statewide had been institutionalized because of poverty alone and that another 933 had been institutionalized because of their mothers' illnesses. The New York Charity Organization Society and the Russell Sage Foundation, two of the nation's most powerful and influential private social agencies, warred with New York's mothers' pension advocates, asserting that relief belonged solely to the domain of private organizations and that government relief would create special interests that would exploit the government. The defeat of these two agencies in 1915 through the enactment of the New York State Child Welfare Law was very significant.

Political Support through Exclusion: The Suitable Home Provision

Social welfare reformers who supported the mothers' pension movement did not believe, however, that all indigent mothers were adequate mothers, worthy of pensions. The "suitable home" condition represented a way to protect the nascent program from criticism and to garner public support. By marketing this program as an "elite" program for worthy mothers, pension advocates attracted support from a public that might otherwise have been alienated by such a far-reaching program. The reformers

chose to focus their campaign on what were often perceived as helpless
and virtuous widows to avoid the stigma associated with deserted wives.
Pension advocates often even justified the "fall" of many widows as a
consequence of being overworked and impecunious. It was easier to sell a
program that protected families that had experienced the tragic loss of
male breadwinners than one that protected so-called indolent or wanton
women. This approach had the unintended consequence of further stig-
matizing single mothers whose husbands had not died. A virtuous single
mother was a widow; single mothers with any other marital status were
suspect. The programs for supporting dependent children in their own
homes were often called interchangeably "mothers' pensions" and "widows' pensions." However, not all widows were considered worthy mothers. Distinctions of worthiness involved not only marital status but also
race and ethnicity.

Suitable Home, Race, & Mothers' Pensions

A covert impetus in the mothers' pension movement was generated by the
fear that birthrates for poor immigrant women were higher than those of
mothers of native stock. One report concluded that at the turn of the century in Massachusetts, foreign mothers averaged 50 percent more children
than U.S.-born mothers. Another study predicted that the poor immigrant population would crowd out the Yankees.[53] It was inaccurately believed in the early part of the twentieth century disproportionate numbers
of deserted or unwed mothers were immigrants. As mentioned in chapter
2, turn-of-the-century immigrants came from different countries and had
different religions than previous immigration waves. This newest arrivals
came predominantly from eastern and southern Europe and were primarily Catholics, Jews, and Eastern Orthodox Christians, making them less
accepted than earlier immigrants. In fact, reports during the Progressive
Era on single mothers made gross ethnic generalizations. A 1904 report on
desertion contended that "with all our . . . Catholics, the wide open door
of our immense institutional system makes it easy for a man to lay down
his obligations. . . . Despite the dogged perseverance of the Hebrew race
[there is] no more flagrant offender than the Jew. If the rent is over-due
he disappears." And a 1920 study alleged that "the most outstanding feature of our Slavic desertion cases seems to be the extreme undesirability
of the women as wives . . . immorality, more or less intemperance, dirti-
ness, wretched housekeeping, quarreling, and defiance of their husbands'

wishes."[54] Other, less racist reports deemed the new conditions of life in America responsible for the high rate of illegitimacy among immigrant populations. Even Theodore Roosevelt wrote extensively in support of contemporary "scientific" theories asserting the inherent inferiority of African-Americans and expressed his concerns about the dangers that higher African-American breeding rates posed to America.[55] The low birthrate among native whites was considered "race suicide," a term favored by Roosevelt. The fertility rate for white women had dropped from the nineteenth to the twentieth century, and many people, including Roosevelt, criticized working women for shirking their responsibilities as mothers and wives. Many supporters of mothers' pensions, again including Roosevelt, hoped that they would encourage native white families to meet the four-child quota that the president had set.[56]

The discourse and actions of many elite, liberal, well-educated reformers echoed the popular negative sentiments about immigrants.[57] One well regarded reformer, Florence Kelley,[58] a mother of the Children's Bureau and daughter of Congressman "Pig Iron" Kelley, commented in 1913,

> it is obvious that every nation profits by welcoming the victims of religious persecution (Huguenots, Waldensians, Pilgrims, Puritans, Quakers, even Mennonites, and Jews). But exactly how can we technically draw the line to get to admit the Russian Jews yet exclude the Catholic Slavs? . . . Surely our Yankee ingenuity ought to enable us to draw the difficult exclusion line above suggested. I am convinced that the Pacific Coast people are right about the Mongolians; and I am sure we are utter fools to endure the ruin of the Atlantic Coast by the invasion of Asia Minor and South Eastern Europe. My record of twenty-one years of intimate contact with the immigrants should safeguard me against any charge of race or religious prejudice in this.[59]

It seems incongruous that Kelley could support civil rights and be a member of the National Association for the Advancement of Colored People yet advocate racial exclusion. And while her comments must be considered relative to those of fellow Progressives, they speak volumes about the spectrum of race and racial dialogue and illuminate the significance of racism at this critical policy-building moment. Racism was so prevalent in society that even Progressive reformers saw no contradiction between racism and social reform.[60] Even if these leaders did not personally subscribe to doctrines of white racial superiority, their advocacy often promoted it.[61] In essence, this entire welfare network functioned within a racial system, and the advocacy of mothers' pensions, either explicitly or implicitly, strengthened that system.

Thus, political support and motivation for mothers' pensions was grounded not only on the sexist division of labor but on racial discrimination. Middle- and upper-class women were expected to maintain the home and the family while their husbands were the breadwinners. Many reformers echoed the public sentiment that women should not be both breadwinner and homemaker: it was important that women receive aid to prevent the disintegration of traditional family values and the contemporary division of labor.

These values applied implicitly to the white middle and upper classes. White U.S.-born, middle-class Protestant women advocated a social welfare policy that reflected their demographic makeup. As already discussed, the coalitions that supported mothers' pensions evolved out of and around various women's organizations that excluded nonwhites and comprised almost exclusively middle- and upper-class Protestant women. They sought to preserve Anglo-Saxon, Protestant values in female-headed white American households and to foster these same values in female-headed white foreign-born households. Neither poor, working-class white women nor African-American women of any class participated in the state-building aspect of this social welfare policy.

Not only did these coalitions of white women reject the African-American women's participation in welfare reform, but the rhetoric that they used in appealing for support for the pension programs was often couched in the context of white race preservation. The national mothers' pension network was homogenous in terms of class, religion, and ethnicity. All the advocates were white, and most were well-to-do. Almost all were of northern European, Protestant background and lived in the Northeast or Midwest.

The white women's welfare movement for the most part also rejected the participation of African-American reformers and women's clubs. White settlement houses and clubs remained largely off-limits to African-Americans, and the few settlements that accepted African-Americans were segregated. Some settlements opened separate branches for African-American reformers, and only a handful, such as the Henry Street Settlement House and Hull House, were open to both races. Many settlement workers decided that segregated facilities would be in the best interests of their African-American clientele.[62] When African-Americans moved into white immigrant neighborhoods, many settlements closed and moved away with the whites, conducted segregated activities, or just outright excluded African-Americans.[63]

African-American reformers such as Josephine St. Pierre Ruffin, the representative of the Woman's Era Club of Boston, were refused admission to GFWC conventions. A leading white reformer, Sophonisba Breckinridge, stated in 1933 that colored women's clubs were not welcome in the GFWC.[64] Although a few welfare reform efforts were interracial—for example, African-American reformers were finally included in the 1930 White House Conference on Children—this was the exception. The Children's Bureau had no African-American employees, and only a few reports even looked at minority groups such as African-Americans or Hispanics.

The African-American Welfare Reform Network

African-American female welfare reformers formed their own welfare movement, partially in response to white rejection and partially in response to developing demands that differed to some extent from those of the white reformers. The National Association of Colored Women (NACW) was the first organization of this developing African-American women's network as well as the first national civil rights organization. The African-American equivalent to the GFWC, the NACW had forty-five thousand members by 1911, and thousands more women belonged to NACW-affiliated clubs. Other African-American women's reform groups included the Federation of Colored Women's Clubs, the Negro Health Movement, the Negro Women's Club, and the National Council of Negro Women.[65] However, African-American women's activism coincided not with increased political and socioeconomic gains for African-Americans but with significant setbacks, including growing segregation and the "repeal" of Reconstruction Era political advances discussed previously. While white women were gaining the right to vote, the majority of African-Americans were disenfranchised.

These African-American reformers resembled their white counterparts in socioeconomic status—many came from prominent or prosperous African-American families and were highly educated. Unlike many of their white counterparts, however, many African-American reformers were married. Their careers did not constitute an alternative to marriage, to some degree as a result of economic necessity.[66] Although they were privileged in comparison to the African-American population as a whole, they were not nearly as well off as white reformers. Often because of fiscal necessity, African-American reformers expressed a favorable view of working women and female professionals while embracing the ideal of the male-breadwinner household.

A considerable difference also existed in the way that white and African-American reformers substantively viewed welfare reform. The first significant distinction between the two groups concerned education. For most white Americans, access to public education developed early; therefore, white reformers did not see education as welfare. African-Americans, however, had few educational opportunities and consequently viewed education as part of welfare or antipoverty efforts. The African-American welfare reformers' emphasis on education is evident in the fact that most of the women in this network had taught at one point and that a significant percentage were professional educators. A great deal of their energy went toward establishing schools from primary levels through college.[67]

The most significant difference between the two reform groups was African-American reformers' advocacy of universalistic welfare programs. Although African-American reformers did not entirely reject the distinction between deserving and undeserving poor, the programs they proposed were, for the most part, open to all. Although many programs were targeted to the "worthy" poor, African-American reformers were more concerned than white reformers about the misuse of funds and about beneficiaries' ability to contribute something. Most welfare programs run by African-American reformers were not means-tested. Furthermore, they were mostly contributory—that is, recipients had to pay monthly dues for a health insurance program.[68] White reformers' predilection for means-testing, supervision, and the distinction between deserving and undeserving poor could no doubt be partially explained by racial distinctions. African-American reformers did not share their white counterparts' view that immigrants and African-Americans lacked morals and proper work habits. African-American welfare reformers distanced themselves from disreputable individuals but did not make condescending distinctions between themselves and those they helped, as the white reformers did. Consequently, participants in the African-American movement had a different attitude about class and the poor than did the white welfare reformers.

Although reformers of both races shared the belief that poor women needed moral and technical support, African-American reformers were likely better to understand the structural origins of poverty. Segregated housing often resulted in middle- and upper-class African-Americans living in close proximity to poor and working-class African-Americans and consequently becoming more familiar with systemic determinants of poverty than their white counterparts. African-American reformers, therefore, did not focus their work on remedying racially tinged individual "character defects." Furthermore, many African-American activists understood that their fate was connected to the fate of the poor masses. According to Mary Church Terrell, a highly educated and wealthy African-American woman, "self-preservation demands that [African-American women] go among the lowly, illiterate and even the vicious, to whom they are bound by ties of race and sex . . . to reclaim them."[69] Progress, defined by culture, education, and opportunity, took on a special meaning for these African-American reformers.

New Deal–era civil rights groups echoed the call for universalist programs rather than means-tested assistance. In particular, these activists believed that means-tested assistance would be regarded as undeserved and that those dependent on it would be stigmatized and considered inferior to those on universal welfare programs such as social insurance. Furthermore, civil rights advocates were concerned that this means-tested assistance would result in the continued dependency and subordination of the African-American population.[70]

Framing the Mothers' Pension Debate in Racial Terms

Reflecting prevailing racist sentiments, a significant number of leading white reformers and white women's organizations framed the debate over mother's pensions in terms of race preservation.[71] Multiple strands of racial rhetoric existed at that time. On the one hand was a discourse against African-Americans, while on the other was a discourse against ethnic or immigrant groups. A great deal of the turn-of-the-century argument in favor of racial purity was aimed at immigrant groups. In many ways, the effective exclusion of African-Americans from mainstream social life was taken for granted; as a result, the subject of African-Americans rarely entered these debates.

Social reformers were well in tune with the philosophy of racial purity, and their positions ran the gamut from veiled to explicit racism. Rheta Childe Dorr said in 1918 that "woman's work is race preservation, race improvement, and who opposes her, or interferes with her simply fights nature, and nature never loses her battle."[72] Beatrice Forbes-Robertson Hale claimed that not all women were equipped to be mothers, saying in 1914 that "there will naturally always be a large number of women in whom the conserving, building quality of the mother is absent. Not every woman is born to be a mother, either physically or socially."[73] Other reformers more explicitly denounced the cultures of other races. Annie Marion MacLean stated that "Americans generally avail themselves of opportunities for self-improvement to a greater extent than the foreigners."[74] She also claimed that the Slavic races "have brought over to this country the manners and customs of a lower civilization and . . . are living under conditions which tend to perpetuate their civilization instead of raising them to a higher level."[75]

The National Congress of Mothers was also both an ardent supporter of mothers' pensions and an active participant in the crusade against the threat of white race suicide. For congress members, the mothers' pension reform offered a neat solution by countering the trend of lower white birthrates while recognizing the public service of motherhood. In an article in the organization's magazine, *Child Welfare*, a member wrote, "the decline in the birth rate may force the time when the state will give honorable recognition to motherhood."[76]

Because of the existing political climate, even those reformers who would have been more inclined to include African-Americans in the purview of mothers' pensions were unable to do so. To guarantee legislative support for these programs, advocates had to stress the respectability and high quality of the recipients. African-American women, for the most part, could not be considered eligible recipients because in the minds of the reformers they threatened not only program standards but essential political and social program support.

One result of the exclusion of African-Americans from the mothers' pension movement was that no real forum existed for communication between white and African-American reformers. Consequently, white reformers remained ignorant of the problems facing the African-American population, resulting in inaccurate and prejudiced conclusions and a national welfare movement designed to impose white, middle-class norms on a population deemed worthy of assistance only if it embraced the superiority of this white middle-class culture. An unavoidable consequence was that the legislation and administration of these programs excluded many who were deemed unfit because of their culture, religion, or color. The effective exclusion of African-Americans, nonwhite immigrants, and the poor from the mother's pension movement reflected the goals of the movement—to assist working- and middle-class white women. The goal of preserving and protecting white, middle-class values was institutionalized in the various state mothers' pension laws that were enacted from 1911 to 1932.

4

Mothers' Pension Legislation

Exclusion by Statute

Children of parents of worthy character, suffering from
temporary misfortune and children of reasonably
efficient and deserving mothers who are without the
support of the normal breadwinner, should, as a rule,
be kept with their parents, such aid being given as may
be necessary to maintain suitable homes for the rearing
of children.
—White House Conference on Children, 1909[1]

I would say that the immorality of the mother has no
rational connection with the need of her children under
any welfare program.
—1968[2]

THE RAPID-FIRE SUCCESS OF the mothers' pension movement is
evident in how quickly states adopted enabling legislation. A few states
had adopted provisions of some form or another to care for dependent
children before the creation of mothers' pensions or widow relief. As
already mentioned, in 1898 the New York legislature passed a bill (later
vetoed) granting an allowance to widowed mothers equal to the state's cost
for institutionalizing their children. Oklahoma provided educational funds
for indigent children of widows in 1908, and Michigan did so in 1911. Missouri became the first state to provide for the care of dependent children
in their own homes using municipal funds.[3] With 1911's Illinois Funds to
Parents Act, that state became the first in the nation to officially accept responsibility for dependent children and to adopt a program to aid poor
children in their own homes,[4] and mothers' pension critics and advocates
alike scrutinized the new program.[5] Lessons learned from the Illinois "experiment," such as refining eligibility requirements, were incorporated
into subsequent legislation in Illinois and other states. No other mothers'
pension programs were established until 1913, when eighteen more states

legislated programs to protect poor children in their own homes. In 1913, twenty-seven of the forty-two state legislatures in session considered a mothers' pension law. By 1920, forty states had enacted legislation; fifteen years later, all states except Georgia and South Carolina had adopted some form of mothers' pension legislation, as had the territories of Alaska, Hawaii, and Puerto Rico.

Regional and state differences existed in the degree of liberalness or stringency of the mothers' pension legislation and were reflected in eligibility, citizenship, and residency requirements; "fitness" and other moral/behavioral criteria; specification of poverty; benefit levels; financing; administration; and the degree of state supervision. Regional differentiation is important for this analysis of the disproportionate exclusion of African-Americans from the benefit rolls. In 1920, 79 percent of the U.S. African-American population lived in the eleven former Confederate states. Any variations in benefit legislation and administration in the South from the national average would have disproportionately affected the African-American population.

This chapter examines the differences in the timing of the adoption of legislation, level of administrative responsibility, benefit levels, and conditions for receiving aid, demonstrating that these variations are explained primarily by the regions' different racial compositions and social status accorded African-Americans. The racial differentiation that characterized the mothers' pension movement manifested itself in mothers' pension legislation. This chapter also considers the timing of the enactment of state mothers' pension laws relative to a state's African-American population and to other factors such as urban population and per capita income. For the purposes of this analysis, unless otherwise noted, the following states are defined as southern: Alabama, Arkansas, Florida, Georgia, Kentucky, Louisiana, Mississippi, North Carolina, Oklahoma, South Carolina, Tennessee, Texas, and Virginia. Oklahoma and Kentucky are included because their mothers' pension legislation more reflects the pattern followed by the southern states than by the midwestern states.

Regional Differences

An examination of regional population data and income measures provides a snapshot of the landscape within which mothers' pension laws were enacted. The Progressive Era should be understood in terms not only of its pathbreaking social welfare movements but also of the unprecedented levels of legal and civil sanctions imposed on the African-American and immigrant communities. Nativist movements occurred primarily in northern, urban regions, and anti-African-American movements prospered primarily in the South. The following data illustrate differences between the South and other regions along important demographic variables, such as child population, urban and African-American composition, and income. These measures illustrate significant differences between the South and other regions in the 1920s, the formative years of mothers' pensions. The tables and regression models are located in the appendix.

During the early 1900s a statistically significant difference ($p < .01$) existed across regions in the percentage of children in the population who were fourteen or younger. The percentage was significantly higher in the South than in other regions. A greater number of children combined with lower per capita income would indicate a greater need for mothers' pension program expenditures in the South than in other regions of the United States.

A statistically significant difference ($p < .01$) also existed in state per capita income among the regions. Mean state per capita income in the South was also statistically lower than in other regions. Alternate hypotheses suggest that a state's wealth was key to the establishment of social welfare legislation. However, as the data discussed later demonstrate, state per capita income did not affect the enactment of mothers' pension legislation.

The mean percentage state urban population in the East was significantly ($p < .01$) higher than in other regions. The South had the lowest percentage urban population. State urbanization did not affect the timing of mothers' pension legislative enactments but did affect the stipulated grant amount. Also compared to other regions, the South had a much lower mean percentage urban African-American population ($p < .01$) than the other regions. The South's African-American population was predominantly rural, affecting African-Americans' access to mothers' pension benefits, since there were fewer programs and lower grant amounts in rural areas. The percentage of the state population that was African-American was significantly higher ($p < .01$) in the South than in other regions. The magnitude of a state's African-American population negatively affected the enactment of mothers' pension laws; the higher the African-American population, the later the laws were enacted.

Table 4 details the African-American population of the southern states as a percentage of the total U.S. African-American population. The distribution of the African-American population in the South is important

TABLE 4.   Southern African-American Population as a Percentage of Total U.S. African-American Population, 1920

	Southern African-American Population	U.S. African-American Population (%)
Alabama	901,000	8.85
Arkansas	472,000	4.64
Florida	329,000	3.23
Georgia	1,206,000	11.84
Louisiana	700,000	6.87
Mississippi	935,000	9.18
North Carolina	763,000	7.49
South Carolina	865,000	8.49
Tennessee	452,000	4.44
Texas	742,000	7.29
Virginia	690,000	6.78
Total Southern African-American population	8,055,000	79.10
Total U.S. African-American population	10,183,131	
African-American population in U.S. (%)		9.60

Source: Data from U.S. Department of Commerce, Bureau of the Census, *Fourteenth Census of the United States* (1920).

Note: Only the eleven Confederate states are included in the tabulation of the southern population here. Kentucky and Oklahoma are not included.

when considering their depressed economic and social position in that region.

Regional Differentiation in Adoption of Laws

Before considering the content of the various mothers' pension laws, the timing of the enactment of mothers' pension legislation is illustrative. Table 5 details the timing of initial mothers' pension legislation by region and state, which is significant for the program's evolution. In particular, states with longer histories of mothers' pension administration were more efficient in the administration of Aid to Dependent Children after that program was created.[6] By 1913, almost all northeastern and midwestern states with significant industrial centers had enacted mothers' pension legislation. Only New York lagged behind until 1915. The first southern states to adopt mothers' pensions were Oklahoma and Tennessee in 1915. Arkansas followed in 1916, Texas in 1917, and Florida in 1919. However, the Deep South states did not pass legislation until at least the 1920s: Louisiana in 1920, Mississippi in 1928, and Alabama in 1931—ten to fifteen years after their northern counterparts. Furthermore, the only two states not to have mothers' pensions by the New Deal were southern: Georgia and South Carolina. Before the first southern state had enacted legislation, almost half of the states in each of the other regions had enacted legislation.

An analysis of variance (ANOVA) finds a statistically significant difference ($p < .05$) among the regions in the mean year in which mothers' pension legislation was first enacted. The mean year for the South is significantly later than the other regions. There is a statistically significant correlation ($.723, p < .01$) between the percentage African-American population in a state and the year of initial legislation for the care of dependent children. This correlation is present when controlling for region ($.658$,

TABLE 5.   Enactment of Mothers' Pension Legislation by Year and Region

Year	South	Midwest	West	East
1911		Illinois		
1913		Iowa	California	Massachusetts
		Michigan	Colorado	New Hampshire
		Minnesota	Idaho	New Jersey
		Nebraska	Nevada	Pennsylvania
		Ohio	Oregon	
		South Dakota	Utah	
		Wisconsin	Washington	
1914			Arizona	
1915	Oklahoma	Kansas	Montana	New York
	Tennessee	North Dakota	Wyoming	
		West Virginia		
1916				Maryland
1917	Arkansas	Missouri	Alaska	Delaware
	Texas			Maine
				Maryland
				Vermont
1918	Virginia			
1919	Florida	Indiana	Hawaii	Connecticut
1920	Louisiana			
1923	North Carolina			Rhode Island
1926				District of Columbia
1928	Kentucky			
	Mississippi			
1931	Alabama		New Mexico	
Never	Georgia			
	South Carolina			

Source: Public Aid, 1934; Mothers' Aid, 1931.

$p < .$ oɪ). At the regional level, this correlation is statistically significant only in the South (.630, $p < .$ o5).

To determine the probabilities of a particular state or region enacting mothers' pension legislation, two logistic regression models were estimated. The results of one model show that the percentage African-American population is significantly correlated ($p < .$ oɪ) with the timing of legislation to aid dependent children. The higher the African-American population in a state, the later legislation was enacted. This model is significant ($p < .$ oɪ) and accounts for approximately 50 percent of the variance in the year of legislative enactment. Alternate hypotheses contend that a state's wealth (measured by per capita income) and urbanization are key factors in social welfare development.[7] This model shows that neither of these factors was significant in the enactment of mothers' pension legislation. It is significant that region, independent of race, is not statistically significant. This indicates that region is important because of race: the meaning of region is deeply racial. In the second model, the percentage African-American proportion of a state was the most powerful independent variable. States with higher percentages of African-Americans had a higher probability of not enacting mothers' pension legislation. Although per capita income is significant, its effect is minimal. The significance of the 1934 data year is that controlling for earlier data periods, the probability of states enacting legislation increased with time.

Legislation

Mothers' aid legislation varied from state to state in terms of eligibility criteria, benefit levels, administration, and financing.[8] The Children's Bureau was very concerned about the variability in state laws, and when communicating with different state entities, bureau personnel encouraged the adoption of certain legislative standards based on the success and failure of mothers' aid laws in other jurisdictions. Evidence indicates extensive communication between the bureau and administering or legislative bodies for the sole purpose of encouraging amendments to existing state legislation that would make the bills conform to the bureau's standards. In some instances, the bureau even drafted legislation on behalf of jurisdictions.[9]

For the purposes of this analysis, I have organized the various provisions in the legislation establishing mothers' pensions into five topics: (1) local administration of programs; (2) eligible recipients of aid; (3) program financing; (4) pension or aid amount; and (5) conditions for receiving aid. This analysis supports the position that the states' mothers' pension legislation provided great latitude for local administrators to implement the programs to reflect local, often prejudicial, norms. The permissiveness of the state legislation resulted in the intrusive and arbitrary monitoring of recipients, nonstandardized grants, arbitrary determinations of eligibility, and the exclusion of poor African-American mothers, who were not considered suitable by local standards.

Local Administration of Programs

Broad variation occurred in the degree to which state mothers' pension laws were enforced or monitored. One significant aspect of the mothers' pension legislation was the extent to which the state laws were compulsory on the counties. In many ways, the essential weakness in the mothers' aid programs lay in the fact that most state laws were permissive instead of mandatory,[10] allowing localities to choose whether they wanted to have mothers' pension programs. Furthermore, most laws did not mandate state supervision. In 1926, only sixteen of the forty-two states with mothers' aid laws required some form of state monitoring.[11] In 1934, on the eve of the Social Security Act, thirty-seven of forty-five states continued to entrust the administration to local units with no provisions for state supervision.[12]

In the beginning, most programs were administered locally by juvenile courts, the agencies in most states with the longest histories of dealing with the care of dependent children. These courts had an existing bureaucracy and responsibility for dependent children that was an outgrowth of other child-saving movements during the Progressive Era. In several states, such as New York, Illinois, Wisconsin, and California, juvenile court judges became important advocates of mothers' pension laws. By 1928, all but two states had established juvenile court systems, facilitating the role of the state as *"parens patriae."*[13] However, many advocates of mothers' pensions opposed the administration of these programs by juvenile courts. In 1912, C. C. Carstens, director of the Child Welfare League of America, conducted an investigation for the Russell Sage Foundation on the administration of mothers' pensions, concluding that having juvenile courts administer these laws was inadvisable.[14] Carstens did not support leaving the administration of the programs to the courts in part because of the difficulty in developing standards for the administration of the same law among different courts.[15] His opinion was echoed by juvenile court judges, including Judge Merritt W. Pickney, often considered the founder of the mothers' pension movement in Illinois. Pickney commented that "the administration of this law by the Juvenile Court was from the very beginning attended with difficulties"[16] because the courts lost sight of the intent of the law—to keep children at home. Nevertheless, the majority of state pension programs in 1914 were administered by juvenile courts or other county courts.[17] In 1926, twenty state programs were administered by juvenile courts. In five states a county or city board with other functions administered the programs. In twelve states, mothers' pensions were handled as part of the local poor-relief system. In Delaware, the program was administered by a state agency, and in New Hampshire, it was administered by the local school boards. In only three of the forty-two states that had programs in 1926 (New York, Pennsylvania, and Rhode Island) was a county board established with the specific function of administering mothers' aid.[18] Delegating the enforcement and administration of the mothers' pension programs to local agencies eliminated the possibility of establishing impartial standards both within and across state lines. However, the trend was away from court administration and toward county and state board administration of the programs with no relationship to the courts.[19] By 1934, only fourteen states gave the responsibility for local administration to the juvenile courts, special local agencies were responsible for administration in seven states, and fourteen states left administration to poor-relief officials.[20]

Another problem in administering mothers' pension programs was individual counties' levels of autonomy. For example, in Illinois in 1926, each county was a separate, independent administrative unit. The courts were autonomous within the counties. Consequently, the judge of the juvenile court had the right to grant or refuse pensions if he disapproved of the law, regardless of whether funds had been appropriated by the county supervisors.[21]

A bivariate analysis of program administration as outlined in the legislation shows significant differences ($p < .01$) among the regions. The majority of programs in the South were administered at the local level. All of the programs in the Midwest and the majority of the programs in the West were also administered locally. The East differs significantly from the other regions, however, with the majority of the programs administered with some level of state participation.

Corresponding to the level of administration, the legislation stipulated the degree of state supervision. Significant regional differences existed in state supervision ($p < .05$). The results of a bivariate analysis show almost all mothers' pension programs in the East had state supervision, whereas the majority of programs in the South, Midwest, and West had either no state supervision or required only that administrative units submit annual reports to the state.

The significance of the locus of administration and the degree of state supervision lies in the leeway with which administrators could implement programs to reflect local, parochial norms. Although the percentage of state supervision in the West and Midwest was small relative to the East, the number of African-Americans in these regions was minimal. In the South, where the majority of the U.S. African-American population lived, 90 percent of mothers' pension programs were administered locally, and 60 percent had no state supervision. Across the nation, this meant that the majority of mothers' pension programs could be tailored to prevailing race relations. In the South, the group primarily affected by this local administration would be African-Americans, while in the West and to some extent the Midwest, Mexicans, Native Americans, and Asians would be affected

The procedures for obtaining aid and regulatory requirements also varied across states and regions. Generally, either a potentially eligible mother or a "reputable" citizen who knew and cared about a particular case was allowed to apply for the benefit.[22] In most states, the law required an investigation of each applicant to determine eligibility, character of the home, and the amount of aid required. In general, oversight of the families that were granted aid was conducted in accordance with the principles of social casework.[23] In most cases, local officials conducted the supervisory visits, which usually occurred between four and twelve times per year. State agent visits occasionally supplemented those by local administrators.[24] These visits sought primarily to determine whether aid was no longer necessary or the home was no longer suitable; they were not conducted to ensure that laws were properly implemented or that adequate relief was being provided.

The local agencies and investigators retained considerable discretion in determining mothers' pension eligibility, grant amounts, and case administration. Selection to receive a pension and to continue on the pension rolls was left to the judgment of the investigator. No mechanism existed, however, for ensuring that the investigators were competent. When the National Resources Planning Board reviewed the mother's pension programs, it claimed that "many were not entrusted to qualified personnel."[25]

In summary, the latitude granted to the local administrative agencies enabled localities to tailor the administration of the program to local norms and prejudices. In many states, especially in the South, this meant that the legislation permitted local administrators to exclude African-American families from mothers' pensions.

Eligible Aid Recipients

A mother's marital status was a mechanism for screening out "undesirable" mothers from the mothers' pension benefit. From the beginning, mothers' pension programs intended to benefit widowed mothers and were often referred to as widows' aid or widows' pensions. According to the Children's Bureau, "the central idea in the theory and early discussion of aid to dependent children in their own homes and the most common inclusion in the earlier laws was aid to widows."[26] However, states varied in their inclusion of other dependent women in the pension programs, and some states permitted guardians other than mothers to receive benefits.

In 1914, Colorado's and Nebraska's mothers' pension laws applied to any "proper" parent. In Nevada, grandparents were considered acceptable guardians, and in Wisconsin aid could go to any parent or guardian. In all other states in that year, aid was available only to the mothers of the children in need.[27] By 1922, eleven states and territories permitted pensions to be paid to dependent children's guardians other than mothers.[28] In 1929, fifteen states plus the territory of Hawaii and the District of Columbia permitted pensions to be paid to other guardians,[29] and by 1934 that number had increased to sixteen states plus Alaska, Hawaii, and the District of Columbia.[30]

In some states, mothers who were divorced; whose husbands were in prison, in insane asylums, or incapacitated; or whose husbands had deserted were also eligible. In 1914, all states required that mothers be married or widowed, except for Michigan, which funded unmarried or divorced recipients.[31] By 1922, only Connecticut, Maryland, New Jersey, Texas, and Utah specified that only widowed mothers could receive aid;[32] by 1934, only Connecticut made that specification.[33]

In 1922, seven states plus the territory of Alaska had laws specifying that divorcées were eligible.[34] In 1929, Florida and North Carolina expanded their laws to include divorced mothers,[35] and New Mexico, Texas, and Utah did so in 1934.[36] In many states where the laws did not specify divorced mothers as eligible, deserted or abandoned mothers were eligible.

Deserted women were eligible for benefits in four states in 1914, seventeen states plus Hawaii in 1922,[37] twenty-two states and territories in 1929,[38] and thirty-six states and territories in 1934.[39] State laws varied regarding the length of time fathers had to have been away from their family before the mothers became eligible, ranging from three months in Kansas and Minnesota to three years in Ohio.[40] Women whose husbands were incapacitated, imprisoned, or in insane asylums were eligible for benefits in twenty-nine states and territories in 1922,[41] thirty-one states and territories in 1929,[42] and thirty-seven states and territories by 1934.[43]

For the most part, legislators saw unmarried mothers as morally unfit and consequently excluded them from the programs. Only Michigan in 1914 and Hawaii, Nebraska, and Tennessee in 1922 specifically authorized aid to unmarried mothers.[44] By 1934, only Alaska had expanded its law to include unmarried mothers.[45] On the eve of the New Deal, therefore, mothers' pensions were available to unmarried mothers in only three states and two territories. In some states, a mother with an illegitimate child could not get assistance for her legitimate children.[46] This eligibility condition affected African-American families more than white families because the former had higher illegitimate birthrates. In 1921, the illegitimate birthrate per 100 live births was 1.4 for whites and 12.5 for blacks; eleven years later, the numbers reached 2.07 and 15.7, respectively. The Bureau of the Census estimated that 84,500 illegitimate births occurred in the United States in 1932, of which 39,000 were white children and the majority of the remainder were African-Americans.[47] In 1940 the illegitimate birthrate per 100 live births for women between ages fifteen and forty-four was 3.6 for whites and 35.6 for African-Americans.[48] Consequently, these provisions had the potential to disproportionately exclude African-American mothers on the basis of their marital status.

Consistent with the primary aim of mothers' pension programs, all states stipulating marital status criteria allowed widows to receive benefits across the years. However, the distributions for the mothers with other marital statuses reveal interesting regional variations. After widows, deserted mothers fared best, receiving mothers' pension benefits in almost half of the states in all regions. Divorced mothers were not allowed benefits in any eastern states and in only thirteen states in other regions. Unmarried mothers received benefits in only six states.

Some states did not specify whether deserted, divorced, or unmarried mothers were ineligible or eligible, enacting laws sufficiently vague that benefits could be awarded according to local administrators' judgments. For example, in 1922 Nevada's and New Hampshire's laws made eligible any mother "who is dependent upon her own efforts to support herself and family." North Dakota made eligible "any woman with one or more children dependent upon her for support." Washington made eligible "any needy mother."[49]

Finally, the definition of "dependent" child varied from state to state. In most states in 1912, "dependent" included neglected as well as dependent poor children. Children considered dependent in some states would have been classified as juvenile delinquents in others.[50]

Program Financing

Most states legislated that the financing of mothers' pensions would come from local taxes. In 1915, all states except for Pennsylvania, Wisconsin, California, and Massachusetts funded the programs out of county treasuries. In 1922, thirty states and territories funded the programs through county/city resources alone, and ten funded the programs jointly by state and locality. Arizona and New Hampshire picked up the entire cost of their programs.[51] By 1926, twenty-seven of forty-two states still financed the programs from county resources alone, and thirteen states shared expenses with localities. Arizona and New Hampshire remained the only two states to finance the entire cost of the programs.[52] By 1934, seventeen states had authorized state contributions,[53] but appropriations were made in only fourteen of these states, and in five the state's contribution was so small that it was insignificant. State expenditures for these fourteen states totaled approximately $5.6 million, while county expenditures in forty-three states added up to six times that amount.[54] In 1934 total expenditures for mothers' aid amounted to $37,487,479, of which only $5,865,522 (16 percent) came from state funds, while the remaining $31,621,957 came from local tax funds. In nine states, states picked up almost half of all costs.[55] Again, only in Arizona and New Hampshire did the state bear the entire cost of the program.[56]

The source of the funding for mothers' pension programs differed significantly ($p < .05$) among the regions. The East had a much lower mean percentage of programs funded only by localities than did other regions. By contrast, the South, Midwest, and West had very few programs funded through state and local collaboration and no programs funded by the state alone.

Pension or Aid Amount

Almost all statutes established a maximum allowable pension. The legislated maximum grant varied greatly across states, as did the formulas used to calculate the allowance. The amount of the total family allowance was determined not only by the number of eligible children in a family but also by what the laws considered other income contributions to the family made by relatives or the earnings of family members themselves.

Other amounts were based on the cost of maintaining a child in a state or county home. Significantly, the variation in pension amount appears to correlate with geographical region. This variation intensified benefit disparities between African-Americans and whites. In 1922, the maximum monthly allowance for one child ranged from eight dollars (Vermont) to forty dollars (Michigan) and for each additional child ranged from four dollars (Texas) to fifteen dollars (Illinois).[57] These grant amounts changed little from 1922 to 1934. In 1934 the range for one child remained the same, while the range for each additional child spread from five dollars (several states) to sixteen dollars (Oregon).[58]

Most states required the pension recipients to submit monthly budget estimates to the courts to test the adequacy of the pension grants. In 1926 the maximum available monthly allowance for a family with three children was fifty to seventy dollars in eight states, forty to forty-nine dollars in seven states, thirty to thirty-nine dollars in ten states, and twenty to twenty-nine dollars in ten states. Eleven states had a maximum for a family of any size that ranged between forty and sixty dollars per month.[59] By 1931, the maximum monthly allowance for a family of three had reached sixty to seventy dollars in four states, fifty to fifty-nine dollars in five states, forty to forty-nine dollars in nine states, thirty to thirty-nine dollars in eight states, and twenty to twenty-nine dollars in seven states. Four states permitted additional funds under certain circumstances.[60]

In 1931 the actual average monthly allowances given to a family ranged from $4.33 in Arkansas to $69.31 in Massachusetts. In the eleven states that had no limitations on the maximum family allowance, the average grant amounts varied from $11.11 in Mississippi to $69.31 in Massachusetts. A 1931 Children's Bureau report concluded that no relation existed between the statutory limitations on the grants and the actual amounts awarded.[61] In most states, the actual grant amount fell below the statutory maximum. A multiple regression confirms that the legal grant limitations did not constitute a statistically significant determinant of the actual grant awarded.[62]

Annual per capita expenditures for mothers' pensions also varied from state to state and region to region. Figure 1 illustrates the clustering of southern state per capita expenditures at the lower end of the spectrum.

A difference of means of regional per capita mothers' pension expenditures indicates a statistically significant ($p < .05$) difference between the South and the other regions. The mean annual per capita mothers' pension expenditure in the South was four times lower than in other regions.

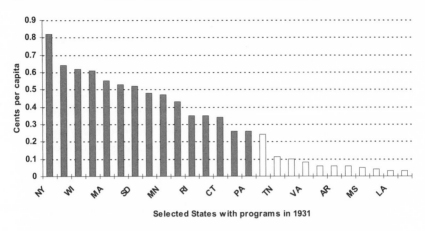

Fig. 1.   Annual per capita expenditure for mothers' pensions. (Data from U.S. Department of Labor, Children's Bureau, *Mothers' Aid—1931*, 15.)

Conditions for Receiving Aid

Another factor that led to the arbitrary and unequal disbursement of aid was the set of legal conditions that a potential beneficiary or recipient had to meet and maintain for eligibility. Mothers' pension benefits were not extended to all mothers or, by extension, all children. States were free to decide who qualified for pension benefits and under what conditions. The criteria included level of poverty or dependency, age of the dependent children, residency and citizenship, and the "suitable home" requirement.

ECONOMIC NEED

Most states stipulated that recipients had to be entirely dependent on their own resources for support and that they had to have no other sources of income. For example, many state laws specifically prohibited ownership of property or had provisions limiting the amount of property that could be owned. For example, a Nebraska mother could not receive aid if she was the owner of real or personal property worth more that two thousand dollars.[63] In 1922, eleven states had laws that specified that mothers could not own real property, specified the value of real property that mothers could own, stipulated that mothers could not have relatives who could provide support, and/or specified that mothers could not be employed in manufacturing occupations.[64] In 1929 the laws of twelve states plus the District of Columbia made these stipulations.[65] In 1934, sixteen states and territories stipulated the amount and value of property a mother could hold.[66] In six states, laws stipulated that eligible children had to be "without property sufficient for own support."[67] Almost all the laws required that mothers be unable properly to support their children.

While acknowledging that the grant amounts were not sufficient to support a family, the state laws gave local administrators the power to approve the type and amount of work mothers could do outside of the home. Advocates saw the explicit purpose of mothers' pensions as to provide grants that enabled mothers not to have to find employment outside their homes and thereby to avoid neglecting their children. However, the laws—specifically, the maximum family allowances—made it almost impossible for a family to survive without the mother seeking outside employment. The eleven states listed earlier (see note 64) recognized this goal and legislated the type of employment permitted.

AGE OF DEPENDENT CHILD

In all states, another condition for eligibility was the age of dependent children. Legislators were eventually compelled to have the maximum age for aid conform with the laws regulating compulsory school attendance and child labor. In 1926, the maximum age limit varied from fourteen to seventeen years. In twenty-five states, aid could be granted until children reached age sixteen.[68]

In 1934, only Colorado set its upper limit at eighteen, while most states and territories permitted benefits for children under sixteen and Florida, Nevada, New Jersey, Ohio, and Wisconsin stipulated that aid could be continued past that age for children who were physically or mentally incapacitated or in emergency/special situations.[69] Arkansas, Idaho, North Dakota, and Washington permitted aid to children under fifteen. Finally, ten states permitted aid only until the age of fourteen,[70] although Kentucky, Maryland, Oregon, Pennsylvania, Rhode Island, and West Virginia permitted aid to continue until age sixteen if the child was ineligible for employment and/or if the child was in school with a satisfactory record.[71] No statistically significant differences existed across regions in the maximum age of qualifying children.

RESIDENCY & CITIZENSHIP

Anti-immigrant sentiment, coupled with strict immigration laws, resulted in rigid citizenship requirements in the various mothers' pension statutes.

A 1926 Children's Bureau study showed that the requirements ranged
from a minimum of one year in the county to citizenship in the United
States together with five years' residence in the state and two years in the
county. In thirty-two of the forty-two states with programs in 1926, residence in the local political unit for periods ranging from six months to
five years was required. In thirty-nine of the forty-two states, legal state
residency was required, although the requirement varied from one to five
years. In five states, the fathers had to have been a resident of the state at
the time of their death or incapacitation for mothers to receive aid. In
California and Illinois, recipients had to be U.S. citizens, while eleven
states provided that recipients either had to be citizens or had to declare
their intention to become citizens.[72]

In 1934, the laws of six states and territories—Arizona, Arkansas, Connecticut, Puerto Rico, Rhode Island,[73] and West Virginia—required that
the applicants be citizens of the United States. Seven states and territories—the District of Columbia, Illinois, Minnesota, Mississippi, Montana,
New York, and North Dakota—required applicants to be citizens, to
have applied for citizenship, or to have legally declared their intention to
become citizens. In addition, all states had some jurisdictional residency
requirement. Many states had state residency requirements, ranging
from one year (Arizona) to five years in the state immediately preceding
the application (Maine). Either in addition or instead, most states had
county residency requirements, ranging from six months (Idaho) to five
years (New Jersey).[74] These residency and citizenship requirements effectively excluded many immigrants and migrants from the mothers'
pension programs.

The Progressive Era saw incredible changes in the distribution of the
nation's population. Many African-Americans were migrating to the North
and the Midwest, and immigrants were arriving en masse on the American
shores. Although many of the eligibility conditions that potentially excluded African-Americans were more prominent in the South, residency
requirements could adversely affect African-Americans and immigrants in
the North and Midwest as much as in the South.

The "Suitable Home" Provision

The legal condition that had the greatest potential to result in the biased
distribution of benefits was the vaguely defined condition related to the
suitability of the recipient's home. Early mothers' pension advocates had
stressed the importance of distinguishing between suitable and unsuitable

homes and fit and unfit mothers. In 1918, Florence Nesbitt articulated this view, stating that mothers' pension programs could

> not possibly be considered worth the expenditure of public funds un-
> less there can be reasonable assurance that children will have a home
> which will provide at least the conditions necessary to make possible
> a moral, physical and mental development. Ill-trained, ill-nourished
> children, predisposed to crime and disease, growing into a stunted,
> ineffective adulthood, are a serious liability, not an asset to society.
> Perpetuating homes which produce such results would be both un-
> charitable and unwise.[75]

Provisions regarding suitability granted administrators the right to subjectively determine applicants' eligibility. In practice, this provision permitted local, parochial norms instead of some standard of economic need
ultimately to determine eligibility. According to the Children's Bureau in
1933, "one qualification for eligibility as expressed in the statutes of all
but one of the States (Maryland) having a mothers' aid law is that the
mother shall be a proper person to have the care of her children, and in
a number of States a further requirement is made that the home shall be
a satisfactory place for the rearing of children."[76] Julia Lathrop, head of
the Children's Bureau, stated that "in most of the laws the requirement is
made that the mother is a fit person, morally and physically, to bring up
her children and that it is for the welfare of the child to remain at
home."[77] Because the concept of a fit mother was outlined only vaguely in
state-level policy, local authorities could apply their own judgments of fitness to reflect the type of mothers to receive assistance. Because mothers'
pensions were financed primarily through local funds, local authorities
were not under any legal obligation to fund mothers that state legislation
deemed eligible. The definition of a "fit" or "suitable" mother was de-
rived from white, middle-class standards and functioned to structure the
behavior of poor mothers.[78]

Independent of parochial norms and prejudices, mothers' pension investigators had difficulty administering the vague "fit mother" and "suitable
home" eligibility condition. Certain aspects of this fitness condition were
more tangible than others. Most state statutes offered two guidelines for
determining eligibility: (1) eligibility was defined in terms of the father and
family unit—whether he was dead, was imprisoned, was mentally ill, was
physically incapacitated, or had deserted his family and whether the parents were divorced, separated, or unmarried; and (2) eligibility required
that the mother be physically, mentally, and morally fit to maintain

custody of her children. By 1934, very similar suitability language appeared in the statutes of all states with mothers' pension programs except Arizona, California, and Maryland.[79] For example, Idaho, Illinois, Missouri, New Hampshire, Ohio, South Dakota, and Utah established that a "suitable" mother could not work regularly away from the home. The amount of time defined as "regular" varied from state to state. Other requirements of moral and physical fitness were more ambiguous. Homemaking abilities and moral character were often the basis for making judgments of a mother's fitness. In some states, a mother's nationality or degree of commitment to American values was thought to reflect her fitness as a mother. Most states kept records on recipients' countries of birth. Minnesota mothers were required to speak English at home.[80] Several states forbade "suitable" recipients from having male boarders or lodgers,[81] and others required mothers to foster their children's religion. Some states, such as Pennsylvania and West Virginia, required satisfactory school reports from dependent children's teachers.[82] Investigators in many states were required to report on the decorations, furnishings, and general condition of potential recipients' homes. One investigator's manual pointed out that "it will be readily seen that the pauper type of woman is not the kind intended for Mothers' Aid."[83]

White advocates of mothers' aid championed standards of the suitable mother and home. Consistent with the intent of mothers' pension advocates, legislators wanted to distinguish the mothers' pension programs from poor relief and therefore sought to aid only those mothers considered respectable and worthy. The ambiguity of the fitness and suitability conditions enabled program administrators to discriminate on the basis of race and class. In the short run, the "suitability" criterion allowed the greatest leeway for program administrators to exclude African-Americans from mothers' pension programs. In the long run, it defined subsequent social welfare policy and institutionally reinforced the distinction between the undeserving and deserving poor.

5

Administration of Mothers'
Pension Programs

De Facto Exclusion

The test of a law is its administration, not whether its
provisions include all the items that might be devised
for a "model law."[1]

MOTHERS' PENSIONS PROTECTED MANY poor children from being
separated from their families, however, many children were legally or ex-
tralegally excluded from its provision. An analysis of the administration
of the mothers' pension laws reveals the extent to which mothers' pensions succeeded or failed in providing for destitute families. It is impossible to assess the impact of the exclusion on individuals of particular
populations because no data exist on women who were refused aid. However, legal and extralegal exclusions clearly were institutionalized in the
administration of the programs, affecting their growth, their future administration and evolution, and their future potential beneficiaries. By
1931, most states had legislated mothers' pension programs, and these
programs had reached a certain degree of administrative stability and development. For this reason, it is interesting to examine precisely who
these programs served and how the funds were distributed. Not surpris-
ingly, an analysis of mothers' pension programs in 1931 reveals significant
regional differences in the races of the populations served and in administrative levels.

In 1923, twelve years after the passage of the first mothers' pension law,
64.2 percent of all dependent children receiving care were receiving it in
institutions. By 1933, this figure had dropped to 48 percent.[2] This finding
indicates that existing mothers' pension programs had failed to keep at
least half of the nation's dependent children in their own homes. Not only
did the rigid eligibility requirements effectively exclude certain classes of

people from receiving aid, but the local implementation of the laws resulted in further exclusion. Local-level administrators interpreted state legislation to reflect parochial values and prejudices on a case-by-case basis. As a result, local implementation often made programs even more restrictive than the law had intended.

These programs were often administered by the same private relief workers and social workers who had opposed the early mothers' pension movement. In fact, not until the 1920s did mothers' pensions gain widespread support from social workers.[3] Only a few reform leaders, such as Jane Addams, Florence Kelly, Julia Lathrop, and Edith and Grace Abbott, considered themselves early proponents of mothers' pensions. Unlike many of their fellow reformers, these five women shared a background as former or active settlement house workers. For the most part, social workers molded the programs that they managed to suit their case-by-case approach. This permitted great subjectivity in determining benefit levels, the fitness of the mother, and economic need. As Barbara Nelson has noted, "this administrative style was characterized by moralistic, diffuse decision criteria, high levels of bureaucratic discretion, and many levels of managerial cross-checking. While it was designed to be efficient and accountable, it was also cumbersome and repeatedly intrusive."[4]

Most of the information on the administration of the mothers' aid programs was collected by the Children's Bureau. In 1931, the bureau sent staff into the field to analyze different aspects of mothers' aid administration. Data were gathered from a survey of administrative units of mothers' pensions conducted by the Children's Bureau. Their study included all reporting agencies in eighteen states and some reporting agencies in twenty additional states. Data were procured for approximately half of the nation's families receiving pensions.[5] For each state, summary data exist regarding the number of local administrative units reporting mothers' pensions, the number and race of families receiving mothers' pension benefits, grants and per capita expenditures, and mothers' marital status. Based on this data, this chapter reviews the following features of the local implementation of mothers' aid programs: (1) administration; (2) marital status; (3) financing; (4) coverage; (5) paternalism; (6) mothers' employment; and (7) racial outcomes. This examination reveals the subjective and discriminatory implementation of the mothers' pension statutes.

By 1931, most U.S. states had mothers' pension programs.[6] This analysis excludes the four states that lacked mothers' pension programs in 1931—Alabama, Georgia, and South Carolina in the South and New Mexico in the West. Those states that had mothers' pension programs show marked regional differences in the number of recipients, amount of benefits provided, and the racial distribution of such benefits.

Administration

Significant regional differences existed in the administrative structure of mothers' pension programs in 1931. The administration of mothers' pension programs in southern and midwestern states was organized differently than in eastern and western states. Whereas only half of eastern states with mothers' pension programs had administrative units with county jurisdiction, all units in the other regions had county jurisdiction. Moreover, the mean number of such administrative units was significantly higher ($p < .05$) in the South and Midwest than in the East and West. The mean percentage of administrative units with county jurisdiction reporting mothers' pension grants is significantly ($p < .05$) lower in the South than in the other regions. This means that, relative to the other regions, mothers' pension programs in the South were more likely to be administered at the local level and that southern administrative units were least likely to report having granted mothers' pension benefits.

Although acknowledging that "no agency of administration is superior in all respects to others,"[7] the Children's Bureau encouraged organizations and state agencies to support the centralization of administration. In correspondence with an Arizona agency in 1930, Florence Hutsinpillar, director of mothers' aid for the bureau, wrote,

> to promote administration of the law throughout the State along fairly uniform standards, it is desirable to have a central agency to make the experience of one locality available to another, to issue standards and policies, and by helpful consultation and visitation to bring the knowledge of the most acceptable social-work practices to all administrators even in the most remote localities.[8]

In another letter suggesting improvements to the existing law in Kansas, Hutsinpillar wrote, "state participation under well-trained social workers offers probably the best method of safeguarding standards and of improving administration throughout the counties."[9]

These letters exemplify the Children's Bureau position, as indicated in its communication with different jurisdictions, that while local agencies were best suited for the actual distribution of grants, a state welfare agency or board was the most appropriate for administering the state law.

The Marital Status of Mothers'
Pension Recipients

Most states' legislation reflected the interest in aiding widows rather than mothers who were divorced, deserted, or unmarried. However, some states statutorily permitted aid to these other classes of mothers. The recipient population confirms this primary interest in serving widowed mothers. Figure 2 presents the results of a study of mothers' pension recipients conducted by the Children' Bureau in 1931: 82 percent (49,477) of the families were headed by widows; 5 percent (3,296) had been deserted by fathers; 4 percent (2,325) had physically disabled fathers; 3 percent (1,596) had fathers in prison; and 3 percent (1,984) had mentally disabled fathers. Only 2 percent (1,369) of the recipient families had divorced parents, and only 55 of the 60,119 families surveyed, .09 percent, had unmarried mothers.[10] By statutorily limiting the benefit to widows, welfare programs distinguished between what were subjectively considered the deserving and undeserving poor.

Financing

Grants & Standardized Budgets

Even states with relatively high benefit levels did not adequately support the dependent families of those women deemed "fit." A 1912 study by C. C. Carstens commissioned by the Russell Sage Foundation reported that of a hundred families investigated, the pension granted was adequate in fifty-nine cases, inadequate in thirty-nine, and most likely inadequate in two others. Furthermore, of 522 pensioned families studied in October 1912, 52 (10 percent) were receiving the maximum amount granted by the court yet were not adequately aided, and many others families receiving inadequate aid were not receiving the maximum grant.[11] A 1915 Children's Bureau study of families receiving mothers' pensions revealed that fewer than half of the 778 Cook County, Illinois, families investigated had income equal to the Chicago Standard Budget for Dependent Families.[12] A 1928 study revealed that in Pennsylvania, which had one of the highest average benefit levels, one-quarter to one-third of mothers' pension grants were inadequate.[13] In 1926, the maximum grants in most of the forty-two states with mothers' pensions were not sufficient, and most families did not receive the maximum grant.[14] A common dilemma was

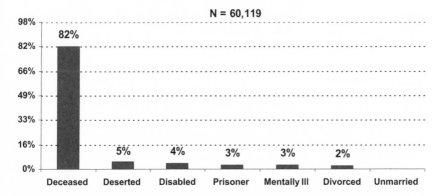

Fig. 2. Status of fathers in families receiving mothers' pensions, 1931 (N = 60,119). (Data from U.S. Department of Labor, Children's Bureau, *Mothers' Aid—1931*, 11–13.)

whether more families should be assisted with smaller grants or fewer families should be assisted with larger grants. Generally, grants were higher in the industrial northeastern states and smaller in southern states. For example, in 1931, the average monthly family grant was $4.33 in Arkansas, $7.29 in Oklahoma, $10.01 in Florida, and $10.06 in Louisiana compared with $69.31 in Massachusetts. Table 6 shows that benefit levels varied along geographic lines. The industrial northeastern states were more likely to have the highest average grants, with the Midwest and West following. The southern states in general placed well below the other regions in average grant amounts. A test of the difference in means of the average monthly grant amount was statistically significant. The East had the highest mean monthly grant amount, while the South had a significantly lower mean grant amount.

Table 7 shows the results of a multivariate model that examined the factors that determined the average monthly grant per family. Several variables are significant in this model. The percentage African-American population had a negative effect on the average monthly grant. Therefore, those states with higher African-American populations, especially the South, had lower monthly grant amounts. The number of families aided per ten thousand negatively correlates with the grant amount. This effect was anticipated, because many administrators were forced to lower grant amounts to provide greater coverage. Furthermore, the fact that 1931 represented the middle of the depression exacerbated the financial capacity of all localities across the nation. Higher per capita mothers' pension expenditures also significantly correlate with grant amounts. The higher the per

capita expenditures, the higher the monthly grants. State urban population also positively correlates with grant amount. Finally, with the South
as the baseline, the East positively correlates with the grant amount. This
means that states in the east were more likely to have higher grant
amounts. Alternate hypotheses argue that a state's financial resources have
a greater effect on benefit levels than does race.[15] However, in this model,
state per capita income is not statistically significant. This model supports
the argument that race is a more significant factor in determining mothers' pension benefit levels than is state wealth. The model also shows that
states that are more urban—specifically states in the North and Midwest—
are more likely to give higher grant amounts than states that are less
urban, such as states in the South.

A comparison of grants in cities to those in rural areas reveals that
urban grants were larger. In all regions, the mean monthly grant was
higher in urban areas than in other areas. The lowest monthly grant was
in the rural South. The percentage difference between the grants in urban

TABLE 6.   Mothers' Pensions: Average Monthly Grant per
Family, 1931

	Average Monthly Grant per Family ($)		Average Monthly Grant per Family ($)
Massachusetts	69.31	Ohio	21.68
Rhode Island	55.09	Wisconsin	21.66
New York	52.62	Oregon	21.35
Connecticut	45.91	Vermont	21.11
Pennsylvania	37.45	Iowa	20.81
Michigan	37.04	New Hampshire	19.77
California	31.40	Washington	19.66
Maryland	30.52	Nebraska	17.81
Maine	30.16	Arizona	17.25
New Jersey	30.03	North Carolina	16.64
Minnesota	29.35	Virginia	16.52
Tennessee	26.78	West Virginia	15.46
Indiana	26.73	Kansas	14.05
Colorado	26.50	Idaho	13.16
Missouri	26.22	Utah	11.77
Illinois	26.11	Mississippi	11.11
Montana	24.78	Texas	10.07
Nevada	24.76	Louisiana	10.06
Delaware	23.69	Florida	10.01
North Dakota	22.93	Oklahoma	7.29
Wyoming	22.55	Arkansas	4.33
South Dakota	21.78		

Source: Children's Bureau, U.S. Department of Labor, *Mothers' Aid—1931.*

and rural areas is considerable. In the South, there is an 83 percent difference between urban and rural grant amounts. This is significant because at that time the majority of the African-American population lived in the rural South. A test for the difference in means in the monthly grant per family in cities of one hundred thousand or more showed that the mean grant in the South was significantly ($p < .01$) lower than in other regions. A similar test for nonurban areas also showed that the mean grant in the South was significantly lower ($p < .01$) than in other regions.

In some states—that is, Connecticut, Massachusetts, New Jersey, and Pennsylvania—the difference between grant amounts in urban and other areas was not as marked because of smaller cities located throughout the state. However, certain states—such as Colorado, Illinois, Maryland, Michigan, and Ohio—had considerable differences in urban and rural grant amounts.[16]

Although mothers' pension grants were larger than the relief grants available through private agencies or other outdoor relief, in even the most generous states the grants remained inadequate when compared to wage labor earnings. In 1930, manufacturing workers earned an average

TABLE 7. Regression Analysis: Average Monthly Grant per Family, 1931

Independent Variables	
Constant	14.689 (unstandardized)
Total state African-American	−.52**
population in 1930 (%)	(−2.513)
Numbers of families aided per 10,000	−.703***
population in 1931	(−6.157)
State per capita income in 1929	−246
	(−1.794)
Annual per capita mothers' pension	1.039***
expenditures in 1931	(8.085)
State urban population in 1930 (%)	.443***
	(4.158)
East	.233**
	(2.499)
Midwest	.007
	(.080)
West	.066
	(.906)
N	38
Adjusted R^2	.888

Note: Dependent variable is average monthly mothers' pension grant per family in 1931. t-statistics are in parentheses.
***$p < .01$ **$p < .05$

of $124 per month.[17] In comparison, Massachusetts, the state with the most generous grant, had a monthly pension amount of $69.31.[18]

Per Capita Expenditures

Most states did not help localities fund mothers' pension programs. By 1934, only sixteen states had authorized the contribution of state funds to the local programs. However, two of these states had appropriated no money, in five other states the state contribution was so small that the assistance was negligible. In fourteen states, expenditures totaled approximately $5.6 million. At the same time, counties in forty-three states spent six times that amount.[19] The result was that grant amounts varied across a state, reflecting the different localities' ability to support the programs. Consequently, the variations in the amount of the grants in a single state were sometimes greater than the variations in grant amounts between states.[20]

A state's annual per capita mothers' pension expenditures significantly ($p <$ .01) correlate with the amount of the monthly grant. Significant regional differences existed in annual per capita mothers' pension expenditures. The mean annual per capita expenditure for mothers' pension programs in the South was significantly ($p <$ .01) lower than in the other regions. Annual per capita expenditures in the East, Midwest, and West were approximately four times higher than the annual per capita expenditures in the South. A test for the difference of means in annual per capita expenditures in rural areas was also statistically significant ($p <$ .01). In this test, the annual per capita expenditures in rural areas in the South were lower than in the other regions.

Although a test for the difference in means for the per capita expenditures in urban areas (cities with populations greater than one hundred thousand) was not significant,[21] notable differences existed among the regions. In the South and the East, per capita expenditures were higher in urban areas. In the East, per capita expenditures in urban areas were 30 percent higher. In the South, per capita expenditures in urban areas were 60 percent higher.

Budget Schedules

Ethnic considerations often skewed the budgets administrators used to calculate grants. In 1922, the Children's Bureau sent a budget questionnaire to a variety of public agencies that administered mothers' aid programs. Eleven of the forty-five agencies surveyed deviated from their budget schedules based on the nationality of the recipients. Eleven agencies calculated that minorities and immigrants needed less money to live on.[22] One agency deviated from the schedule because it "had a Mexican problem which affected the use of the schedule."[23] Another agency deviated from its budget schedule by calculating lower food and clothing allowances for foreign families, and another agency gave lower allowances for Italian and Czechoslovakian recipients. One reporting agency added 10 percent to the food budget for "high type" families.[24] Finally, Washington, D.C., had two standard budgets, a lower one for African-Americans and a higher one for whites. White caseworkers reportedly called African-American mothers by their first names but used more formal forms of address for other mothers and discouraged African-American mothers from educating their children. These arbitrarily constructed budget schedules gave officials more license to administer mothers' pension programs in a manner that reflected local, parochial norms and prejudices.

Coverage & the Extent of Implementation of Mothers' Pension Laws

By 1921, ten years after the first law was passed, mothers' pensions were being granted in eleven hundred counties in forty states. By 1931, these numbers had increased to sixteen hundred counties in forty-five states. By 1934, three hundred thousand children were being supported by mothers' pensions.[25] However, because the state statutes were permissive, mothers' pension programs did not necessarily operate statewide. Not all states with mothers' pension laws established units to administer the programs, and many localities chose not to provide the benefit. State reports of the numbers of mothers' pension recipients were not readily available, so the Children's Bureau conducted questionnaire studies that showed that 45,825 families received aid in 1921, while ten years later, 93,620 families received aid. This growth resulted primarily from an increase in the number of counties offering the program rather than from new state laws; however, 242 counties in seventeen states did not provide reports.[26]

Administrators of state social welfare agencies across the nation and employees of the Children's Bureau and Department of Labor expressed concern about the limited availability of mothers' pensions. The state superintendent of the Children's Home Society of Florida wrote in a letter to the Children's Bureau, "There is some likelihood that Florida may want to change its Mothers' Allowance Law, which is not a mandatory law, and which I am sorry to say is not being carried out in very many counties of the State."[27] Correspondence in 1931 between the mothers' aid adviser in Portland, Oregon, and Hutsinpillar reveals a similar problem of coverage in that state. Hutsinpillar wrote, "I am so glad that you are going to alter your mothers' aid law again. I have never felt very happy over the tone of the law which has seemed to emphasize restrictions upon the fund rather than more constructive child welfare features." Hutsinpillar described at length several administrative problems in the Oregon law that limited greater coverage, noting in particular a problem with the administrative agency that oversaw implementation.[28]

In response to a 1932 inquiry from Michigan, an official in the Social Service Division of the Department of Labor wrote about the implementation of mothers' pension laws across the nation:

> Although 45 of the States have mothers'-aid or mothers'-pension laws on their statute books, this does not mean that the law is being administered in all parts of these states. A recent survey made by this office shows that less than one-tenth of the counties are granting mothers' aid in the following States: Kentucky, Mississippi, Missouri, Tennessee, Texas and Virginia.[29]

Although nationwide coverage clearly did not extend to all jurisdictions, the mean percentage of administrative units reporting grants in the South was radically lower than in the other regions. The difference among the regions is statistically significant ($p < .01$). Edith Abbott commented at the 1917 National Conference of Social Work, "mothers' pensions do not interfere with any great vested interests . . . since the laws are largely optional, and local authorities are not required to appropriate for them or may make their appropriation as niggardly as they please."[30]

During the early 1930s, Georgia's American Legion became interested in promoting child welfare legislation such as mothers' pensions. In correspondence with legion representatives, the Children's Bureau's Hutsinpillar expressed concern that this legislation would not operate in most of the state unless a state agency provided assistance. She suggested that the state's Board of Public Welfare assist in this exercise: otherwise, "under a permissive mothers' aid law with sole responsibility vested in the county the prospect does not seem bright for nearly three-fourths of the State."[31] Undoubtedly recognizing the trend in southern states, Hutsinpillar's response to an inquiry about establishing mothers' aid in South Carolina emphasized the importance of providing the most inclusive coverage possible: "the law should be inclusive enough to provide for any mother who is deprived of her husband's support." She also stressed the importance of state supervision by using as example the poor coverage in other states that had no state participation, listing Florida, Tennessee, Louisiana, and Virginia as examples of administrative structures not to be emulated.[32]

A 1922 Children's Bureau study revealed that in thirteen of the thirty-eight states studied, only .5–33 percent of the needy children were receiving help through mothers' aid. In fourteen states, only 33–50 percent of the needy children were helped. In only eleven states were 66 percent or more of these dependent children being helped.[33] The 1931 Children's Bureau study revealed that aid was being given in only 1,490 of the 2,723 U.S. counties (55 percent) authorized to administer the benefit. In 1934 mothers' pension programs functioned in 5 percent or fewer of all counties in Kentucky, Louisiana, Tennessee, and Texas.[34] Although authorized, programs did not operate at all in Arkansas, Mississippi, and New Mexico.[35] At no point during the existence of mothers' pensions did more than half the counties in the United States provide mothers' pensions. Furthermore, programs predominated in the northern industrial states and were relatively absent in the southern agrarian states.

Every region had scores of families on waiting lists. For example, in January 1935, Cook County, Illinois, had 1,434 families receiving mothers' aid but 7,942 mothers on the waiting list. Furthermore, 3,870 families on relief rolls were entitled to mothers' aid but could not get it because of the lack of funds.[36]

For the most part, programs were more developed in urban centers.[37] By 1934, 51 percent of the families aided lived in cities of fifty thousand or more, and the majority of these urban recipients lived in nine cities: Boston, Chicago, Cleveland, Detroit, Los Angeles, Milwaukee, New York, Philadelphia, and Pittsburgh.[38] The underrepresentation of the rural poor disproportionately affected potential African-American recipients in the South. Many counties in southern states with high African-American populations, such as Louisiana and Tennessee, did not offer mothers' pension programs. Four southern states with high percentages of African-American residents—Arkansas, Georgia, Mississippi, and South Carolina—either had not legislated mothers' pension programs or lacked operating programs. As late as 1935, Georgia and South Carolina had still not passed mothers' pension legislation.

The effort to combine relief and "social treatment" in a single public agency intensified the defects arising from local administration of the laws.

Frustration and disappointment resulted when skimpy local appropriations made neither adequate assistance nor casework services possible. Significant ($p < .05$) regional differences existed in the number of families receiving mothers' aid in 1931. The overall distribution of mothers' pension benefits was significantly lower in the South than in the other regions. The East and Midwest had much higher means than the West and South. The same statistically significant regional differences existed for the mean number of children benefiting from mothers' pensions, mean per capita mothers' pension expenditures, and mean average monthly grants per family.

These regional differences are also reflected in the number of African-American families receiving mothers' pension benefits relative to the total African-American family population. A statistically significant difference ($p < .01$) existed among the regions in the ratio of African-American families receiving mothers' pension benefits to the total number of African-American families. The mean percentage of African-American families receiving mothers' pensions was significantly lower in the South than in other regions. Although the mean percentage of white families aided was also lower in the South, the difference between the percentage African-American aided and the percentage white aided was greater in the South than in the other regions.

Paternalism: Expense Accounts
& Investigations

Regular expense accounts, whereby recipients were obliged to record and itemize their expenditures, became popular with local administrators. These accounts were a powerful supervisory tool available to both social workers and legislators trying to evaluate whether mothers' aid recipients were putting public funds to good use. Localities varied in their requirements for recording expenses. Accounting was done on a monthly, quarterly, or even semiannual basis. The forms were organized so that the mother could report her daily expenditures on food, household supplies, fuel, and clothing. Some localities required mothers to break down these categories even further—that is, by type of food or clothing. If a case supervisor disapproved of the products that the mother purchased, aid could be discontinued. This monitoring device enabled local administrators to impose biased standards of acceptable housekeeping, food preparation, and dress.

Reports from the Children's Bureau illustrate caseworkers' and supervisors' paternalistic disdain for potential pension recipients. For example, many mothers were assumed to have limitations with regard to managing homes and being mothers. One report stated that "a large percentage of the women needed help in the care and training of their children, and in managing their incomes and their household affairs."[39] Another report claimed that "in concentrating on the welfare of the child the workers tried not to forget that the mother was frequently a young woman who had had small chance for training and development, and she was placed in touch with every neighborhood agency that could help her to become a better home maker and mother."[40]

Contemporary reports further indicate that caseworkers/probation officers often conducted intrusive and injurious investigations to determine the eligibility or continued eligibility of mothers' pension recipients. Carstens's study of mothers' administration in four cities gave him little

confidence in the kind of investigation that the probation officers make. In many instances the probation officer presented certain facts which were wholly inadequate for determining whether or not a pension was advisable, and the case was then referred back to the probation officer for additional inquiry on certain specific points. The committee's work was delayed, their time was spent in mere technical criticism, and the families were kept from a week to a month longer without the definite, and prompt answer which they anxiously awaited and to which they were entitled.

Moreover, Carstens claimed that the investigation methods were

found to be made frequently with a brutality to which no applicant for assistance should be exposed. Insinuations were made regarding immoral conditions in the neighborhood inquiry about the widow which were based upon neither facts nor suspicions, but which the county representative threw out to arouse interest in his inquiry, and by means of which he hoped to get incriminating information. . . . The probation officer's investigation . . . seemed to develop into espionage instead of friendly supervision.[41]

Carstens's analysis, however, did not compare the condition of the families pensioned by the court for mothers' pensions with the condition of the families pensioned by private agencies.

Whereas current racial distinctions focus on different ethnic groups or individuals' skin colors, early-twentieth-century racial ideas distinguished

Anglo-Saxon immigrants from other immigrant populations. In particular, the dominant Anglo-Saxon Americans viewed southern and eastern Europeans, Latinos, and African-Americans as in need of uplift to the supreme Anglo-Saxon values and standards. Some even viewed people who were not white, Anglo-Saxon, and Protestant as "irremediably inferior," while others regarded members of these groups as inferior but with the potential to rise up to American standards. Because mothers' pension legislation was permissive with regard to imposition of local norms by these administrators, African-American women and immigrant women could be deemed unsuitable on very private or personal grounds—for example, for failing to attend acceptable churches, to eat appropriate foods, to have suitable neighbors, or to read proper literature. Supervision was essentially geared toward the adoption of American values. A variety of the supervisory measures reflected this racial bias. For example, mothers were expected to take English classes and were told to avoid cooking with garlic, which was considered an aphrodisiac. Pension advocates and administrators in urban areas used the pension benefits as carrots to entice immigrants who allowed themselves to be Americanized. Consequently, in several cities, immigrants could receive benefits that were off-limits to African-Americans.

The schedule used in a 1923 Children's Bureau's study of the administration of mothers' pensions reflected the degree to which these mothers' personal competence and lifestyles were questioned. In addition to asking about place of birth, nationality, employment, and education, the schedule had a section on "standards of living." In addition to questions on "surroundings" (type of neighborhood and character of the home), "rooms and furnishings" (household linens, dishes, piano, and cooking utensils), and "food and housekeeping" (amount and kind of food items purchased), the section included information on "recreation and education" that evaluated church and Sunday school attendance, reading of daily and weekly papers and magazines, and frequenting of picture shows, clubs, and classes.[42] Failing to attend church, smoking, refusing to move out of a particular neighborhood, and cooking the "wrong" foods were considered evidence of being an "unfit" mother and often resulted in the loss of benefits.[43]

The Massachusetts Mothers' Aid Law had typical intake, decision-making, and monitoring procedures.

> The mother makes application of the overseer of the poor in her place of residence. He investigates her need, fitness and resources, filling out a blank form which the board has prepared of the purpose,

and ending with his recommendation. This information and advice he sends to the state board [of charities]. The supervisor then assigns one of the five women visitors to make a second independent investigation, and reviews the recommendation of the overseer in the light of the two findings. The result of her study of the case, whether approval, disapproval or suggestions on treatment, she embodies in a letter to the overseer in question. In the course of her work she is in constant conference with the superintendent of the adult poor division, a man who has the advantage of many years acquaintance with the individual cases that present some deviation from the usual types, while the committee itself considers special cases and all general questions of policy.[44]

This intake process differed substantially from the process used for other public welfare benefits. For example, workers seeking workers' compensation needed only to notify their employers of their injuries. The employers then sent claims to the commission controlling the program, a straightforward and standardized process unlike that followed for mothers' pensions. The mothers' pension program functioned as both public welfare and social control, a means to structure and define the values and behavior of hundreds of thousands of people in ways that reflected Anglo-Saxon, middle-class norms. The paternalist nature of the mothers' pension administration resulted in a welfare benefit based not on economic need but instead on recipients' behavior. This focus on the suitability of the mother eclipsed pension advocates' original idea that mothers' pensions constituted a right. Mothers' pension advocates had argued that the problems of dependent mothers originated in poverty arising from the loss of breadwinners rather than from the mothers' failures. Consequently, economic need was the most salient issue. However, as implemented, mothers' pensions located eligibility within a framework that distinguished between the worthy and the unworthy, and ambiguous moral criteria replaced economic need in the administration of this legislation.

Employment

The mothers' pension laws were predicated on the theory that a mother's services were worth more at home raising her children than in the outside labor market. However, mothers' pension grants were on the whole not

sufficient to provide for the pensioned families without the mother working for wages. Many of the recipients had to work to supplement the insufficient grants. One study showed that 84 percent of recipients in
Philadelphia, 66 percent in Chicago and San Francisco, and 57 percent in
Los Angeles had to continue working.[45] A 1919 study revealed that 67 percent of mothers' pensioners in Illinois were employed.[46] A 1918 study in
Harrisburg, Pennsylvania, showed that 75 percent of 116 pensioned mothers worked, as did 95 of the children of these mothers. Mothers' pensions
did little to prevent child labor. According to a 1923 study, 52 percent of
942 mothers receiving grants in nine cities were also working to support
their families.[47] The author of this 1923 study, Florence Nesbitt, warned
about the toll on these mothers, who were "overly weary," and their children, who were not being supervised.[48] Nesbitt's study also showed that
67 percent of the mothers receiving pensions in Denver were employed, as
were 69 percent in Westchester County, New York; 59 percent in Min-
neapolis; and 57 percent in St. Louis.[49] These figures likely drastically un-
derrepresent the number of employed pension recipients, many of whom
did not report their employment.

In 1928, Emma Lundberg, a leading advocate of mothers' pensions and
an employee of the Children's Bureau, stated that "mothers' aid administration offers the most obvious evidence of the seriousness of placing laws
on the statute book but failing to make them practically effective through
adequate appropriation and proper administration. It is recognized that
the chief problem at present is . . . to obtain adequate appropriations and
to raise the standard of administration so that the laws may mean adequate care for the children they are intended to benefit."[50]

An obvious conclusion is that mothers' aid programs were never intended to allow poor mothers to stay home and raise their children. In
fact, expectations for middle-class mothers differed than those for poor
mothers. Middle-class women were expected to stay home and raise their
children, but poor families were expected to provide for themselves. Although some evidence disputes the validity of this claim, in some localities mothers' pension applications were rejected for families that had children capable of working. Furthermore, in some places, pension terms
required mothers to make up the difference between the grant amount
and the amount needed for subsistence. Certain social workers recognized
the need for the mothers to work simply because of the inadequacy of the
grants and assisted women in arranging their home lives to accommodate
work schedules and child rearing.

Mothers' pension plans stipulated the types of employment suitable for recipients. Many administrators prohibited mothers from seeking full-time employment that took them out of their homes. Instead, women were restricted to seasonal, part-time employment or homework, such as cleaning, sewing, or laundry. A 1923 Children's Bureau study revealed that of the wage-earning mothers receiving mothers' pensions, 59 percent worked by the day, 9 percent reported doing laundry and sewing, and only 16 percent were working in factories.[51] According to a Kansas City caseworker, "we expect and require the mother to earn all she can at home by pursuits which are compatible with her position, such as washing, sewing, baking bread for neighbors, teaching music, or doing work supplied from the mercantile houses."[52] Unfortunately, these employment opportunities were often the most exploitative because they were the lowest-paid occupations available to women. Caseworkers often pushed mothers from more protected employment opportunities into the unprotected workforce that part-time work and homework created. Rhode Island's mothers' pension law stipulated that "no mother shall receive the benefits of this act who shall be employed in any factory, manufacturing, mechanical, business or mercantile establishment."[53] Although other states lacked such legal stipulations, departments of public welfare and overseers of mothers' pension programs limited the employment opportunities available to pensioned mothers. Furthermore, the pay from day or part-time work combined with a pension often totaled less than women could earn in factories or mills, making women reluctant to give up factory or mill employment. Caseworkers reported that pensioned mothers gave up their allowances and went to work in the steel industry, in mills, or with the railroads because doing so resulted in more job security and higher pay than pension and day work afforded.[54]

Factory and mill employment opportunities were available almost exclusively to whites, however, restricting African-American mothers to day work and part-time seasonal work. A 1922 Children's Bureau study reported that the "opposition to day work on the part of mothers has increased greatly in the past few years with the increased demand for women in factories. The tendency has been more and more for white women to leave this work for the colored women, for whom industrial openings have become more limited."[55]

By failing to provide adequately for these dependent families, mothers' pensions had effects resembling those of other forms of outdoor relief. Recipients were forced to pursue other avenues of economic support while being subjected to pension administrators' invasive and often offensive scrutiny.

Racial Outcomes

Social welfare scholar Winifred Bell has noted "the discriminatory treatment of recent immigrants and African-Americans in the small Mothers' Pension programs organized in the first quarter of the twentieth century. African-Americans were rarely admitted to this elite program for fatherless families, and as late as 1922 social workers reported that 'low-type' families like Mexicans, Italians and Czechoslovakians were seldom helped. If they were, they usually received lower grants than 'high-type' Anglo-Saxons."[56]

Responding to concerns about racial differentiation in mothers' pension administration, the 1930 White House Conference created a Children's Charter and set forth additional standards and principles of child saving and child welfare.

> Mothers' Aid should everywhere be available, and should not be niggardly.
> The needs of children born out of wedlock, good care and education, are the same as those of other children.
> Every effort should be made to meet the needs of Negro, Mexican, Puerto Rican, and Indian children.[57]

Contrary to the intent of the Children's Charter, mothers' pensions were not available everywhere, children born out of wedlock were for all intents and purposes excluded, and the needs of African-American children were not met. The racial discrimination that characterized the pension movement and was discernible in the mothers' pension legislation became more apparent in the administration of the programs. According to Bell, "it is apparently true that most 'fit and deserving' widows were also white."[58] The vagueness of the "suitable" home condition ensured its adaptability to local and regional norms and prejudices. As Gunnar Myrdal observed, "according to popular belief in the South, few Negro low income families have homes which could be called 'suitable' for any purpose."[59] Local administrators were responsible for defining these conditions, and as Bell put it, "in doing so, they tended to restrict the programs to nice Anglo-Saxon widows and to move separately but in concert to protect their young programs from Negro and unmarried mothers who might well attract criticism."[60] Table 8 illustrates the great difference in the distribution of mothers' pension benefits across race in the different regions. In the East, the mean percentage of African-American families receiving mothers' pensions was higher than the mean percentage of

African-American families in the reporting area. In the Midwest and West, the means of the percentages of families receiving aid roughly corresponded to the mean percentages of the African-American population in the area. In the South, however, a gross disparity existed between the mean percentage of African-American families receiving aid (3.9 percent) and the corresponding mean percentage of the African-American population (29.0 percent).

Unlike the national Civil War Veteran pension program, mothers' pensions and other maternalist benefit programs were run at the local level. Many scholars have claimed that the most important factor in explaining the exclusion of poor African-Americans was the states' inability to fund the programs.[61] It is true that in areas that had low mothers' pension expenditures, many poor mothers, both African-American and white, could not get benefits. However, this does not explain underfunding's disproportionate effect on the African-American population, especially considering the fact that African-Americans were much more likely than whites

ABLE 8.   Distribution of Mothers' Pension Benefits by Region, 1931

	East	Midwest	West	South	Total
•an number of families receiving mothers' pension aid	1,259	1,853	829	480	1,165
•an number of white families receiving mothers' pension aid	1,198	1,788	799	461	1,119
•an number of African-American families receiving mothers' pension aid	60	52	9	17	36
an percentage of African-American families receiving aid as a proportion of total families aided	4.8%	2.8%	1.1%	3.5%	3.1%
an number of African-American families in all reporting areas	20,327	11,516	1,560	43,688	18,717
an percentage of African-American families in all reporting areas	6.5%	2.6%	0.9%	29.0%	9.1%
an percentage of African-American families receiving aid as a proportion of total families in the area	8.5%	3.3%	0.7%	3.9%	4.2%
an percentage of African-American families receiving aid as a proportion of all African-American families in the area	.30%	.45%	.58%	.04%	.19%

ote: Population in reporting areas refers to the population in the administrative units that reported the race of the her in the 1931 Children's Bureau survey.

to be poor, with much lower average incomes. The results of a regression model further undermine this other explanation, as table 9 details. A state's income, a proxy for the economic ability to fund the programs, does not significantly correlate with the percentage of African-Americans receiving mothers' pensions. Annual per capita mothers' pension expenditures are significantly correlated, however. The higher the annual expenditures, the higher the percentage of African-Americans aided. Therefore, African-Americans are more likely to receive mothers' pensions in northern states than in southern states.

Although there is no racism variable per se, discrimination against African-Americans can be illustrated in qualitative ways. Caseworkers' descriptions and characterizations of potential recipients illustrate prejudice toward African-Americans and immigrants. Caseworkers described African-American women as "primitive," "limited," "not nearly as talkative as many of her race, but apparently truthful," and "fairly good for a colored woman." Immigrants were described as "a typical low-grade Italian woman," "typical Puerto Ricans who loved fun, little work and were dependent people."[62] Although after 1920 a movement arose in favor of replacing caseworkers' informal judgments with scientific intelligence testing, categories describing clients remained very unscientific and biased,

TABLE 9.   Regression: Percentage of African-American Population Receiving Aid, 1931

Independent variables	
Constant	−1.50
	unstandardized
State per capita income	−.106
	(−.338)
Total percentage urban population	.218
	(.856)
Annual per capita mothers' pension expenditure	.415**
	(2.396)
East	−.064
	(−.334)
Midwest	.451
	(2.783)***
West	.093
	(.580)
N	37
Adjusted R^2	.333

Note: Dependent variable is percentage of African-American population receiving mothers' pension aid, 1931. *t*-statistics are in parentheses.
*** $p < .01$ ** $p < .05$

with clients called "shiftless," "coarse," "low-type," "uncouth," "immoral," "feebleminded," "lazy," "worthless," "low-grade," "of weak character," "ignorant-type," "degenerate," and "of low mentality."[63]

In her 1934 study of mothers' pensions, Grace Abbott explained that "some local administrative agencies, in order to limit the intake to a number which can be cared for with reasonable adequacy, have set up rules to exclude certain classes. . . . Many exclude women with only one dependent child; others exclude certain groups of the disabled . . . and some have even drawn racial lines. As a result, large numbers of eligible families are not receiving mothers' aid. It is probably safe to say that at least 75 percent more than are now in receipt of assistance are eligible and in need."[64] Many of the poor excluded from mothers' pensions went on emergency relief rolls. According to a report on mothers' pensions in Florida, "out of 100,000 families who were on the emergency relief rolls as of January 1, 1934, 5,914 (2,714 white and 3,200 African-American) were of the same general types as families eligible for mothers' pensions."[65] Only two northern states acknowledged that the need among African-American families was comparable with the need among white families.[66] In 1931, Pennsylvania and New Jersey accounted for about half of the nation's African-American mothers' pension recipients, while mothers' pensions remained rare in the southern states, where approximately 80 percent of the African-American population lived.

Recipients' demographic characteristics offer conclusive evidence of this discrimination. Scattered pre-1930 studies examined the racial makeup of the recipient pool. In 1914 in Cincinnati, four of the hundred recipients were African-American. In Chicago, no African-Americans received mothers' pensions in 1911, and in 1917 only 2.7 percent of the aided mothers were African-American. By contrast, in 1911 German immigrants received 20 percent of the mothers' pensions but comprised 7 percent of the population, Irish-Americans (3 percent of the population) got 22 percent of the pensions, Italian-Americans (2 percent of the population) got 8 percent of the pensions, and Polish-Americans (6 percent of the population) got 14 percent of the pensions. Only one African-American woman in St. Louis received aid in 1923, and only five of four hundred North Carolina recipients were African-American in 1928.[67] Localities across the nation excluded African-Americans from the recipient rolls.

The Children's Bureau conducted the first and only systematic nationwide study of the racial composition of mothers' pension recipients in 1931. Many earlier reports or studies of mothers' aid programs did not even mention African-Americans or include them as a category. The 1931 study included all reporting agencies in eighteen states and some report-ing agencies in twenty others, procuring data for approximately half of the nation's families receiving pensions. Of the 46,597 families for which information was reported, 96 percent were white, 3 percent were African-American, and 1 percent were of other races.[68] Half of the African-Amer-ican recipients in the study lived in Ohio and Pennsylvania. In Toledo, Cleveland, Pittsburgh, and Philadelphia African-American families con-stituted a larger share of the caseload than did other populations. In North Carolina, the only southern state that had more than scattered pen-sion programs, only one African-American family received a pension.[69]

Obvious regional differences exist in the means for percentage of African-American families receiving pensions in a particular county and for percentage of African-American families in the county. Whereas in the East, the African-American representation on the mothers' pension rolls was higher than the population, the opposite held true in the South. While an average of 20 percent of the population in the southern areas was African-American, only 1 percent of African-American families re-ceived benefits. Because the mean percentage African-American popula-tion in the South was significantly higher ($p < .01$) than in the other re-gions, this disparity is even more significant.

The Children's Bureau reported that "comparison of the percentage of Negro families in the total population of the counties reporting race, with the percentage of the families aided that were Negro, shows that provi-sion for Negro families was limited in a number of states. The dispropor-tion between probable need and provision is even greater when the lower income level of Negro families is taken into consideration."[70] In most counties nationwide, few or no African-American families received aid. According to the 1931 study, only one African-American family received aid in Florida. Only one African-American family received aid in Lake County, Indiana, although African-Americans constituted 10 percent of the population there. In Houston, Texas, where African-Americans con-stituted 21 percent of the population, and Marion County, Indiana (11 per-cent), no African-Americans received mothers' pensions.

Table 10 illustrates that the proportion of African-American families re-ceiving mothers' pensions was significantly lower ($p < .01$) in the South than in other regions. An alternative hypothesis is that the significantly lower annual per capita expenditures in the South constitute the key ex-planatory factor of this low inclusion. However, this hypothesis cannot explain the difference in the percentage of whites aided relative to African-Americans.

Table II illustrates the significant difference in the percentage of African-American population aided relative to the white population. Whereas in every region the percentage of the white population aided was higher than the percentage of the African-American population aided, the differences in the percentages is the greatest in the South. Whereas the percentage of the white population aided is on average double that of the African-American population in the East, Midwest, and West, the number of whites aided the South is four times greater than the African-American population aided. Even if per capita expenditures are significant, they cannot explain this variation.

Mothers' pension legislation and program implementation resulted in the grossly disproportionate exclusion of poor African-American mothers from the mothers' pension rolls. With the advent of mothers' pensions, many counties significantly reduced their budgets for general poor relief. As the mothers' pension programs and poor relief budgets diminished, African-Americans had even less recourse to assistance. The care of dependent

TABLE 10. Mean Percentage of African-American Families Receiving Mothers' Pension Aid as a Proportion of African-American Families in the Population, 1931

		Subset for α = .05		
	N	Group 1 (%)	Group 2 (%)	Group 3 (%)
South	9	.09		
East	10		.25	
West	8		.45	
Midwest	12			.78
Total	39			

TABLE 11. Percentage Population Aided by Race, 1931

	N	White Population Aided (%)	African-American Population Aided (%)
South	9	.36	.09
East	10	.59	.25
West	8	1.17	.45
Midwest	12	1.89	.78
Total	39		

"colored" children was subjected to the standard set by *Plessy v. Ferguson:* such care would be separate and most likely private. Although some mothers' aid administrators probably attempted to maintain clear policies for determining eligibility, it was not easy to specify those policies because of the vagueness of the legislation and the number of variables in the application process. Consequently, African-Americans constituted an obvious group of dependent mothers who were excluded from the mothers' pension programs. These women were victims of both a social culture that deliberately marginalized this population and a political culture that was more interested in protecting support for this nascent program than in considerations of equality.

Conclusion

By the 1930s, criticism of the mothers' pension programs was growing for several reasons. Only half the counties in the United States provided mothers' pension assistance, and less than half of the states had functioning mothers' pension legislation. Furthermore, the amount of aid varied widely across states and across counties. The criteria for determining eligibility were equally unstandardized. Finally, the program subjected applicants scrutiny that was often humiliating, as if they were somehow responsible for the loss of their families' male breadwinners. Instead of focusing on objective need, these mothers' pension recipients were evaluated in terms of their suitability. Their dependent condition, in the eyes of program administrators, justified the scrutiny and humiliation. Becoming a hallmark of subsequent social welfare provision in the United States, especially Aid to Dependent Children, objective determinations of need were overlaid with subjective determinations of worthiness.

The Great Depression exacerbated these problems because of the lack of resources and the increased demand for help from families with unemployed males. The depression forced many officials to discontinue mothers' aid programs. At a December 1933 conference, state officials reported that mothers' aid had been discontinued in thirty-three Michigan counties, ten in Illinois, six in Wisconsin, four in Pennsylvania, and two in New York.[71] The government established the Federal Emergency Relief Administration (FERA), which provided assistance to poor Americans, including children. Consequently, many families who were eligible for mothers' pensions had to rely on FERA money to survive. In fact, FERA relief supported 3.5 times as many dependent families as mothers' pensions did.[72] In 1931 mothers' pensions assisted less than 0.7 percent of the nation's children. In 1933 FERA was assisting one-seventh of all children under eighteen years of age.[73]

While mothers' pensions successfully challenged the traditional forms of social welfare and outdoor relief, these programs did not live up to expectations and failed to modernize the provision of social welfare. Instead, the emphasis on local administration perpetuated the stigma of outdoor relief and the Elizabethan poor-law tradition. Instead of redefining relief as a right, mothers' pensions created a social welfare program that not only failed to defend economic assistance as a legitimate goal in itself but also established the groundwork for using moral criteria to evaluate a potential beneficiary's worthiness.

6

Mothers' Pensions, the New Deal, & ADC

A Racialized Legacy

> At this time, I recommend the following types of
> legislation looking to economic security: . . . federal aid
> to dependent children through grants to States for the
> support of existing mothers' pension systems.
> —Franklin Delano Roosevelt, "A Message to the
> Congress on Social Security," January 17, 1935

ON AUGUST 14, 1935, Franklin D. Roosevelt signed the Social Security Act into law. Within a relatively short period, the United States had progressed from having a nonexistent national welfare state to boasting relatively expansive welfare programs. On June 8, 1934, President Roosevelt had appointed the Committee on Economic Security to develop a national social security program. In the fall of that year, the president appointed an advisory council to assist in the committee's fact-finding process. On January 15, 1935, the committee reported its recommendations to the president, who submitted it to Congress two days later, when the Wagner-Lewis Economic Security Bill (S. 1130 and H.R. 4120) was introduced in the House and Senate. Committee hearings were held in January and February, and six months later, a U.S. welfare state was inaugurated.

There is no doubt that the New Deal and its signature legislation, the Social Security Act, ushered in revolutionary changes in the relationship between the state and society. It is important, particularly for this analysis, that whereas the reforms in certain areas of social welfare provision represented uncharted waters for the United States, others, such as Aid to Dependent Children (ADC), developed based on existing institutions. The Social Security Act had a significant impact on the existing mothers' pensions programs, especially in terms of the number of children aided. In addition, however, the existing mothers' pension programs had formidable impacts on the institutional and ideological development of ADC. In fact, these state programs defined the federal program and contributed to the way welfare came to be seen in this country. Most social scientists have paid little or no attention to the early state and local welfare policy developments. However, these processes were central to the shaping of federal social welfare. The states, not the federal government, were at the center of early debates on health insurance, unemployment insurance, workers' compensation, and mothers' pensions during the Progressive Era.

The institutional and ideological lineage between mothers' pensions and ADC and the role of race in that lineage needs to be more clearly delineated. On the one hand, these programs provided a blueprint from which subsequent efforts to aid dependent families were created. On the other hand, the debate surrounding mothers' pension laws introduced questions that continue in contemporary debates about social welfare provision. This research demonstrates how mothers' aid became the model for ADC and all other "assistance"[1] programs. By providing a model for the development of national welfare policy, mothers' pensions transferred principles embodied in mothers' pension legislation and administration into federal legislation and administration. In the end, ADC inherited a structural legacy of discrimination against African-Americans that defined not only the parameters of ADC's development as a national social welfare program but also the contours of the American welfare state. The Social Security Act established a bifurcated U.S. welfare state: a national social insurance program for retired workers and their dependents and "federally organized" public assistance programs for others, including families with dependent children. In the case of the former, the worthiness of the beneficiaries was taken for granted; in the case of the latter, beneficiaries were forced to prove both their need and their worthiness. The administrative styles of the two welfare streams reflected that bifurcation. In the case of public assistance, states could participate, at their own discretion, in programs that had certain national guidelines and requirements but left the administration up to the states. The national social insurance program guaranteed an administration that was insulated from the moralistic and subjective eligibility criteria characteristic of the state-run public assistance programs such as mothers' pensions.

The stratification of social welfare programs institutionalized in the New Deal era reproduced and deepened already existing social inequalities. Just as labor market forces and cultural changes were allowing women and African-Americans to move onto the main track of citizenship, the Social

Security Act created a new hierarchy of social citizenship in which they were again relegated to last place. Through the legislative process, existing inequities were intensified and other inequities were established.

From Mothers' Pensions to ADC

Single mothers had no unified voice during the New Deal era. Furthermore, African-American reformers were excluded from New Deal welfare planning. Mothers' aid recipients were not an activist group, and no group championed their cause, as groups had during the 1910s and 1920s. The early-twentieth-century agitation for mothers' pensions completely disappeared in the 1930s. Although the same women's organizations were functioning in the 1930s and many leaders of the mothers' aid movement remained active in the government, these groups did not lend their support to single mothers at this critical juncture. Consequently, the original coalition that advanced mothers' pensions—in particular, the women's federations and clubs, the Children's Bureau, and other public figures—did not attempt to make ADC into a program more inclusive than mothers' pensions. No federal institution other than the Children's Bureau had any interest in programs to aid dependent children. Dramatic changes in the existing programs could have threatened the inclusion of an aid to dependent children program altogether. Therefore, the modest changes that were made focused on expanding assistance to areas where the program previously did not operate. However, a few dedicated mothers' pension supporters wanted to see the federalization of these state programs. Although many of the earlier mothers' pension advocates had ceased their activity, a new generation of welfare reform leaders remained active in transporting principles of mothers' pensions to ADC.

Some of ADC's shortcomings can be attributed to the failures of these new reform leaders to create strategic alliances. Specifically, they failed to ally with the poor and the African-American welfare reform networks or the civil rights organizations. In *The Dual Agenda*, Dona Cooper Hamilton and Charles V. Hamilton outline the social welfare and civil rights agendas of the civil rights organizations, especially their emphasis on a universal social welfare system that did not distinguish between assistance and insurance and federal hegemony over program administration. The dual agenda of federal civil rights organizations mirrors the agenda of the Progressive Era African-American welfare reform networks and arrives at the same conclusions—that is, both groups argued that social welfare programs that are not universal trap African-Americans in the "assistance" tier (tier 2) and channel whites into tier 1. Hamilton and Hamilton also argued that when there is state hegemony instead of federal hegemony in administration, African-Americans will be excluded from the programs.[2]

The New Deal reformers adopted the Progressive Era's reform legacy and ignored the social welfare agenda of the civil rights organizations and the African-American reform networks, instead adopting a social welfare strategy that created distinctions among the poor. When the Social Security Act was passed in 1935, ADC was the only program that required recipients to be "needy." Furthermore, ADC was the only program that subjected potential recipients to a morals test to determine if they were "suitable" to raise children. These reformers supported the creation of a needs-based welfare program within a larger welfare system that provided better benefits for one group over another, thereby preempting the opportunity to create a universalistic welfare state. The result was the creation of a bifurcated welfare system that channeled whites and the middle class into one benefit stream and single mothers, minorities, and the poor into another stream.

The Legislative History

When reviewing the legislative history of Title IV, it becomes apparent that it was tied, or rather bonded, to mother' pensions. In his January 1935 message to Congress before the passage of the Social Security Act, the president called for federal grants to states in support of "existing mothers' pension systems." Furthermore, during the congressional debate over the act, the House Ways and Means Committee chairman argued for federal aid to "permit the mothers' pension type of care to become nationally operative."[3]

Two female social welfare reformers, Julia Lathrop and Grace Abbott, were primarily responsible for bringing mothers' aid into the Social Security Act. At the end of 1934, Katherine Lenroot, a Vassar graduate and daughter of a former senator from Wisconsin, was serving as chief of the Children's Bureau, with Martha Eliot, a physician trained at Harvard University Medical School, as assistant chief. These two women, working with an advisory committee on child welfare, wrote the final report on security for children for the Committee on Economic Security.[4] Abbott, Lenroot, and Eliot drafted the ADC title.[5] The proposal submitted to Edwin Witte, chairman of the Committee on Economic Security, allocated

$25 million for "mothers' pensions." Their request was based on the 109,000 families currently receiving mothers' aid and an additional 179,000 families estimated to be eligible for but not receiving mothers' pensions. However, this total remained significantly lower than the 358,000 female-headed families receiving poor relief in 1934. The original proposal also called for the program to be half federally funded; the final act provided for only one-third federal funding.

Although children's interests clearly did not constitute the core of the Social Security Act, the council and the administration attempted to show how various parts of the act directly or indirectly affected child welfare.[6] As Witte acknowledged, Congress had little interest in aid to dependent children. Witte recounted a story that illustrated Congress's indifference to providing for dependent children: Congressman Frederick Vinson (D-Ky.)[7] added a restriction that would have kept the aid limit below what was recognized as sufficient for a widow and children to live on. According to Witte, he and others protested Vinson's proposal, and although it encountered "justified criticism . . . there was so little interest on the part of any of the members in the aid to dependent children that no one thereafter made a motion to strike out the restriction."[8]

Reflecting the interests of its drafters and the legislators who passed the bill, the Social Security Act favored select groups of individuals, offered some conciliatory programs to others, and outright excluded many. Mothers' pension recipients, or future ADC recipients, lacked the political and/or economic resources to garner sufficient attention. Dependent women were poor, they were an unimportant voting bloc, and their children could not vote.

After drafting ADC, the Children's Bureau suffered numerous defeats in getting its preferred version of the bill passed. The Committee on Economic Security and Witte did their best to defend the Children's Bureau's version of ADC but were forced to accept certain congressional amendments to get the bill through Congress. Two significant sources of opposition pushed through the congressional changes—southern congressmen and patronage politicians. The bill was first referred to the House Ways and Means committee, chaired by Robert Doughton of North Carolina, instead of going to the liberal Labor Committee. Doughton and his constituents had substantial agricultural interests and were fully intent on protecting them. The bill then went to the Senate Finance Committee, which was chaired by Senator Byron Patton Harrison of Mississippi. The support of both of these southern committee chairmen was essential to getting the bill passed. Therefore, amendments that suited them were added to the bill. The "southern" amendments affected two significant aspects of ADC: the agency and experts that would administer the program and the level of centralized control.[9]

Administering Agency

Four entities engaged in a considerable struggle for jurisdictional control over ADC: the Children's Bureau, the Federal Emergency Relief Administration (FERA), the Public Health Service, and the group that became the Social Security Administration. The Children's Bureau and its many supporters expected that administrative responsibility for Title IV would go to the bureau, which saw itself as the organization best suited for administering the program because of its long history of working with state officials in the administration of the Sheppard-Towner Act and the mothers' aid laws. Furthermore, various government officials had decided that the Children's Bureau was going to administer a child welfare program authorized by Title V of the Social Security Act. FERA wanted to administer a program completely outside of the existing forty-five state mothers' pension laws. The Children's Bureau and mothers' pension advocates argued that moving administration to FERA would take the program outside the existing mothers' aid apparatus and that FERA would "necessarily pull down the carefully built standards of the Mothers' Aid program and virtually result in giving children aid which was little better than local poor relief."[10] The Children's Bureau wanted mothers' aid clients to be distinguished from the stigma and humiliation of general public assistance to which they would be subjected if the program were lumped together with other nonselective assistance programs.

A political shuffle ensued that bounced administration of ADC to various agencies. The Roosevelt administration's bill called for placing control of ADC with FERA. However, the House Ways and Means Committee gave the responsibility to the Social Security Board. The Senate Finance Committee returned ADC to the Children's Bureau and placed the Social Security Board within the Department of Labor. In the end, all of the assistance programs, including ADC, went to the Social Security Board, and legislators created within the board a Bureau of Public Assistance. Witte's final attempts to place the Social Security Board in the Department of Labor, the home of the Children's Bureau, failed.

From a purely institutional perspective, ADC recipients were denied the most logical defender of their interests. Before the depression, the Children's Bureau of the Department of Labor had distinguished itself as the most important federal agency involved in welfare activities.[11] Created in 1912, the Children's Bureau establishment coincided with the first mothers' pension laws. Congress mandated that the bureau "investigate and report . . . upon all matters pertaining to the welfare of children and child life among all classes of our people."[12] One of the bureau's primary responsibilities had been to research and conduct field studies of all aspects of child health and welfare. The bureau also advised the state governments on every conceivable aspect of mothers' pension programs, working particularly closely with the state departments of welfare with responsibility for child care and protection, including child labor, child health, and juvenile delinquency. The Children's Bureau had been responsible for administering the first Federal Child Labor Law in 1917–18 and the Federal Maternity and Infancy Act from 1921 to 1929.

Locating ADC within the Children's Bureau would not have prevented the exclusion of African-Americans. In fact, as discussed earlier, the Children's Bureau built up mothers' pensions as a privileged program for "deserving" mothers that resulted in the exclusion of African-Americans. From an institution-building perspective, the problem with the separation of ADC from the Children's Bureau was its association with other income-maintenance programs. This association had a negative effect on the program's development. Lumping these programs together only perpetuated and strengthened the distinction between social insurance and "welfare." ADC recipients would now be affected by the same stigma as the recipients of other noncontributory programs. The separation of the public assistance programs from the other welfare benefit streams institutionalized on a federal level a stratified state welfare system. The push to integrate the administration of aid to children, the aged, and the blind and of general relief resulted in the further isolation of children's interests from mainstream concerns.[13]

The battle between FERA and the Children's Bureau played out even on the issue of how the new legislation would define "dependency." In FERA's proposal,

> "dependent children" shall mean children under the age of sixteen in their own homes, in which there is no adult person, other than one needed to care for the child or children, who is able to work and provide the family with a reasonable subsistence compatible with decency and health.

This definition provided for a standard of decency and health and, more importantly, determined eligibility based on the family's needs, not just those of the child or children. Eligibility was to be based on the provision of subsistence, not on the absence, presence, or disability of a family member. For FERA, ADC meant general relief or assistance for families with children under age sixteen.

In the end, the FERA definition was rejected and the definition of "dependent children" in the Social Security Act resembled that in mothers' aid legislation. Title IV defined a dependent child as a child under the age of sixteen "who has been deprived of parental support or care by reason of the death, continued absence from the home, or physical or mental incapacity of a parent."[14] Child welfare leaders saw the federal legislation as an opportunity to expand and strengthen existing mothers' pension programs. They did not support any changes that would create a general assistance program. These leaders wanted to continue the standards of mothers' pension legislation, selecting one group for aid. They feared that the broader aid suggested by FERA would destroy the standards established by the mothers' pension programs.

Centralized Control

The second conflict in designing ADC was the level of centralized control over the local ADC programs and the implicit racial implications. Congressmen and state politicians, particularly from the South, argued and fought against federal standards for ADC administration. The Social Security Act threatened to change the relationship between employers and 5.5 million African-American workers—2 million who were in agriculture and 1.5 million in domestic service. Opponents of federal standards were concerned that if ADC freed poor African-American women from the burden of supporting their children, employers would be forced to raise the wages they paid to such women. Southern congressmen did not want federal benefits based on northern standards to undermine the existing southern race and labor relations.[15] As Teresa Amott reminds us, "at the time of the establishment of AFDC, the southern racial caste system was firmly in place. Southern congressmen, determined to maintain a supply of cheap labor to interests in the South, insisted that authority to set benefit levels and administer eligibility under the AFDC system be set at the state level."[16] Local politicians also feared the loss of patronage jobs in the local assistance programs, which would happen if the federal standards proposed by the Children's Bureau were adopted. The result was the well-known exclusion of agricultural and domestic laborers from social insurance. Ten years after the legislation was passed and after numerous amendments, one-third of African-American male workers and two-thirds of African-American female workers remained excluded. Passage of the final Social Security bill passed required the sacrifice of federal standards for the assistance programs. Although happy to have resources provided by the federal government, southerners did not want either federal controls or welfare programs that might undermine the existing southern race relations.

Without federal control, the state and local agencies were free to exclude—or continue to exclude—whomever they wished. The AFDC's design thus ensured that African-Americans could be left off the benefit rolls. In essence, African-Americans in the South could be excluded from welfare assistance, and southern economic interests were free to maintain a labor force that enabled them to remain competitive with the North.[17] Had ADC been structured differently—that is, if federal standards had been attached and enforced—the shape of our entire welfare state might be different. Federal standards would have reduced the variation in state programs and would most likely have resulted in wider inclusion, particularly among African-Americans. Although it is impossible to estimate, it is reasonable to assume that if the African-American population had had access to ADC during the 1930s and 1940s, no intense and rapid inclusion of African-Americans would have occurred during the 1960s, and without that rapid expansion, there would have been no backlash from the establishment and in public perception.

By federalizing existing mothers' pension programs, ADC federalized the existing racial patterning and disparities inherent in mothers' pensions. In fact, the Social Security Act as a whole reinforced the existing racial balance. During the congressional hearings on the Social Security bill, testimony regarding racism in ADC fell on deaf ears. Charles Houston, a representative of the National Association for the Advancement of Colored People, testified before the Senate Finance Committee that his group had considered testifying in support of the bill, but the more it was studied, the more it began to look "like a sieve with the holes just big enough for the majority of Negroes to fall through."[18] Houston called for an equitable distribution of ADC resources even in communities that were segregated.[19] George Haines, representing the Federal Council of Churches Department of Race Relations, offered the committee further testimony that raised the problem of racism. Detailing numerous instances of racism in existing public policies, Haines called for a clause that would prohibit discrimination and would deny benefits to states that demonstrated the equitable distribution of benefits.[20] Neither of these men represented powerful organizations or powerful interests, so their appeals fell on deaf and even hostile ears.

Instead of promoting racial equity, the New Deal policies marginalized African-Americans even more and in a more symbolic way than policies of previous eras.[21] Instead of compensating for the racialized policies of different states and localities, New Deal policies institutionalized that racism at a national level. The early New Deal programs treated African-American men and women differently than their white counterparts. Prevailing racial prejudice, combined with limited employment opportunities, resulted in assistance for poor whites but not for poor African-Americans. Many African-Americans were denied employment on the grounds that they were accustomed to poverty and did not have the same needs as whites. Minorities generally did not have access to higher-skilled and therefore higher-paid jobs. They were often fired from their low-skill jobs to make room for whites. Dual wage scales often existed for the same jobs. Some local and state administrators had pay scales that paid African-Americans up to 50 percent less than whites for the same job. And in some localities, specifically in the South, work and other relief programs were completely off-limits to African-Americans.[22]

The stratification of Social Security programs reproduced and deepened these existing social inequalities. In the end, the federal legislation was not broadened, and the administration of ADC went to the Social Security Board rather than the Children's Bureau. The new program was saddled with the institutional legacy of the local agencies that administered mothers' pensions but was denied the protection of the federal agency that had advocated and supervised these local mothers' pension programs.

Title IV Provisions & Requirements

Title IV of the Social Security Act was enabling legislation that left the initiative for developing and/or maintaining an ADC program up to the individual states. If a state wanted federal funds, it was required to operate the program throughout the state, to have a single state agency administer the program, and to share in the cost. All states interested in participating had to submit plans to the Social Security Board for approval. The federal government left itself only one check on the states. The federal agency had the responsibility to approve the state plans and, in the event that they violated the Social Security Act, to withhold funds. If any state failed to "comply substantially" with the plan that had been approved or violated any of the act's other prohibitions against citizenship or residence discrimination, it would be sanctioned. This meant that federal payments would stop until the board was satisfied that the state was complying.[23]

General conditions for receiving ADC were broader than under the local mothers' pension programs. States had to meet a variety of requirements to qualify for funding under the ADC program as specified in the Social Security Act.

> A state plan must (1) provide that it shall be in effect in all political subdivisions of the State, and, if administered by them, be mandatory upon them; (2) provide for financial participation by the State; (3) either provide for the establishment or designation of a single State agency to administer the plan, or provide for the establishment or designation of a single State agency to supervise the administration of the plan; (4) provide for granting to any individual, whose claim with respect to aid to a dependent child is denied, an opportunity for a fair hearing before such State agency; (5) provide such methods of administration (other than those relating to selection, tenure of office, and compensation of personnel) as are found by the Board to be necessary for the efficient operation of the plan; and (6) provide that the State agency will make such reports, in such form and containing such information, as the Board may from time to time require, and comply with such provisions as the Board may from time to time find necessary to assure the correctness and verification of such reports.[24]

Those states that wished to take advantage of the federal funds had to broaden the existing mothers' pension eligibility requirements to be in line with the Social Security Act. For example, the definition of dependency was much broader under the Social Security Act then in most state mothers' pension laws. Title IV defined a dependent child as a child under the age of sixteen "who has been deprived of parental support of care by reason of the death, continued absence from the home, or physical or mental incapacity of a parent."[25] Children could reside in the homes of various relatives, including parents, grandparents, siblings, aunts, uncles, stepparents, and stepsiblings. However, the title still limited eligibility in accordance with the predominant mothers' pension philosophy. In other words, the eligibility of a dependent child to receive benefits was directly correlated to the absence of one or both parents. A poor child with both parents was ineligible for assistance. However, defining incapacity and absence more broadly and permitting children to live with a broader range of relatives made the funds available to more children than the narrower mothers' pension statutes.

The suitability requirement, which was deeply rooted in mothers' pensions, continued under ADC. Title IV did not specifically mention certain conditions for the home or a parent's morality; however, Congress sanctioned the consideration of "moral character" in defining eligibility. This provision, combined with a state's license to define eligibility, ensured the continued use of the suitable home provision.[26] More importantly, the inclusion of moral character as a criteria meant that the intended beneficiary was white. As one of ADC's first directors stated, "The ADC example we always thought about was the poor lady in West Virginia whose husband was killed in a mining accident, and the problem of how she could feed those kids."[27] This statement implied that the poor lady was white.

As with other programs under the Social Security Act, the maximum grant to be matched and the proportion of this amount that the federal government would reimburse were specified. However, these amounts were much lower for children than for the elderly. The federal proportion of the children's aid was limited to one-third, with a maximum total payment of eighteen dollars for the first child and twelve dollars each for subsequent children. These limits were the same dollar limits on payments to the children of servicemen in World War I. During committee hearings, one congressman argued successfully that ADC limits should mirror the limits set for the children of veterans' widows. He did not call attention to the fact that the veterans' widows received thirty dollars a month in addition to the pensions for the children.[28] The federal government would match a third of these amounts. For the elderly, however, the maximum grant was thirty dollars per month, with the federal government reimbursing half of that amount. The federal government also reimbursed states for part of the costs of administering the programs—one-third for ADC and half for old-age insurance. No funds for the dependent child's caretaker or parent were provided until 1950, and not until the 1961 amendments to the Social Security Act could states receive matching federal funds for extending Aid to Families with Dependent Children (as the program was then called) to needy children with able-bodied but unemployed parents.

Title IV left most administrative details to the state's discretion, including the standard of need, the amount of the pension, and the personnel. A single standard was believed to be unrealistic considering the vast differences in the American landscape. The states were not obligated to provide assistance that met any health standard. Although a statewide standard of assistance had to be set, actual grants in different localities could vary because of the variation in cost of living. The actual servicing or administration of the programs also varied depending on personnel. The qualifications, selection, and compensation of personnel to administer the program were also left completely to the states' discretion. Caseloads varied, as did educational qualifications.

Transfer to ADC

Before the depression, mothers' aid programs commanded the largest proportion of all state and local aid—a bigger share than appropriations for aid to the elderly and the disabled and general relief combined. The depression saw a multifold increase in other state-sponsored relief efforts, such as work relief.[29] The depression caused dependent children and single mothers to exhaust the resources of mothers' aid programs as well as other outdoor poor relief. The depression also made it impossible for localities to develop new mothers' aid programs. In 1934, Georgia and South Carolina still had not passed mothers' pension legislation, and the mothers' aid programs in Arkansas, Mississippi, and New Mexico were eliminated because of lack of resources. The same year, reports showed that 171 counties in twenty-six states had discontinued aid. Therefore, on the eve of the passage of the Social Security Act, less than half of the authorized counties were administering benefits.[30]

The passage of the Social Security Act in 1935 brought the national and state governments together to finance, administer, and supervise local programs to aid dependent children in their own homes. ADC had an immediate and significant impact on existing mothers' pension programs, as caseloads increased dramatically. Figure 3 demonstrates the change in the number of children aided when mothers' pensions became nationalized. Within one year of implementation, a significant number of dependent children were receiving ADC benefits. The one regional exception to this was the South, where coverage remained low or nonexistent for several years. During this period, Mississippi had no ADC program, and Texas's program provided benefits for fewer than one child per thousand.[31] Furthermore, the number of children aided per one thousand population in Florida, Georgia, North Carolina, South Carolina, Tennessee, and Virginia remained significantly below the national median. Among the southern states, only children in Alabama, Arkansas, and Louisiana were aided at a rate close to or above the national median.

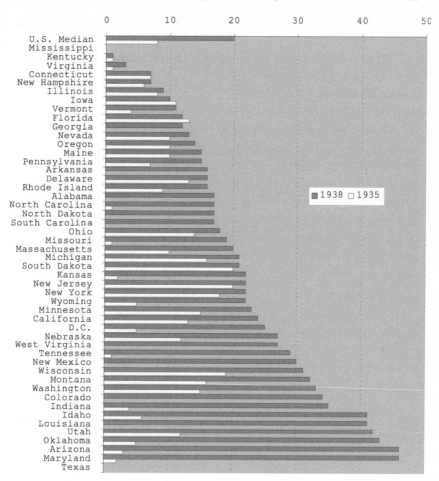

Fig. 3. Number of children on whose behalf payments for mothers' aid and ADC were made per one thousand population under sixteen years of age, by states, 1935–38. (Data from Dorothy R. Bucklin, "Public Aid for the Care of Dependent Children in Their Own Homes," *Social Security Bulletin* 2 [April 1939], as reported in Brown, *Public Relief*, 30–31.)

Even accounting for the paltry number of children aided in the South, ADC magnified the existing mothers' pension programs and expanded the number of dependent children being served. Pennsylvania went from having a mothers' aid program with 8,286 recipients in December 1935 to an ADC program with 30,245 families in December 1939 and 48,778 families by December 1940. Other states that lacked functioning mothers' aid programs were also affected. In 1935 Alabama did not have a program, but by December 1936, 5,316 families received ADC.

Table 12 compares the number of families and average grant amount under mothers' pensions and ADC for nineteen states.[32] The table shows the dramatic increase in the number of families aided under ADC compared with the number of families aided under mothers' pensions. The chart also shows a moderate increase in grant amounts in some states, a comparable grant amount in several states, and a grant reduction in a few states under ADC. The most startling change is the increase in the number of families assisted under ADC.

Many local communities had not established mothers' pension programs for a variety of reasons, including the desire to exclude certain populations from assistance. These same communities were now forced to participate in a federal-state program intended to serve a broader community than that intended by mothers' pensions. This development had

TABLE 12.   Comparison of the Number of Families and Average Grant per Family for ADC in Nineteen States in June 1931, June 1936, and June 1940

	Number of Families			Children under 16 Aided in 1940, per 1,000 Population	Average Grant per Family ($)		
	1931	1936	1940		1931	1936	1940
Alabama		4,911	5,914	17		8.86	14.13
Arizona		465	2,544	55		27.98	32.31
Arkansas	131	2,301	4,654	18	4.33	6.98	12.00
Colorado	650	997	5,960	49	26.50	26.87	30.02
District of Columbia	161	1,533	933	22	65.83	37.5	37.27
Idaho	230	1,390	2,894	46	13.16	25.94	28.70
Maine	608	1,185	1,527	17	30.16	35.69	38.74
Maryland	121	5,494	7,326	44	30.52	29.50	31.15
Nebraska	1,453	1,422	5,428	31	17.81	23.26	27.36
New Hampshire	175	346	673	13	19.77	34.92	44.78
New Mexico		32	1,888	38		29.28	25.17
New York	18,423	24,727	36,058	23	52.62	41.72	45.07
Oklahoma	1,896	15,311	18,554	52	7.29	8.84	14.49
Rhode Island	388	569	1,210	18	55.09	53.17	45.57
Utah	628	1,901	3,392	48	11.77	29.07	35.41
Vermont	90	291	569	16	21.11	17.31	32.83
Washington	2,517	4,370	4,979	30	21.66	28.21	38.01
Wisconsin	7,052	8,047	12,303	31	21.66	28.21	38.01
Wyoming	95	502	747	27	22.55	28.99	31.89

Source: Data from Children's Bureau, U.S. Department of Labor, *Mothers' Aid–1931;* Social Security Board, *Public Assistance* (Washington, DC: Government Printing Office, 1936); Social Security Board, *Social Security Bulletin III* (Washington, DC: Government Printing Office, 1940).

a significant impact in the South where many mothers' pension programs had not operated or operated in only select counties. According to the Committee on Economic Security's 1935 report to the president,

> laws for aid to dependent children should be mandatory upon the local units, and state equalization funds should be made available to counties for aid purposes, in amounts sufficient to bring this aid throughout the state at least to a minimum level of adequacy, both as to number of families aided and amount of grant. If well administered, state aid will act as an effective powerful lever in raising administrative standards of investigation, budgetary practices and other procedures.[33]

Although qualifying ADC programs were mandated to operate statewide, a requirement intended to prevent discrimination and patronage from determining who got benefits, the rule was vitiated. States circumvented the requirement by varying grants across counties based on subjective cost-of-living variations and by awarding fewer per capita grants in certain counties, specifically those with a higher percentage African-American population.

Even the requirement that a single state agency be responsible for administering or supervising the program was flexible. Some states had infrequent and loosely structured state supervision, while others had tightly controlled central state administration.[34] In states where authority was decentralized and strong local autonomy existed, the county essentially controlled the program. Some states had problems with the establishment of ADC because it required tremendous changes in intergovernmental relations. In particular, certain localities wanted to ensure that program implementation reflected local values and consequently resisted ceding control of social welfare administration to the state governments. Local control translated into the exclusion of African-Americans.

States that had well-institutionalized mothers' aid programs required only minor changes to meet the conditions necessary for participating in ADC. In particular, states in the Northeast such as Connecticut, Maine, New Hampshire, Rhode Island, Vermont, New Jersey, Delaware, Massachusetts, Pennsylvania, and New York were more likely to have centralized mothers' aid programs. Most of these states made the transition from mothers' aid to ADC without much difficulty. Connecticut was the only New England state that waited to adopt ADC, which was not put into place until 1941.

States that had well-developed but decentralized mothers' aid programs had problems with the national government agencies. For example, the Social Security Board would not accept judicial authorities as ADC administrators, which created problems in Michigan, where the probate judges in charge of the juvenile courts administered mothers' aid. Illinois, the first state to have a statewide law for mothers' aid, did not adopt ADC until 1941 because of court opposition. States that institutionalized mothers' aid as a county option were laggards in implementing ADC, specifically because these local agencies and local governments had difficulty accepting state administration.

Michigan provides one example of how the Social Security Act's Title IV affected existing legislation. Prior to Title IV, Michigan had an operative mothers' pension program, but the Social Security Act stipulated a much broader group of relatives or guardians who could receive assistance for the care of dependent children than Michigan's Mothers' Pension legislation had permitted. Furthermore, under Title IV, specific causes of dependency were not enumerated, as was the case under Michigan's Mothers' Pension Act. However, Michigan added two additional requirements to those enumerated in Title IV: (1) no mother receiving a pension from the probate court would be considered eligible for ADC; and (2) the moral suitability of the custodian of the child must be established. The latter requirement was undoubtedly inherited from the mothers' pension plan, which required the mother to be a "fit and proper guardian for her child or children." In 1936, ADC went into effect in all counties in Michigan. While mothers' pensions had been administered through probate courts, ADC was administered under state supervision, ensuring a greater standardization of payment and procedures for establishing eligibility. In addition, a commission developed procedures by which families denied benefits under ADC or unhappy with the program could petition for hearings.[35]

Administration of ADC

ADC was often underfunded because the program did not serve a politically important constituency, unlike old-age assistance. In some cases, ADC payments remained smaller than what the law authorized. Too few resources remained after supporting old-age pensions. Extreme cases, such as Texas, had no ADC programs yet spent significant amounts on old-age assistance.[36] By 1938, every state had an old-age assistance program, whereas eight states (Connecticut, Illinois, Iowa, Kentucky, Mississippi, Nevada,

South Dakota, and Texas) plus the Alaska territory still lacked ADC programs. State and local investment in old-age assistance ($205,289,000) to-
taled nearly three times more than that for ADC ($71,912,000).[37]

Where the state bore responsibility for funding ADC programs, it could
make whatever investment in the program it wanted to as long as it met
the federal statewide operation requirement. States had different fiscal
capacities to maintain programs, different proportions of families below
the poverty line, and, most importantly, different racial populations. Consequently, residence often determined whether a child received benefits;
children in the South received the least coverage. In June 1938, 243,000
families with more than 600,000 children were receiving ADC. By 1939,
that number had increased to 298,000 families and 718,000 children. The
total cost of the program was $103 million, with the federal government
reimbursing $34 million of that amount. Even though these figures
quickly met and surpassed the Children's Bureau's initial estimates, the
Bureau of Research and Statistics continued to believe that a great number of eligible dependent children—at least 1 million and more likely
closer to 2 million—still lacked assistance, although the data necessary to
statistically prove that belief were not available.[38] One of the obvious reasons for this gap in coverage was several states' failure to establish ADC
programs, although a few of these states continued giving out assistance
through their mothers' pension programs.

The South experienced more problems than did other regions, in particular because it was least able to finance public assistance. Many southern states had had no mothers' aid programs, so a welfare state had to be
built upon a political and administrative vacuum. Furthermore, the region's preoccupation with the effects of welfare on wage levels also re-
tarded the establishment of ADC. Conditions in the South must be understood in terms of the prevailing racial order and the related interest in
maintaining a large cheap labor pool. During his unsuccessful 1936 senatorial campaign against Richard Russell, Georgia Governor Eugene Talmadge attacked the Social Security Act, claiming that it would destroy
the supply of African-American farm labor and tax Georgia's white
people while giving 90 percent of the benefits to African-Americans. As
governor, Talmadge vetoed the Georgia legislature's efforts to enact laws
necessary to establish the Social Security Act's public assistance programs. Talmadge also opposed the renomination of President Roosevelt in
1936. Talmadge lost his senatorial bid and his veto was overturned, but
only after a significant battle.[39]

Many southern states did not want to finance relief but instead relied on localities to fund it. Consequently, southern mothers with dependent children who did not have access to ADC were forced to rely on FERA. Since FERA was federally administered, African-Americans were able to get FERA relief. Unlike mothers' pension benefits, where African-Americans comprised only 3 percent of the total beneficiary population in 1931, FERA was more equitably distributed. In regions outside of the South, the percentage of African-Americans on relief in urban and rural areas was equivalent. In the urban South the percentage of African-Americans receiving assistance was higher than the percentage of whites receiving assistance. In the rural South, however, the percentage of African-Americans receiving assistance remained very low. Furthermore, the ratio of African-Americans to whites on assistance in the South remained lower than in the East and Midwest. Many southern states saw nationally financed work programs as a preferable alternative to ADC and consequently hesitated to establish ADC programs.[40]

The Suitability Condition: From Mothers' Pensions to ADC

After the passage of the Social Security Act, the "suitable home" or "fitness" policies that characterized state mothers' pension laws prevailed in most state ADC plans. States' ability to set eligibility requirements for ADC recipients formalized at the national level the state "fitness" or "suitable home" policies. In January 1934, thirty-nine states required that mothers receiving aid be "fit and proper" or "mentally, morally and physically fit." In preliminary reports and debates on Title IV, Congress revealed its desire that the "moral character" of the dependent child's caretakers or parents be considered in eligibility determinations.[41] The suitability sentiment had prevailed within the Children's Bureau from 1911 to 1935, and advocates reaffirmed their support of it after the act was passed. A few years after the passage of Title IV, some states repealed their suitability laws but continued to use them in eligibility determinations. In other states, such laws were not widely used but remained on the books. Other states "so strengthened [suitability requirements] that in time they pervaded and influenced all aspects of the ADC program."[42] Overall, the "suitable home" condition achieved widespread acceptance, as is reflected in the fact that the requirement was present both in states that wanted to extend public aid as broadly as possible and in those states with small and very limited programs.

By October 1, 1939, half of the states had incorporated either a provision suggested by the American Public Welfare Association that children should live in a "suitable family home meeting the standards of care and health, fixed by the laws of this state and the rules and regulations of the State Department there under" or a requirement that the home or parent be "fit" or "proper." In fact, seven states and the District of Columbia retained requirements that the parent, the home, or both parent and home be fit. A footnote in the American Public Welfare Association's document explained the purpose of this "suitability" provision: "the maintenance of proper home environment for dependent children is vital to the success of any child welfare program. The provision for assistance under this Act affords a unique opportunity to raise the standards of home care. This feature should be stressed in the drafting of this legislation."[43]

One effect of the suitability provision was ADC's continued exclusion of dependent children of unmarried women. A 1939 study of ADC recipients revealed that only 3.5 percent of those children living with their mothers had unmarried mothers. Five states had no children born out of wedlock receiving ADC, and eleven other states had fewer than fifty children of unmarried mothers receiving benefits. The report's author, Mary Larabee, attributed this exclusion to the "suitable home" provision.[44] Jane Hoey,[45] the director of the Bureau of Public Assistance from 1936 to 1953, reported that only 2 percent of children living with unmarried mothers were receiving benefits.[46]

Several welfare reformers protested the inclusion of "suitability" provisions in the state ADC plans. Grace Marcus, for example, noted the negative effects of carrying over the mothers' pension philosophy to ADC, stating that certain ambiguities in ADC "would seem to have [their] roots in the 'suitable home' philosophy of Mother's Aid, in which the agency assumes a quasi-authoritative role, undefined in its responsibilities or powers."[47]

Hoey also spoke out against the practice of denying benefits to dependent children because of the actions of their parents. Hoey set herself apart from many advocates of mothers' pensions and ADC, including Edith Abbott, in claiming that "denying children this form of aid because their parent's behavior does not conform to a certain pattern is coming to be recognized as not a solution of such problems. Yet transfer from general relief to aid to dependent children is still frequently made on a basis of promoting the nice families."[48] Also distancing herself from the accepted parochialism with which mothers' pensions and ADC were being administered, Hoey argued that state and local administrators should implement objective standards established by the federal and state laws to guarantee equitable assistance for all families with dependent children.

Hoey was particularly concerned that racial discrimination would make insuring equitable assistance a challenge. She noted the "deep prejudices towards minority groups that you find in every community, the intolerance towards the different points of view about the essentials of living that you find in every community."[49] In a 1965 interview, Hoey spoke in detail about the blatant exclusion of African-American, Mexican, and Native American children from different state ADC programs and about the problems she faced in documenting and ending racial exclusion by state boards. In one instance, she sent staff members to different counties to study a cross-section of cases to verify rumors of racial quotas. In Mississippi,

> I got word that in that state a quota had been put in every county— but nothing in writing—that there was to be 10 percent quota for Negroes. . . . Some would be 50 percent, or 60 percent Negroes in a county, and 10 percent quotas.[50]

Hoey also talked about the exclusion of Native Americans from the benefit rolls, describing how Native Americans in New Mexico were reluctant to even come into the offices to apply and how in Arizona applications had been accepted but not acted on. Nevada was so reluctant to assist Native American children that the state did not implement an ADC program until 1955, becoming the last state to do so. Finally, she discussed how Texas's and New Mexico's citizenship requirements were intended to exclude Mexicans from ADC benefits.

The intentional use of the "suitable home" provision to selectively exclude people from ADC became more apparent during the late 1930s, when there was an attempt by social welfare reformers to shift the meaning of "unsuitable" or "unfit" to define only those homes where children were abused or neglected. Although a few states accepted this new definition, most others preserved exclusion based on race. In some areas neglectful parents received no punishment, and certain reports indicate that abuse and neglect were more common among white families.[51] This reveals the overtly discriminatory nature of this provision. Fearing that white families would be dropped from ADC because of neglect and replaced by African-American families, most localities rejected this move to define suitability in relation to neglect and abuse.

Because of the vagueness of the suitability provisions, many families who were interested in applying for ADC were determined to be ineligible before they had even gone through an application process. While we

know that many families were denied applications, it is impossible to
know how many families were denied or even to determine demographic
information about these families because records were created only for
those families who went through the application process.[52] Most states
have records only for approved applicants, limiting the data available on
the ineligible families and the official determinations about why they
were ineligible. Furthermore, it is impossible to estimate the number of
families that would have applied for aid but chose not to because they
thought that they would not be accepted or, even worse, feared reprisals
for applying.

The Social Security Board's third annual report questioned the policy
of terminating aid in "unfit" homes.

> In some places it has been the traditional practice to give mothers'
> aid only to selected applicants and to leave to the overseer of the poor
> or other local official the families in which serious social problems
> exist. Modern practice in the States recognizes that the major consid-
> eration must be the welfare of the children rather than the conduct
> of the parents and that the existence of social problems in a family
> group usually indicates the need for more intensive service rather
> than for curtailment of aid.[53]

Although such reports signal national-level administrators' recognition of
the deleterious effects of the suitability condition, these officials could do
little to counter this seemingly intrinsic program component.

Nevertheless, from 1943 to 1945, the Social Security Board attempted to
compel states to repeal suitable home requirements and to provide aid to
all needy children. As a result of the board's efforts, fifteen states repealed
the suitability condition.[54] However, during the same period, five other
states incorporated the suitable home provision into their programs.[55] Although suitable home provisions already existed informally in most
states, between 1952 and 1960, nine states, mostly in the South, added formal suitable home requirements.[56] The national administrators' efforts
were countered by states' and localities' determination to limit the program to suitable, white families.

One of the biggest challenges in addressing the use of a suitability provision lay in changing the philosophy of the individuals running the state
and local ADC programs, many of them the same people who had administered the mothers' pension programs. In seven of eight states that had
mothers' pension programs in 1935 and immediately adopted ADC, the
same person served as administrator of both programs.[57] The continuity

in personnel clearly indicates that a change in funding and legislation did not signal a shift in administration—aid to dependent children, whether under mothers' pension laws or the Social Security Act, would be administered as the localities saw fit. Employees at the Bureau of Public Assistance clearly understood that the local administrators of ADC had well-defined ideas about how the program would look. Bureau officials also knew that they were powerless to influence the local administrators because the federal law restricted bureau operations to the state level.

Winifred Bell's examination of the history of ADC, especially the development of that program vis-à-vis mothers' pensions, focuses greatly on the "suitable home" provision. According to Bell,

> the evidence shows that their primary functions [of such provisions] were (1) to restrict the growth of the case-load and (2) to inhibit ADC coverage of Negro and Illegitimate children who because of their family composition were more apt to qualify than were white children with two able-bodied parents in the home. The desire of states to restrict their programs selectively is also shown by the appearance of a series of closely related eligibility conditions which primarily affected nonwhite and illegitimate children.[58]

Bell and legions of reformers and scholars demonstrate the deliberate and thinly veiled attempt to create a welfare state for whites.

The Racial Legacy of Mothers' Pensions

In theory, the advent of the ADC federal legislation in 1936 would mark a new era in the history of aid to mothers with dependent children. However, the permissiveness of the state mothers' pension legislation and lack of state funding and supervision allowed localities to implement programs according to local desires, mores, and prejudices. In practice, officials denied benefits to African-American mothers in both systematic and arbitrary ways. Although poor African-Americans fared better under ADC than under mothers' pensions, the improvement is significant only when compared to the almost universal exclusion of African-Americans from the earlier programs. In 1939, the director of the Bureau of Public Assistance reported that states and communities often established procedures or requirements that caused a particular hardship on certain groups, such as African-Americans and unmarried mothers. A 1942 report from the Social Security Board analyzed programs in sixteen states and acknowledged,

Practices in the administration of aid to dependent children in some States apparently result in assistance to fewer Negro and Indian children than white children in relation to the number of needy children in the respective populations.[59]

Although now a federal program, ADC mirrored many of the negative features of state mothers' pension programs, especially the racial composition of the recipient pool.

Decentralized administration, the lack of federal standards, and the perpetuation of the suitable home standard meant the continued imposition of the norms and prejudices that had kept African-Americans off the mothers' pension rolls. Furthermore, the disjointed administration of two child-welfare programs, one through the Bureau of Public Assistance and one through the Children's Bureau, left many children, especially African-Americans, in an administrative vacuum. With federal leadership of these two programs divided, control devolved to state and local administrators. The administrators of the federal child welfare programs either adopted or were handicapped by the same parochialism and prejudice that resulted in the scarcity of resources for African-American families under mothers' pensions. Modeling ADC administration on the decentralized mothers' pension programs perpetuated the disproportionate exclusion of African-American families from the benefit rolls. More than anything else, the "suitable home" requirement resulted in the almost wholesale exclusion of African-Americans and other ethnic minorities.

When African-Americans were included in ADC benefit streams in the South, the benefit amounts were lower. Table 13 shows the average monthly ADC grant for children. Grant amounts for African-Americans and whites were approximately the same or were higher for African-American families in the East and Midwest. In the United States as a whole, grant amounts for African-Americans were 3.2 percent higher than for whites. However, grant amounts for African-Americans in the South were significantly lower than those for whites, ranging from 7.3 percent less in Washington, D.C., to 37.6 percent less in South Carolina.

At the time, African-Americans and other minority groups had higher rates of poverty and mortality, indicating those populations' higher need for economic assistance. Table 14 illustrates the stark differences between the white and African-American population in levels of income, death rates, and life expectancies.

If ADC were reaching all eligible children, the percentage of African-American children on the ADC rolls should have mirrored the group's overall percentage of the population in states with large numbers of African-Americans. However, a 1942 Bureau of Public Assistance study of sixteen states revealed that of states with high concentrations of African-Americans, particularly in the South, only the District of Columbia showed a comparatively high ratio of African-American ADC recipients. In other states, notably in the Northeast and Midwest, relatively more African-American children appeared on the ADC rolls. The percentage of African-Americans on the rolls in Arkansas, Louisiana, and North Carolina was lower than their representation in the general population. A study of ten states where more than five thousand African-American children were receiving ADC showed an alarming discrepancy in grant distribution among races. Consequently, the Bureau of Public Assistance "expressed certainty that at least in West Virginia, Louisiana, Arkansas and North Carolina, needy African-American children were suffering from discrimination."[60]

TABLE 13. Racial Differences in ADC Payments, 1939–40, in States with African-American Populations over 100,000 in 1930

	African-American ($)	White ($)	Difference in Payments between African-American and White Families ($)	Percentage Difference
United States	13.09	12.68	0.41	3.2
Pennsylvania	18.13	14.42	3.71	25.7
Ohio	15.18	12.39	2.79	22.5
Indiana	15.03	12.5	2.53	20.2
Michigan	14.2	12.92	1.28	9.9
New York	24.15	22.08	2.07	9.4
Missouri	13.09	12.08	1.01	8.4
West Virginia	8.05	7.66	0.39	5.1
Tennessee	7.38	7.23	0.15	2.1
Maryland	11.34	11.65	−0.31	−2.7
Oklahoma	5.37	5.74	−0.37	−6.4
Washington, D.C.	12.24	13.2	−0.96	−7.3
New Jersey	12.45	13.44	−0.99	−7.4
Louisiana	8.55	9.58	−1.03	−10.8
Alabama	12.87	14.44	−1.57	−10.9
Virginia	5.78	6.56	−0.78	−11.9
North Carolina	5.93	7.03	−1.1	−15.6
Arkansas	3.52	4.24	−0.72	−17.0
Florida	7.3	10.61	−3.31	−31.2
South Carolina	4.03	6.46	−2.43	−37.6

Source: Data from Lieberman, *Shifting*, 128.

TABLE 14.   Income and Population Statistics by Race

	Median Annual Salary, Families and Individuals, 1939 ($)	Distribution of Families with Annual Income under $3,000, 1947 (%)	Death Rate, Age-Adjusted, per 1,000 Population, 1940	Life Expectancy at Birth (in years), 1940
White	1,325	24.1	10.2	62.9
African-American	489	62.4	16.3	53.1

Source: U.S. Department of Commerce, Bureau of the Census, *Historical Statistics*, ser. G 353–371 (median annual salary), ser. G 16–30 (income distribution), ser. B 167–180 (death rate), and ser. B 107–115 (life expectancy).

The results of a multiple regression (significant $p < .01$) illustrate a statistically significant correlation between race and the number of ADC cases in southern counties. The percentage of African-American population in a county negatively correlates with the number of ADC cases in a county: the higher the percentage African-American population in a county, the fewer ADC cases per one hundred population. This supports the hypothesis that ADC benefits, like mothers' pensions, were awarded less in counties with large percentages of African-Americans. Alternative hypotheses have argued that per capita income positively correlates with monthly grant amounts and the number of the population aided. This model shows the opposite effect. Per capita income negatively correlates with the number of ADC cases: the higher the per capita income, the fewer the ADC cases. The percentage of a state's population in the county, an indicator of urbanization, was not statistically significant.

Analysis of ADC Benefits in Southern Counties

Since African-American exclusion from ADC occurred primarily in the South, county-level analysis of ADC benefit provision in nine southern states is illuminating. Counties with higher percentages of African-Americans had fewer ADC cases per population. Furthermore, the percentage of the African-American population aided was significantly lower than the percentage of the white population aided. Alternate hypotheses argue that a state's wealth and/or urbanization are the primary explanatory factors in determining benefit distribution and benefit levels. This county-level analysis demonstrates otherwise: not only are these variables not statistically significant, but race is the primary explanatory factor.

The data for the county-level analysis were compiled from the 1940 U.S. census and the annual reports of state departments of welfare responsible for administering ADC. The data consist of population and ADC case summary data for all 814 counties in nine southern states.[61]

African-American Representation & ADC

Table 15 is sorted in descending order by the percentage of the state population that is African-American. With the exceptions of Florida, Arkansas, and Virginia, as the African-American population decreases, the number of ADC cases in the state increases. Mississippi, the state with the highest African-American population, has the lowest mean number of ADC cases per ten thousand population. Tennessee, the state with the highest mean number of cases per ten thousand population, has the lowest percentage African-American population.

When the percentage of the state African-American population is correlated with the number of ADC cases in a state, a statistically significant negative correlation appears $(-.429, p < .01)$ between these two variables. The same is true when controlling for the size of the total state population $(-.374, p < .01)$. This was a general effect in the South, present after the advent of ADC. At the county level, a similar effect occurs. Summarizing county data by using means, however, hides an important cor-

TABLE 15. ADC Cases and 1940 Census Population

	State Population	Mean Percentage State African-American Population (%)	Mean Number of ADC Cases per 10,000 in County	Total ADC Cases
Mississippi	2,183,845	49	0.05	1,011
Virginia	2,671,925	25	0.05	1,136
Alabama	2,833,251	35	0.14	4,816
Arkansas	1,949,387	25	0.16	3,116
Florida	1,897,444	27	0.18	2,581
Georgia	3,123,703	35	0.20	5,613
North Carolina	3,571,623	27	0.26	8,431
South Carolina	1,899,804	43	0.27	4,922
Tennessee	2,915,821	17	0.40	10,789
Total	23,046,803	31	0.19	42,415

relation. At the county level, a statistically significant negative correlation $(-.299, p < .01)$ exists between the percentage of the county population that is African-American and the number of ADC cases per hundred of population in the county. This correlation exists for the region overall and in each individual state with the exceptions of Florida, South Carolina, and Virginia. When controlling for the size of the total county population, this correlation $(-.298, p < .01)$ continues to exist for the overall region. At the state level, however, the correlation does not exist for Florida, Mississippi, and Virginia. These exceptions are related to the within-state distribution of the African-American population.

Exclusion through the 1950s

Only five years after its inauguration, the ADC program appeared to be suffering the same fate as its predecessor. Coverage remained low relative to need, and assistance payments were insufficient to enable mothers to stay home and raise their children. As with mothers' pensions, most mothers had to work outside the home to survive. In fact in 1941, 75 percent of ADC mothers were employed, working as clerks, in factories, as waitresses, or as domestic servants.[62] The newly created Social Security Board was occupied with the development of what were considered more important programs, such as old-age security, and consequently did little to promote ADC. Unlike the beneficiaries of other Social Security Act provisions, such as old-age security and unemployment compensation, the beneficiaries of mothers' pensions/ADC lacked the money and political power to reconstitute the mothers' pension legislation.

The 1939 amendments to the Social Security Act exacerbated the situation. These amendments separated widows from mothers lacking male breadwinners for reasons other than death, subjecting the latter to ADC's means-tested protocol while awarding the former survivor benefits. As Chris Howard has pointed out, "the 1939 amendments to the Social Security Act inadvertently diminished the primary political resource left to ADC recipients, their ability to generate sympathy among voters and legislators. . . . [T]hese amendments moved the original constituency of mothers' pensions, worthy widows and their children, to the tier of social insurance programs. . . . [T]hese amendments improved the lot of all families in the short run but left ADC with a more politically vulnerable constituency—families in which the father had deserted or been imprisoned or the parents had never married or were divorced."[63] The widows, all along the intended beneficiaries of mothers' pensions, became part of the nonstigmatized U.S. welfare system. The remaining ADC recipient pool comprised mostly unmarried, deserted, or divorced mothers, who had historically been deemed unworthy or unfit. As Linda Gordon has stated, "ADC recipients, already stigmatized as poor single mothers, grew politically weaker because of their continuing poverty and increasing discouragement. Their indigence and stigmatization in turn undercut their ability to organize to create political pressure, and their lack of organizational strength further weakened the respect they could evoke."[64]

Throughout the late 1930s, African-Americans comprised 15 percent of ADC recipients.[65] In 1940, 17 percent of all ADC recipients were African-American. However, this figure hides the disparities between the northern and southern states. In seven southern states, the proportion of African-American recipients remained substantially smaller than the proportion of African-Americans in the population.[66] Some southern states, such as Georgia and Louisiana, tried to minimize the extension of public aid to African-American families through statutes. The most significant finding of the Bureau of Public Assistance's 1942 study of sixteen states was the wide divergence in the attitudes of welfare workers toward assisting illegitimate and nonwhite children. Ten of the states had more than five thousand African-American children receiving ADC; however, the inclusion rates for African-American children ranged from only 14 per 1,000 in North Carolina to 173 per 1,000 in Illinois.[67]

A field supervisor in one southern state attributed the fact that there were so few African-Americans on the rolls to the

> unanimous feeling on the part of the staff and board that there are more work opportunities for Negro women and to their intense desire not to interfere with local labor conditions. . . . [T]he attitude that "they have always gotten along" and that "all they'll do is have more children" is definite. . . . [T]here is hesitancy on the part of lay boards to advance too rapidly over the thinking of their own communities, which see no reason why the employable Negro mother should not continue her usually sketchy seasonal labor or indefinite domestic service rather than receive a public assistance grant.[68]

She noted that 250 African-American families in one southern county received grants, but only because program officials feared that the families would starve without assistance.

Georgia had a quota system in effect in 1938, granting assistance not on the basis of need but based on a fixed ratio of white and African-American recipients. The state's director of public welfare rescinded this rule only after he was served with federal sanctions.[69] Nevertheless, African-Americans subsequently remained disproportionately underrepresented on Georgia's ADC rolls. Although in 1940 38 percent of children under the age of fifteen were African-American, African-Americans represented less than 12 percent of the ADC recipients between 1937 and 1940.[70]

In Louisiana in 1943, the state agency responsible for managing ADC adopted a policy whereby applicants would be denied assistance if they were needed in the cotton fields. One parish applied this policy to children as young as seven. This policy disproportionately affected African-American families since most cotton field laborers were African-American.

Although significant gains occurred in the number of African-American ADC recipients between 1942 and 1948, states still varied considerably in the racial composition of their caseloads. In 1948 in Arizona, Georgia, Mississippi, and New Mexico, twenty of every thousand African-American children received aid, compared with a hundred of every thousand nonwhite children in Florida, Illinois, Missouri, Nebraska, New York, North Dakota, Oklahoma, Pennsylvania, and Rhode Island.[71] As a 1944 Bureau of Public Assistance document recognized, some families could do nothing to try to qualify for assistance because color was their primary fault.[72]

The exclusion of African-Americans was so commonplace that only the most extremely discriminatory laws raised concern. For example, Louisiana had long excluded African-Americans from the benefit rolls, but when the state implemented a new "suitable home" policy in 1960 that resulted in the dropping of 22,500 children from ADC, the move drew significant attention to the statute's overtly discriminatory impact. The birth of an illegitimate child was the reason why 90 percent of the families affected by the statute were deemed ineligible; 95 percent of these ineligible families were African-American.[73]

Localities and states had at their disposal many extralegal ways of restricting access to ADC. One method used in several states during the 1950s was a "substitute parent" provision. To exclude otherwise eligible families yet avoid federal sanctions, various states redefined *parent* and *parental support*. Children became ineligible if their mothers had relationships with men for any period of time, regardless of the type of relationship and its duration. According to the new eligibility conditions, the men became "substitute parents" and, therefore, the children were no longer "deprived of parental support" or "needy." Even though this "substitute parent" had no legal obligation to support the children and could not be prosecuted under general statutes for failure to do so, his presence in a mother's life rendered her children ineligible. By 1960, Arkansas, Georgia, Louisiana, Michigan, Mississippi, Texas, and Virginia had added this eligibility condition to their suitable home provisions.[74] Just like the suitability provision, the substitute parent provision disproportionately affected African-American families.

Gunnar Myrdal summarized the dilemma faced by poor African-Americans in states where there were special eligibility requirements such as the "suitable home" policy.

> [S]uch regulations, of course, may easily lend themselves to rather arbitrary interpretations whereby, in particular, many Negro families can be cut off from any chance of receiving this kind of assistance. According to popular belief in the South, few Negro low income families have homes which could be called "suitable" for any purpose . . . and since practically all Negroes are believed to be "immoral," almost any discrimination against Negroes can be motivated on such grounds.[75]

The permissiveness and vagueness of the "suitable home" provision resulted in different definitions of suitability that, when applied, excluded the majority of poor African-American mothers and their children across many jurisdictions. In localities across the nation, eligible African-Americans who were fit parents were excluded from ADC, while neglectful and/or abusive white mothers—some of whom did not meet all criteria for eligibility—received ADC. The exclusion of African-Americans across the country cannot be reduced to a conspiracy on the part of all local administrators. This racially based exclusion was permitted by a much more insidious condition: American society and culture had been and remained so embedded with racial differentiation that the application of a suitable home provision could not escape the racialized norms and values prevalent at that time.

The institutionalized exclusion carried over from mothers' pensions to ADC defined the federal effort for more than thirty years. Even though these programs sought to keep families together, the eligibility rules were used to deliberately exclude certain classes of individuals from the benefit stream. Everything from the law itself to the program implementation was designed so that states and localities had the ability to administer the programs as they saw fit. This administration by parochialism was not overturned until the 1960s. In the interim, hundreds of thousands of needy African-Americans were denied benefits solely for reasons of race.

The End of Legislated Discrimination

The arbitrary and extralegal exclusion of African-Americans from ADC continued until the 1960s, when two events—the Flemming Rule and subsequent amendments to the Social Security Act and the U.S. Supreme Court's decision in *King v. Smith* (1968)—successfully challenged this exclusion and finally opened the ADC benefit rolls to African-American children.

The first challenge to this racial bias occurred thanks to the Louisiana government. Although other states had executed similar actions, Louisiana in 1960 removed twenty-three thousand children from the welfare rolls because they were born out of wedlock, and Arthur Flemming, secretary of the Department of Health, Education and Welfare, which administered AFDC, stepped in. In 1961, the department issued what is now known as the Flemming Rule, which made eligibility conditions that denied assistance to children because of their mothers' behavior sanctionable. According to the rule, "A State plan may not impose an eligibility condition that would deny assistance with respect to a needy child on the basis that the home conditions in which the child lives are unsuitable, while the child continues to reside in the home." The department advised state agencies administering ADC that "after June 30, 1961, grants to states would not be available if the state terminated assistance to children in a home determined to be unsuitable unless the state made other provisions for the children affected." Congress modified the Flemming Rule under the 1961 and 1962 amendments to the Social Security Act that provided that states were allowed to remove children from homes determined by a court to be so unsuitable as to be "contrary to the welfare" of the children.[76] The amendments also provided that states could terminate assistance to a child in an unsuitable home if they provided other adequate assistance to the child under general welfare provision.

King v. Smith challenged state welfare regulations that disqualified dependent children from ADC because of their mothers' behavior. As Chief Justice Earl Warren wrote for the Court,

> A significant characteristic of public welfare programs during the last half of the 19th century in this country was their preference for the "worthy" poor. . . . This worthy-person concept characterized the mothers' pension welfare programs which were the precursors of AFDC. Benefits under the mothers' pension programs, accordingly,

were customarily restricted to widows who were considered morally fit. In this social context it is not surprising that both the House and Senate Committee Reports on the Social Security Act of 1935 indicate that States participating in AFDC were free to impose eligibility requirements relating to the "moral character" of applicants. . . . As applied, these suitable home provisions frequently disqualified children on the basis of the alleged immoral behavior of their mothers. In the 1940s, suitable home provisions came under increasing attack. Critics argued . . . that they were habitually used to disguise systematic racial discrimination. . . .

In light of the Flemming Ruling and the 1961, 1962, and 1968 amendments to the Social Security Act, it is simply inconceivable, as HEW has recognized, that Alabama is free to discourage immorality and illegitimacy by the device of absolute disqualification of needy children. Alabama may deal with these problems by several different methods under the Social Security Act. But the method it has chosen plainly conflicts with the Act. In denying AFDC assistance to appellee on the basis of this invalid regulation, Alabama has breached its federally imposed obligation to furnish "aid to families with dependent children with reasonable promptness to all eligible individuals."[77]

In *King v. Smith*, the Court determined that states could not add additional requirements for eligibility if the intended recipients were below the established poverty level. This ruling eliminated the quasi-legal basis for discrimination that legislators and administrators had had at their disposal in the form of "suitability" and "fitness" requirements. Together, the Flemming Rule and *King v. Smith* attacked the foundation on which discriminatory ADC programs had been built. By rendering illegal the suitability condition as well as other behavior-related sanctions, the Court had opened the doors for many African-American as well as other dependent children and their families to receive benefits. However, a fifty-year history of programmatic exclusion of African-Americans from the mothers' pension and ADC benefit rolls remained, as did a fifty-year history of widespread public acceptance of that exclusion. Consequently, the ensuing rapid and intense inclusion of African-Americans on the ADC rolls resulted in a public and government policy backlash that continued until ADC was dismantled in 1996. After African-Americans had access to this benefit stream, welfare adopted a new image.

7

Conclusion

Building a White Welfare State

The word "charity" does not enter into the category of
the movement. The very foundation of the Mothers'
Pension idea is to eliminate the thought of public alms
giving. In assisting the Mother to rear her fatherless
offspring it has grown to be regarded by the greatest
thinkers that in so doing the State is only performing
its duty in protecting its future citizens.
—1915[1]

So I think it is time for us to limit the amount of time
that people can be on welfare. . . . You have to be
responsible for what you are doing. We are not going to
continue to support you in a way in which you
abdicate, you simply run from, you hide from, your
responsibility as a citizen.
—John Ashcroft, 1996[2]

MOTHERS' PENSIONS WERE INSTITUTIONALLY and ideologically
successful. They provided an institutional legacy and framework on
which subsequent welfare policy for dependent children was built. The
politics, principles, and administrative processes entrenched in mothers'
pensions created a history of social welfare provision within which the
New Deal legislation itself is located. This book demonstrates not only the
need for the reperiodization of American welfare state development but a
reconceptualization of U.S. welfare state development that acknowledges
the central role of race.

Why a Reperiodization?

Most analyses of the American welfare state fail to comprehensively examine U.S. welfare policies prior to the 1930s and the impact of nascent

state-level welfare development on national policy-making. The failure to appropriately consider the role of Progressive Era state and local welfare policy leaves a void in the lineage and evolution of American welfare state development. Ignoring this critical moment in welfare state development is antithetical to historically based institutional theories of state development. The Social Security Act does not mark the beginning of U.S. welfare policy; consequently, it should not be interpreted as the beginning of the institutional and political legacy of the U.S. welfare state. The twenty-six years prior to the act's passage constitute an institutional and legislative history in which the New Deal legislation itself is located. Only through an examination of the ideological and institutional history of mothers' pensions can the development of the U.S. social welfare state be fully understood.

A reperiodization that places the Progressive Era and specifically mothers' pensions at the root of the development of the modern welfare state enables scholars to see how welfare state development in the United States was very much tied to the policies and institutions created at this critical juncture in U.S. state-building history. The policy and administrative legacies inherited from the mothers' pension era shaped and limited the options available to New Deal welfare reformers and thereby shaped the development of the American welfare state.

One of the distinguishing features of this early welfare state period was the stratification of welfare benefit recipients. The defined legal, rigid tests of benefit eligibility were made even more restrictive by the incorporation of the "suitable home" standard. The ideology of differentiation became a distinctive characteristic of the U.S. welfare state. The mothers' pension principle of distinguishing between deserving and undeserving poor became embedded in U.S. welfare policy-making. The U.S. social welfare state was created with a bifurcation between the provision of social insurance for "deserving" employed, nondependents and the provision of public assistance or relief for dependents, who might or might not be worthy of such assistance, and the unemployable. This built-in bifurcation is both symbolic and programmatic. This distinction has been carried over from one social welfare policy agenda setting to another, from local and state policy-making and policy administration to national policy-making and policy administration. Instead of redefining relief as a right, mothers' pensions left in their wake a social welfare program that not only failed to defend economic assistance as a legitimate goal in itself but also established the groundwork for using moral criteria to evaluate a potential beneficiary's worthiness. An unavoidable consequence was that the legislation and administration of these programs excluded many who were deemed unfit because of their culture, religion, or color.

Another distinguishing feature of mothers' pensions were their decentralized and parochial administration. State governments were free to choose whether to legislate mothers' pension laws, the scope and content of mothers' pension legislation, and whether to fund mothers' pension programs. Those states that legislated mothers' pension programs often left the implementation of the programs and policies to the counties or localities, often with minimal or no state supervision. The decentralization of mothers' pension administration, coupled with ambiguous statutory requirements, permitted the exclusion of certain groups from the mothers' pension rolls. Just like mothers' pensions, Aid to Dependent Children (ADC) policy-making and administration were decentralized and fragmented. ADC policy was made at both the national and state/local levels, meaning that thousands of administrative units across the country were involved in this process. As with mothers' pensions, ADC plans varied from state to state, and these variations never disappeared. Different streams of welfare provision reflected different levels of social welfare policy-making. While Social Security was designed and administered at the national level, ADC was administered locally and therefore parochially. The emphasis on local administration with ADC only perpetuated the stigma of public relief.

Subsequent amendments to the Social Security Act, including those passed in 1962, only increased local administrators' power and thereby strengthened ADC's parochial nature. Because localities had administrative discretion, local norms and values had always been embedded in the implementation of mothers' pensions. ADC inherited this feature, and instead of centralizing policy-making and administrative power, ADC merely institutionalized this parochialism. The state mothers' pension programs that developed during the Progressive Era significantly affected the institutional design of the modern American welfare state. Early welfare policy developments at the state and local levels defined the policy contours and ideological direction in which the national U.S. welfare state grew.

Why a Reconceptualization?

A reconceptualization is necessary to counter the erroneous yet widespread belief that "welfare" and the U.S. "welfare" state evolved to support ethnic and racial minorities, who have been and continue to be perceived as the primary beneficiaries of noncontributory social welfare benefits. The welfare state evolved and continues to exist to benefit whites. Policies were and continue to be enacted to limit the scope of social welfare provision to those considered deserving, Throughout welfare state development, *deserving* is a code word for "white." The mothers' pension movement sought to aid native-born white women and immigrants willing to adopt white, middle-class norms. The goal of preserving and protecting white, middle-class values became institutionalized in the various state mothers' pension laws enacted from 1911 to 1932. The effective exclusion of African-Americans, nonwhite and non-Americanized immigrants, and the poor from the mothers' pension movement reflected its goals—assisting working and middle-class white women.

Although it is difficult to prove the racist intentions of mothers' pension advocates, legislators, and administrators, it is a fact that African-Americans were excluded from every facet of this nascent welfare program. Beginning with the women's pension movement and continuing through the implementation of subsequent legislation, mothers' pensions were based on differentiations among women of different races. The value of motherhood was not universally upheld but instead was upheld only selectively with respect to women considered racially superior. Racial differentiation, which was inextricably tied to the prevailing political culture and which defined political, social, and economic relations during the Progressive Era, became irrevocably woven into the fabric of the nascent American welfare state through mothers' pensions.

Institutionalized Racism & Building a White Welfare State

The current U.S. welfare state reflects the racism institutionalized during the Progressive Era. The distinction between deserving and undeserving has defined how policymakers and administrators have perceived welfare rights and, more importantly, how potential recipient groups perceive their rights to social welfare provision. This bifurcation has determined the status of African-Americans in the American welfare state. Specifically, it has placed African-Americans into unstandardized, stigmatized streams of public assistance that remain outside mainstream American social welfare policy.

This study offers the first systematic analysis that demonstrates the disproportionate exclusion of African-Americans from mothers' pension advocacy, policy-making, administration, and benefit awards and the federalization of that exclusion in ADC. In this particular history of institutional inheritance, race was critical because it defined the development of social welfare policies in the United States. At the moment of their birth, the first U.S. social welfare policies were developed for whites to the exclusion of African-Americans and others, and these groups' small representation at each stage in the development and implementation of the programs reveals this institutional exclusion.

ADC mirrored African-Americans' exclusion from mothers' pensions. Whereas mothers' pensions reinforced the political, social, and economic isolation of African-Americans, ADC's design institutionalized that isolation and exclusion in the American welfare state. This sixty-year institutional history of excluding certain classes of otherwise eligible poor helped define the current U.S. welfare state. In particular, this history begat a welfare system that in 1996 continued to distinguish between deserving and undeserving, worthy and unworthy poor. Because ADC's structure was based on the mothers' pension programs, the opportunity to make the program more inclusive and less racially stratified was lost. The institutionalization of parochial norms in the administration of ADC meant that changes to the policy could be made at the discretion of the local administrators. Until the termination of ADC in 1996, policy changes almost never resulted in greater racial inclusion but instead often resulted in removing African-Americans from the program's benefit rolls.

The Beginning of the End of ADC

In the 1960s, when it became very difficult for administrators to exclude on the basis of race, the rapid influx of African-Americans into ADC, or the "welfare" rolls, resulted in the growing negative association of race with ADC.[3] By 1961, 43 percent of all families receiving ADC were African-American.[4] The intended beneficiaries of ADC, as with mothers' pensions, had been white, widowed mothers, so the increase in the number of African-American mothers and unwed mothers receiving ADC began to generate negative publicity. The effort to reduce the ADC rolls—specifically, the effort to reduce the number of African-American participants—resulted in the implementation of laws and rules, including work rules, man-in-the-house rules, and unannounced visits, that disproportionately affected African-American families. The public image of ADC mothers became increasingly negative and focused on racist stereotypes.

The public perceived ADC recipients as substance abusers and neglectful mothers who deliberately became pregnant to increase their benefits. In reality, studies conducted during that time showed that the only 3 percent of ADC recipients resembled this stereotype and that no outright cases of fraud had been discovered.[5]

From the 1960s through the 1990s, the racialized welfare discourse escalated, reaching its apex in the termination of Aid to Families with Dependent Children (AFDC), as the program had become known, in 1996. Two intertwined yet distinct phenomena led to this escalation. First, the word *welfare* became synonymous with AFDC. Second, welfare became inextricably tied to race.

The United States has a robust welfare state comprising different types of programs, including but not limited to public education, unemployment insurance, health care, worker's compensation, veterans' programs, Social Security, and public assistance. For the purposes of analysis, these programs can be grouped into three benefit categories: education, social insurance (Social Security, Medicare, public employee retirement, unemployment insurance, veterans' programs, medical research and hospital support, and worker's compensation), and public assistance or means-tested programs (Medicaid, food stamps, housing, Supplemental Security Income, AFDC, and general assistance). While the first two categories, education and social insurance, disproportionately benefit the middle and upper classes, the third benefit category targets the nation's poor. According to the Statistical Abstract, in 1996 24 percent of all social welfare spending in the United States across all levels of government was for education. Social insurance spending made up 55 percent of all spending, while means-tested programs comprised only 17 percent of all spending.[6] Table 16 provides a breakdown of the means-tested programs.[7] Less than 3 percent of all U.S. social welfare spending went to AFDC, yet this program became symbolic of irresponsible and wasteful U.S. government

TABLE 16.   Means-Tested Programs as a Percentage of Total Social Welfare Spending, 1996

Medicaid	9%
Welfare (AFDC/General Assistance)	3%
Supplemental Security Income	2%
Food Stamps	2%
Housing	1%

Source: U.S. Bureau of the Census, *Statistical Abstract 1997*, 313.

spending. The term *welfare* assumed a pejorative meaning and became synonymous with AFDC. The entire movement to "end welfare as we know it" was directed toward a program that comprised less than 2 percent of all government spending.

The racialization of welfare evolved concurrently with and partially explains the conflation of AFDC with "welfare." Serving whites primarily, Social Security, unemployment insurance, and other social welfare programs were exempt from the pejorative "welfare" categorization. Different actors in the policy-making arena, from the media to elected officials to the public at large, contributed to and inflamed the racial rhetoric. AFDC was an easy and acceptable target for negative profiling. Racial stereotyping of AFDC recipients became common, and the image of "welfare queen" became the rallying symbol for most people who came to reject welfare. The demand for welfare reform represented a thinly veiled racist call to remove African-Americans and other minorities from social welfare programs.

The Growth of AFDC

Coinciding at first with President Lyndon Johnson's War on Poverty, the mid-1960s to the mid-1970s saw the greatest growth in AFDC. From 1965 to 1975, the proportion of all American families receiving AFDC climbed from 2.2 percent to 6.4 percent. This proportion declined in the late 1970s and early 1980s before increasing slightly in the early 1990s. However, benefit amounts began to decline in real terms after 1970, and by 1995 benefits had lost half of their purchasing power when adjusted for inflation. In 1995, the year before AFDC was eliminated, the average annual benefit per family was five thousand dollars. During this period, enrollments in social insurance programs also grew—in the case of Social Security, at a much faster rate than AFDC.[8] Nevertheless, the growth in the AFDC rolls generated the greatest controversy, and this controversy remained constant for the last thirty years of the program's existence.

The controversy existed because of the growing belief that AFDC recipients represented the undeserving poor. In this view, able-bodied parents were receiving benefits to stay home and take care of their children, an irresponsible and wasteful expenditure of taxpayers' money. Ironically, however, staying home and taking care of one's children was considered service to the nation from the early 1900s through the 1950s, but welfare recipients came to represent something very different during the 1960s. Whether the argument was that welfare recipients were lazy, had no work ethic, committed fraud, were drug addicts, and/or had more children to receive more money, AFDC recipients were considered undeserving. Several surveys administered prior to the passage of the Personal Responsibility Act revealed that at least two-thirds of the respondents believed that welfare recipients were taking advantage of the system and could get along without the money.[9]

As AFDC caseloads increased, criticism grew that any public assistance, especially AFDC, created disincentives for recipients to work. In response, in 1967 Congress passed and President Johnson signed into law the Work Incentive Program (WIN), the first measure of its kind. WIN sought to tie welfare benefits to participation in a training or workforce development program. This program failed for many reasons, most importantly because only 2 to 3 percent of eligible AFDC recipients obtained jobs through WIN. In 1971 Congress passed WIN II, which focused on job placement rather than training. Although more successful than its predecessor, WIN II helped to remove only an estimated 2 percent of recipients from AFDC benefit rolls.[10] This trend of tying work to the receipt of benefits gained more momentum during the 1980s under the Reagan administration. States were encouraged to develop job training programs for welfare recipients, and the most successful state programs became models for the development of the Job Opportunities and Basic Skills Training Program (JOBS), which replaced WIN II in 1990. Again, the premise behind these programs was that AFDC recipients were lazy or lacked the incentive to work and that these programs could make otherwise irresponsible AFDC recipients responsible.

None of these national programs achieved their ultimate goal of permanently reducing the AFDC benefit rolls. State programs, conversely, had been more successful in restricting access to welfare. Applying for waivers from AFDC, various states developed their own varieties of welfare beginning in the 1980s. These waivers gave states latitude to develop more restrictive eligibility requirements and to implement time limits and employment requirements designed to make recipients more responsible. Right before the passage of the Personal Responsibility and Work Opportunity Reconciliation Act (PRWORA) in 1996, almost every state was implementing its own type of welfare reform. The antiwelfare rhetoric that emerged in the 1960s reached its apex in the early 1990s, along with a growing movement to radically reform welfare.

Support for dismantling the welfare state—which, again, accounted for less than 3 percent of all social welfare expenditures—was widespread. In 1992 President Bill Clinton had promised to "end welfare as we know it," echoing the popular belief that existing programs were no longer tenable. Although a clear division existed in Clinton's administration regarding the contours of the new welfare state, it was generally agreed that existing welfare policy was a problem. The Republicans seized the opportunity to push their own welfare agenda, which was advanced in the infamous "Contract with America." Led by Newt Gingrich, the movement to dismantle welfare, specifically AFDC, focused on the so-called pathologies that existing welfare programs created. Republicans were joined by Democrats in advocating discipline, or "tough love," for welfare mothers. These policymakers argued that without discipline, these mothers would continue to be unemployed and bear more children without consideration of the larger costs involved.

Anti-AFDC rhetoric focused on the irresponsibility of the recipient mothers who were content to stay home and raise their kids. This rhetoric represented an enormous departure from that of decades earlier, when mothers receiving pensions were championed for preserving home life by staying home with their children. Policymakers in the 1990s depicted AFDC recipients as lazy or negligent for staying home with their children and not holding outside jobs. In a 1995 speech in College Station, Texas, Senator Phil Gramm stated, "I want to ask the able-bodied men and women riding in the wagon on welfare to get out of the wagon and help the rest of us pull. We've got to stop giving people more and more money to have more and more children on welfare."[11] Representative E. Clay Shaw (R-FL), chairman of the House Human Resources Subcommittee responsible for writing PRWORA, commented that the current welfare system was "pampering the poor."[12] Representative Phil English (R-PA) commented during the House debate on the Personal Responsibility Act, "we have offered here, in my view, a tough love approach to welfare reform. It is a sound one. Our reform plan has a tough work requirement that will reintroduce many families to the dignity of work. Our bill stops subsidizing out-of-wedlock births."[13]

Policymakers also portrayed AFDC recipients as drug addicts, cheaters, and child abusers. To these legislators, these benefits were supporting abusive behaviors and habits. Former drug czar William Bennett testified before a House committee, "I think any police sergeant in the country will tell you that the day the welfare checks go out is a big day for drug buys."[14] John Ashcroft, a senator from Missouri, commented, "we are literally living with a system which has taught people to value children for the kind of incomes those children could attract to the family through the welfare system."[15] Merely receiving AFDC stigmatized mothers.

These legislators also deemed mothers who had children out of wedlock as unfit parents. Failing to marry and raising children in households without fathers made these mothers subject to the accusation that they were harming their children. Criticism against unwed teenage mothers became even more pronounced. Even though the number of teenage girls receiving AFDC in 1995 represented only 2 percent of all parents on AFDC, these mothers were blamed for the "crisis of illegitimacy." Senator Byron Dorgan (D-ND) commented at length during the welfare reform debates about how casually elected officials rely on stereotypical images to implement policy:

> [T]o talk about welfare reform, you have to talk about two truths. One is often used by those of us in public office, regrettably, to talk about welfare. That is, the stereotypical notion of who is a welfare recipient. It is some bloated, overweight, lazy, slovenly, indolent, good-for-nothing person laying in a Lazy Boy recliner with a quart of beer in one hand and a Jack Daniels in another hand, with his hand on the television changer watching a 27-inch color television set and unwilling to get up and get out and get a job and go to work, munching nachos all day long watching Oprah, Geraldo, and Montel. That is the notion of the stereotypical welfare recipient. . . . In public debate we all too often use stereotypes, and the stereotype is the notion that there is someone out there having 16 babies because producing babies allows them to get a lot of welfare. The average size of the welfare family is nearly identical to the average size of the average family in our country.[16]

Very rarely were AFDC recipients portrayed in a sympathetic light, and if they were, the racialization of poverty influenced which mothers were castigated for their irresponsibility and abusive behavior and which were pitied for the burden of poverty they carried.

Regardless of the validity of the claims against AFDC recipients, the antiwelfare movement gained enormous momentum. Because of state programs' success in reducing welfare rolls, many people argued that welfare administration should be returned to the states. Arguments for this devolution varied, but the general consensus was that localities would best be able to address the pathologies of their poor. Since the federal government had failed to encourage welfare mothers to be responsible and independent, the prevailing sentiment was that the states would succeed. In essence, the federal government was willing to wash its hands of welfare and of the welfare rolls filled with what were overwhelmingly perceived as the undeserving poor. Representative William Martini (R-NJ) summed up the anti-AFDC rhetoric when he stated, "No longer will the Government reward children for having children. No longer will we reward families for having a second baby when they cannot afford the first. No longer will the taxpayers pay to support addiction. No longer will Washington impose top-down solutions to problems they do not understand."[17]

PRWORA passed in 1996, terminating AFDC and ending a sixty-year history of federal responsibility for needy children and their parents. AFDC was replaced by Temporary Assistance for Needy Families (TANF), which would operate by giving block grants to states. Under this new program, states would have more freedom in the implementation and administration of "welfare" but had to work within numerous federal mandates aimed at reducing the welfare rolls in all states and changing the perceived pathological behavior of the poor.[18] What followed was the rapid-fire spread of new state policies that strove to limit access to the TANF rolls and alter the behavior of those recipients on the rolls. Policymakers had devoted a great deal of time and effort to dismantling a welfare program that, relative to other social welfare programs, was minimal in terms of cost and in total number of recipients but that came to symbolize to the American people all that was wrong with social welfare.

The White Welfare State

How did a program that had been championed for preserving the values of home life and the service of the mother in raising future citizens become a publicly denigrated program that stigmatized its recipients and catalyzed a national movement for its elimination? What can explain the mobilization of political and social forces to eliminate a program that represented only a small fraction of all social welfare expenditures? How can the American people simultaneously castigate "welfare" and welfare recipients while reaching for increases in other social welfare programs? What made AFDC recipients undeserving? The answer is the same as it was in 1911, in 1935, and in 1966: race. What made African-Americans undeserving under mothers' pensions and under ADC is the fact that they are African-American. The anti-African-American rhetoric changed little from the early 1900s. But when African-Americans were actually receiving social welfare benefits, the rhetoric reflected a different goal on the part of policymakers—program elimination. After exclusion of

African-Americans was no longer tenable, the dissolution of the program became the ultimate objective.

What emerged in the 1960s was more than just a "white backlash," as Kenneth Neubeck and Noel Cazenave argue.[19] The elimination of AFDC as a national program represented business as usual in the evolution of the U.S. welfare state. Although periods of white backlash clearly occurred throughout the twentieth century and represent an integral part of a larger process of racial conflict, the significance of the elimination of AFDC is that the institutionalization of racism in the early 1900s was a determinant of its demise. It is not just the moments of the backlash themselves that are critical, but the embeddedness of race in U.S. state development that enable racial backlash to occur in the first place.

Coinciding with an increase in AFDC recipients in the 1960s was the changing face of the welfare recipient. The mass media no longer portrayed the poor as the unfortunate white family, and "poverty took on a black face."[20] As different studies of the mass media have shown, welfare recipients were usually depicted as African-American, regardless of the group's actual representation on the AFDC rolls. Furthermore, poverty was and continues to be portrayed as a "black" problem. The media coverage of poor African-Americans was usually negative compared with that of whites; in positive stories on welfare, the faces of the poor are typically white.[21] While a white mother on AFDC received sympathy for her poverty and hardships, an African-American mother receiving AFDC was labeled as undeserving, irresponsible, and/or criminal. Certain high-profile media stories exacerbated the racialized reform dialogue.

In 1994 major television networks and national newspapers covered a story about a drug raid in a Chicago apartment that allegedly revealed the neglect and abuse of nineteen children by five welfare mothers and one African-American man. The image of the "Chicago Nineteen" became a powerful backdrop for the welfare reform debate.[22] As James M. Avery and Mark Peffley conclude in their study of race, public opinion, and the media, the media's racial portrayals of poverty matter. Their study demonstrates the media's tendency racialize welfare policy through the disproportionate use of images of African-Americans in stories on poverty. Furthermore, Avery and Peffley show that this racialization affects the way whites respond to the articles.[23] The media stories reinforced popular perceptions and created an environment in which policymakers could take this racialized discourse to the next level.

Just as public discourse vilified AFDC mothers, many policymakers capitalized on racial divisiveness to push through a social policy agenda.

As discussed previously, legislators criticized AFDC generally for the dependency it created and pathologies it reinforced. However, numerous policymakers used and reinforced racist stereotypes of minorities, especially African-Americans. The image of the "welfare queen" emerged with the help of Ronald Reagan[24] and spurred on by depictions of the typical AFDC mother as an irresponsible, lazy drug addict. Reagan's iconic representation of the African-American AFDC recipient was just one in a long line of pejorative representations of African-Americans on public assistance. In the eyes of these legislators, black AFDC recipients did not want to work, used their welfare money to buy alcohol and drugs, and neglected or abused their children.[25] In comparison to the sympathy white welfare recipients generated, policymakers blamed African-Americans for welfare abuse and administrative mismanagement. During the 1995 debates about the Personal Responsibility Act, congressmen did not try to hide their associations of race, welfare, and the "pathologies of the poor." Representative Martin Hoke (R-OH) commented,

> [W]e know that in the minority community among blacks two out of every three births is now out of wedlock. . . . [W]e also know being raised in a family dependent on welfare dramatically reduces a child's intellectual abilities and life prospects. . . . And teenage girls who grow up in fatherless families are far more likely to have early intercourse, pregnancies and abortions than those from two parent families.[26]

In his congressional testimony, Representative Adam Smith from Washington added to the stereotype by stating incorrectly that 80 percent of all births in "black inner city poor neighborhoods" occurred out of wedlock.[27]

Representative Major R. Owens from New York summed up how welfare stereotypes have contributed to the continued racialization of welfare: "when people think of welfare, the media, the political leadership, have handled the problem and issue in ways which have led to an association of welfare with African-Americans, with black people. So it becomes a demonization."[28] The fact that welfare reform seemed a poorly veiled attack on minorities did not go unrecognized during the welfare reform debates. Congressman Gary Franks of Connecticut asked very pointedly, "As we continue to address these issues, the question is, Mr. Speaker, are we, as a Congress, looking at constructive changes or merely attacks toward African-Americans and the poor? Sadly, Mr. Speaker, at this point I am not quite sure."[29]

Just as race is significant in explaining why a state was late in adopting mothers' pension legislation during the 1920s, why some counties did not implement the programs at all during the 1930s, and why ADC benefit amounts varied from family to family during the 1940s, race is also significant in explaining why some states adopted restrictive AFDC waivers during the early 1990s[30] and why the national government abolished AFDC and replaced it with TANF in the 1996 reforms. Race has influenced not only different policies adopted at the state and local levels but also the levels of public support for these policies. Even after the adoption of PRWORA, state policies remained influenced by race. The strictest welfare reforms were more likely to be adopted in states where minorities made up a larger proportion of the welfare caseload.[31] The devolution of welfare to the states has not eliminated racial prejudice in welfare provision but has merely reinvented the parochialism emblematic of the state mothers' pension programs. Returning to the mothers' pension philosophy of a previous century, state TANF programs can reflect local values and determinations of deserving, fit parents.

The United States began its path of welfare state development with a particular deserving recipient in mind—white women. In a class by themselves, white women have been endowed with the right to stay home and raise their children without suffering the pejorative stereotypes imposed on mothers of other racial or ethnic backgrounds. With such strong racist currents running through society, it was ultimately predictable that the United States would generate public policies that perpetuated the racial hierarchy.[32] At different points in U.S. state development, different ethnic and racial groups were deliberately excluded from social welfare provision. However, unlike most other racial/ethnic groups, African-Americans never had a legitimate right to "welfare." Paradoxically, as this book has shown, mothers' pensions and ADC evolved from relatively small social welfare programs institutionally designed to exclude African-Americans into a sprawling program perceived by the public as dominated by unworthy African-Americans. The decentralization and fragmentation of policy-making resulted in the following pattern of African-American participation and status in the American welfare state: initial exclusion, conditional inclusion, stigmatization and political isolation, and finally exclusion through devolution.

At various junctures in the development of this social policy, opportunities arose to institutionally challenge the racialization of aid to dependent children. The state-building process is not linear. "Its character depends on choices taken at pivotal historical moments," write Ira Katznelson and Bruce Pietrykowski, "when fundamental questions about ties between the state and the economy, or between the state and civil society, enter the political agenda."[33] During the passage of the Social Security Act, legislators could have fought for provisions that did not hand to the states a bill that guaranteed the continued exclusion of African-Americans from the benefit rolls. During the War on Poverty, Johnson's advisers argued for a national standard for AFDC, but the administration never proposed such a standard to Congress.[34] Furthermore, the Johnson administration did nothing to counterbalance the growing rhetoric linking race to the "welfare problem." When the PWRORA was being debated, legislators could have raised the level of debate beyond the inflammatory racial discourse but instead chose to embrace this discourse to their advantage. By bestowing the administration of this program on states, the national government implicitly accepted the fact that the TANF would be implemented according to local norms and values, which, if the Progressive and New Deal eras are lessons for us, easily translate into racial and ethnic discrimination.

Since TANF has been implemented, different studies have demonstrated that white recipients are more likely than members of other ethnic groups to be encouraged to get an education, less likely to be sanctioned for policy violations, and more likely to receive child care subsidies. Studies have also shown that the agencies administering TANF are the least helpful to African-Americans in providing job-readiness skills and are least likely to provide basic academic skills or tutoring services to African-Americans. These mothers are not receiving the assistance needed to successfully transition out of welfare. Finally, white women are more likely than African-American women to receive benefits for children born out of wedlock. Some of these disparities are more noted in southern states, such as Virginia and Mississippi.[35]

Throughout its history, the path of this social policy has never deviated. Welfare policy constitutes one of many examples of state-building in a racialized society. Because race is woven into the American economic, social, and political fabric, any analysis of welfare policy should be considered within this larger institutional and policy context.[36] We can see how mothers' pensions and ADC contributed to and strengthened existing civil, political, and social inequalities by mirroring existing social and racial cleavages. Mothers' pensions became the vehicle through which racial differentiation permeated U.S. welfare state-building. The racialization of U.S. welfare policy has resulted in a welfare state that stigmatizes and/or penalizes African-Americans and other ethnic minorities while providing nonstigmatized entitlements to white citizens. This book provides a new lens through which to view and understand the development of America's welfare state at both the state and national levels but is just a starting point in what will be a scholarly reconsideration and reconceptualization of the role of race in the evolution of U.S. social welfare policy and state-building.

Appendix

Additional Data

Data for tables A.1 to A.5 come from U.S. Department of Commerce, Bureau of the Census, *Historical Statistics; Fourteenth Census of the United States* (1920); and *Fifteenth Census of the United States* (1930).

TABLE A.1. Mean Percentage State Population Aged Zero to Fourteen, 1920

		Subset for $p < .01$	
	N	Group 1 (%)	Group 2 (%)
Midwest	13	32	
West	13	31	
East	12	28	
South	13		37
Total	51		

TABLE A.2. Mean State per Capita Income, 1929

		Subset for $p < .01$		
	N	Group 1	Group 2	Group 3
East	12	884.33		
West	11		662.82	
Midwest	13		618.69	
South	13			380.15
Total	49			

**TABLE A.3.   Mean Percentage State
Urban Population, 1920**

| | N | Subset for $p < .01$ | |
		Group 1 (%)	Group 2 (%)
Midwest	13	41	
West	11	39	
South	13	25	
East	12		69
Total	49		

**TABLE A.4.   Mean Percentage State
Urban African-American Population, 1920**

| | N | Subset for $p < .01$ | |
		Group 1 (%)	Group 2 (%)
Midwest	13	75	
West	13	53	
East	12	74	
South	13		26
Total	51		

**TABLE A.5.   Mean Percentage State
African-American Population, 1920**

| | N | Subset for $p < .01$ | |
		Group 1 (%)	Group 2 (%)
Midwest	13	2	
West	13	.7	
East	12	6	
South	13		30
Total	51		

The data in tables A.6–A.25 and tables A.27–A.29 come from data sets that I created using the census records cited for tables A.1–A.5 as well as the following: *Sixteenth Census of the United States* (1940); Childrens Bureau records: *Mothers' Aid*, 1931; *Public Aid*, 1922, 1929, and 1934; Standards, 1923; and Children, 1926; and state welfare reports.

TABLE A.6. Regression Model: Year Legislation to Aid Dependent Children First Enacted

Independent Variable	Coefficient
Constant	1912.82 (unstandardized)
State African-American population in 1920 (%)	.759*** (3.793)
State urban population in 1920 (%)	.212 (.675)
State per capita income in 1929	−.288 (−.852)
State African-American urban population in 1920 (%)	−.102 (−.395)
State income as percentage of U.S. income in 1929	−.104 (−.742)
State population age 0–14 in 1920 (%)	.058 (.240)
East	.313 (1.246)
Midwest	.181 (.767)
West	.258 (1.089)
N	49
Adjusted R^2	0.492

Note: Dependent variable is the year legislation was enacted. *t*-statistics are in parentheses.
***$p < .01$

TABLE A.7. ANOVA: Mean Year Mothers' Pension Legislation First Enacted

	N	Subset for $p < .05$	
		Group 1	Group 2
Midwest	13	1,914.08	
West	13	1,915.54	
East[a]	12	1,916.67	
South[b]	11		1,921.27
Total	49		

[a]Includes Washington, D.C.
[b]Does not include Georgia and South Carolina because they never had mothers' pension programs.

TABLE A.8. Regression Model: Enactment of Mothers' Pension Legislation

Independent Variable	Coefficient
Data year 1929	1.57 (3.3)
Data year 1934	2.64** (6.12)
State African-American population (%)	−13.06*** (7.6)
State per capita income	.0135** (4.3)
Midwest	8.9 (.049)
West	−.03 (.0004)
South	3.9 (3.2)
N	144
R^2 (Nagelkerke)	.54

Note: Dependent variable—mothers' pension law enacted (yes or no). Wald statistics are in parentheses.
***$p < .01$ **$p < .05$

TABLE A.9. Level of Agency Administering Mothers' Pension Programs by Region, 1934

| Level of Agency | Region | | | | Total |
	East (%)	Midwest (%)	West (%)	South (%)	N
Local	33.33	100	69.23	90	35
State	33.33	0	15.38	0	6
State and local	33.33	0	15.38	10	7
Total N	12	13	13	10	48

TABLE A.10. Bivariate Analysis: State Supervision of Mothers' Pension Programs by Region, 1934

| State Supervision | Region | | | | Total |
	East (%)	Midwest (%)	West (%)	South (%)	N
No	8.33	38.46	46.15	50	17
Report only	0	30.76	15.38	10	7
Yes	91.67	30.76	38.46	40	24
Total N	12	13	13	10	48

TABLE A.11. States Stipulating Qualifying Marital Status by Region, 1934

| | Widow | | Deserted | | Divorced | | Unmarried | |
	Yes (%)	No.	Yes (%)	No.	Yes (%)	No.	Yes (%)	No.
East	100	8	63	5	0	0	0	0
Midwest	100	12	92	11	50	6	17	2
West	100	10	60	6	30	3	30	3
South	100	8	88	7	50	4	13	1
Total	100	38	76	29	34	13	16	6

TABLE A.12. Source of Mothers' Pension Program Funding by Region, 1934

	East (%)	Midwest (%)	West (%)	South (%)	Total
Local	25	84.6	69.2	70	30
State	16.7	0	15.4	0	4
State and local	58.3	15.4	15.4	30	14
Total N	12	13	13	10	48

TABLE A.13. Mean Annual per Capita Mothers' Pension Expenditure, 1931

	N	Subset for $p < .05$	
		Group 1 ($)	Group 2 ($)
East	11	.33	
Midwest	13	.32	
West	10	.30	
South	9		.08
Total	43		

TABLE A.14. Maximum Age of Child to Qualify for Benefits by Region, 1922 and 1934

	Age of Child						Total
	Under 13	Under 14	Under 15	Under 16	Under 17	Under 18	
1922							
East		3		7			10
Midwest	1	5		4	2	1	13
West		1	2	7	1		11
South		2	1	4			7
Total	1	11	3	22	3	1	41
1934							
East		3		9			12
Midwest		2	1	8	2		13
West		2	2	7		1	12
South		3	1	5	1		10
Total		10	4	29	3	1	47

Note: In 1937, ADC law permitted children under sixteen to qualify for benefits.

TABLE A.15. Mothers' Pension Programs by Region, 1931

	Existing Mothers' Pension Programs		Total
	No	Yes	
East[a]		12	12
Midwest		13	13
West[b]	1	10	11
South	3	10	13
Total	4	45	49

[a]Includes Washington, D.C.
[b]Does not include Alaska and Hawaii because they were not states at that time.

TABLE A.16. Administrative Units in States by Region, 1931

	Number of States Having Mothers' Pension Programs	Number of States with Administrative Units Having County Jurisdiction	Mean Number of Administrative Units per State	Mean Number of Administrative Units Reporting Mothers' Pension Grants per State	Mean Percentage Administrative Units Reporting Mothers' Pension Grants per State
East	12	6 (50%)	29.0	23.0	83
Midwest	13	13 (100%)	85.5	63.6	76
West	10	10 (100%)	37.9	30.1	78
South	10	10 (100%)	105.8	22.4	25
Total	45	39 (87%)	69.8	38.2	65

TABLE A.17. Mean Monthly Grant per Family, 1931

		Subset for $p < .05$		
	N	Group 1	Group 2	Group 3
East	11	$37.79		
Midwest	13		$23.20	
West	10		$21.32	
South	9			$12.76
Total	43			

TABLE A.18. Mean Monthly Grant per Family in Urban and Other Areas, 1931

	Mean Grant in All Areas ($)	Mean Grant in Cities of 100,000 Pop. ($)	Mean Grant in Rural Areas ($)	Percentage Difference between Grant in Cities and Rural Areas	Percentage Difference between Grant in Cities and All Areas
East	37.79	48.32	35.18	+37.35	+27.86
Midwest	23.20	32.38	18.80	+72.23	+39.57
West	21.32	27.38	20.38	+34.35	+28.42
South	12.76	18.85	10.35	+82.13	+47.73
Total N	43	29	43		

TABLE A.19.   Mean Annual per Capita
Mothers' Pension Expenditures, 1931

	N	Subset for $p < .01$	
		Group 1 ($)	Group 2 ($)
East	11	.33	
Midwest	13	.32	
West	10	.30	
South	9		.08
Total	43		

TABLE A.20.   Mean Annual per Capita Mothers' Pension
Expenditures in Urban and Other Areas, 1931

	All Areas ($)	Areas with Cities of 100,000-plus Population ($)	Other Areas ($)
East	.33	.43	.26
Midwest	.32	.33	.31
West	.30	.28	.32
South	.08	.13	.08
Total N	43	29	43

TABLE A.21.   Mean Percentage of
Administrative Units Reporting
Grants, 1931

	N	Subset for $p < .01$	
		Group 1 (%)	Group 2 (%)
East	12	83	
West	10	78	
Midwest	13	76	
South	10		25
Total	45		

TABLE A.22. Distribution of Mothers' Pension Benefits by Region, 1931

	East	Midwest	West	South	Total
Mean percentage of administrative units reporting grants	83	76	78	25	65
Mean number of families receiving aid	3,094	3,068	1,079	576	2,079
Mean number of families aided/ 10,000 population	7.45	11.77	12.20	6.33	9.63

TABLE A.23. Percentage of Families Receiving Mothers' Pension Benefits by Race and Region, 1931

	Mean Number of African-American Families Receiving Aid	Mean Number of African-American Families in Reporting Areas	Mean Percentage of African-American Families Receiving Aid by African-American Family Population	Mean Number of White Families Receiving Aid	Mean Number of White Families in Reporting Areas	Mean Percentage of White Families Receiving Aid by White Family Population
East	60	20,327	.25	1,198	454,055	.59
Midwest	52	11,516	.78	1,788	329,772	1.89
West	9	1,560	.45	799	175,003	1.17
South	17	43,688	.09	461	137,305	.36
Total	36	18,717	.41	1,119	285,476	1.06

TABLE A.24. Mean Percentage of African-American Families in Area Receiving Aid and of African-American Families in Area, 1931

	Percentage of African-American Families in Area Receiving Aid	Percentage of African-American Families in Area
South	1	20
East	8	6
Midwest	5	4
West	1	1

Source: Data from U.S. Department of Labor, Children's Bureau, *Mothers' Aid—1931.*

TABLE A.25. Mean Percentage
African-American Family Population
in Reporting Areas,[a] 1931

| | *N* | Subset for $p < .01$ | |
		Group 1 (%)	Group 2 (%)
East	10	6.5	
West	9	.9	
Midwest	12	2.6	
South	9		29.0
Total	40		

[a]Population in reporting areas refers to the population in
the administrative units that reported the race of the mother
in the 1931 Children's Bureau survey.

TABLE A.26. Percentage of Persons on FERA to Total Population in
Urban and Rural Areas in the 12 Confederate States

| | Percentage of Persons on Relief | | | | | |
| | Urban | | | Rural | | |
States	White	African-American	Ratio African-American to White	White	African-American	Ratio African-American to White
Tennessee	6.3	11.2	1.78	7.7	3.2	0.42
Arkansas	13.7	26.9	1.96	8.9	4.7	.53
Mississippi	12.0	18.4	1.53	14.1	7.6	.54
Louisiana	10.7	33.0	3.08	17.3	9.6	.54
Georgia	8.7	22.4	2.58	8.7	6.1	.70
Texas	8.5	18.3	2.15	3.3	2.9	.88
Alabama	11.4	22.4	1.96	18.0	17.7	.98
Virginia	3.3	9.8	2.97	1.6	1.6	1.00
Florida	15.1	46.7	3.09	26.6	26.9	1.01
North Carolina	6.4	19.6	3.06	6.7	8.3	1.24
South Carolina	18.8	39.1	2.08	19.8	25.1	1.27

Source: Table adapted from Coll, *Safety Net*, 32; data from "The Negro and Relief," FERA Monthly Report, March 1936, #12. Persons on Relief: FERA, Unemployment Relief Census of October 1933 Population Statistics: 1930 Census of Population.

TABLE A.27.   Regression Model: Number of ADC Cases in County by One Hundred Population

Constant	
Percentage African-American Population in County	$-.321$***
	(-9.492)
Percentage State Population in County	$-.049$
	(-1.485)
Per Capita Income	$-.132$***
	(-3.891)
N	814
R^2	.33

Note: Dependent variable is ratio of number of ADC cases in county by 100 population. *t*-statistics are in parentheses.
***$p < .01$

TABLE A.28.   ADC Cases by State and Data Year

	Year of State Data						
	1936	1937	1938	1939	1940	1941	Total
Alabama		67					67
Arkansas	75						75
Florida					67		67
Georgia		159					159
Mississippi						82	82
North Carolina				100			100
South Carolina				46			46
Tennessee			95				95
Virginia				123			123
Total	75	226	95	269	67	82	814

Source: Bureau of the Census, 1940 Census; State welfare reports; Ward database.

TABLE A.29.   Mean Percentage of Population and ADC Cases per County

	Number of Counties in State	Mean Number of ADC Cases per County	Mean Percentage of State ADC Cases per County	Mean Total Population per County	Mean Percentage of African- American Population per County	Mean Number of ADC cases per 100 Population per County	Mean Percentage of Total State African- American Populatio per Coun
South Carolina	46	107	2.17	41,300	48.36	.27	2.17
Mississippi	82	12	1.22	26,632	45.50	.05	1.22
Georgia	159	35	0.63	19,646	36.62	.20	0.63
Alabama	67	72	1.49	42,287	35.13	.14	1.49
Florida	67	39	1.49	28,320	28.81	.18	1.49
North Carolina	100	84	1.00	35,716	27.07	.26	1.00
Virginia	123	9	0.81	21,723	26.79	.05	0.81
Arkansas	75	42	1.33	25,992	20.37	.16	1.33
Tennessee	95	114	1.05	30,693	10.75	.40	1.05
Total	814	52	1.11	28,313	30.24	.19	1.11

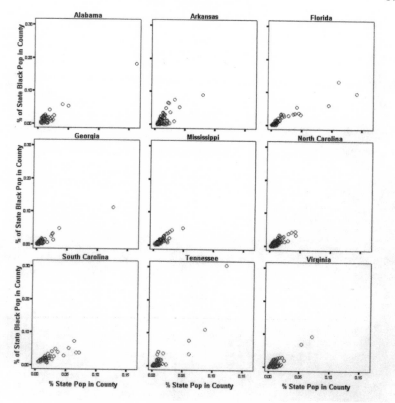

Fig. A.1.   Percentage of state population in county by percentage of state African-American population in county

These figures plot the percentage of the state population in a county by the percentage of the state African-American population in the county. As illustrated, for most states the shape of the plot is roughly a positively sloped line. This means generally, that as a county's percentage of the state population increases, so does the county's percentage of the state African-American population. However, significant differences exist among the states in the spread of the counties and in the slope of the line. This means that significant differences exist among the southern states in how the African-American population is distributed in relationship to the overall population.

Notes

1. The reference to "pensions" for mothers came from reformers and policymakers who likened mothers to soldiers, performing a duty for the good of the nation.
2. U.S. Department of Labor, Children's Bureau, *Mothers' Aid—1931*, 8.
3. Ibid., 7–8.
4. For a compelling and comprehensive analysis of the role of race in nation-building, see Marx, *Making Race and Nation*.
5. See Gordon, *Pitied;* Orloff, *Politics of Pensions;* Skocpol, *Protecting;* Howard, "Sowing"; Hanson, "Federal Statebuilding"; Nelson, "Origins"; 1990; Bane, "Politics and Policies"; Moore, *Mothers' Pensions;* Lopata and Brehm, *Widows;* Quadagno, "Welfare Capitalism"; Vandepol, "Dependent Children"; Trattner, *From Poor Law to Welfare State;* Leff, "Consensus"; Bell, *Aid.*
6. See Boris, *Home to Work;* Evelyn Glenn, *Unequal Freedom;* McDonagh, "Welfare Rights State"; Mink, "Lady"; Mink, *Wages;* Wendy Sarvasy, "Beyond"; Sterett, *Public Pensions.*
7. Skocpol, *Protecting*, 32.
8. See S. Thernstrom and Thernstrom, *America;* A. Thernstrom and Thernstrom, *Beyond.*
9. See Davies and Derthick, "Race," for their complete contribution to this debate.
10. Poole, "Exclusion."
11. See Gordon, *Pitied.*
12. See Quadagno, *Color.*
13. See Mink, *Wages;* Mink, *Welfare's End.*
14. See Abramovitz, *Regulating.*
15. Neubeck and Cazenave, *Welfare Racism*, 12.
16. Katznelson, *Liberalism's Crooked Circle*, 178–79.
17. E. Swift and Brady, "Common Ground," 86.
18. Lieberman, *Shifting*, 149.
19. Hanson, "Liberalism," 96.
20. Nelson, "Origins," 126.
21. Nelson, "Gender, Race, and Class," 416.
22. See Gilens, *Why Americans Hate Welfare.*

23. The Department of Labor's Children's Bureau acted as a research center for gathering information on child health and welfare. The bureau conducted field surveys and investigations into every aspect of child welfare, including child labor, child health and nutrition, education, and juvenile delinquency. In that capacity, the Children's Bureau collected a great deal of information on the laws and administration of the state mothers' pension programs from the early 1900s until the late 1930s. The bureau also wrote numerous reports specifically on mothers' pensions, including studies of state benefits, comparisons of state/local laws and administration, and surveys of beneficiary demographics.

24. These documents are contained in Record Group 102, "Records of the Children's Bureau" at the National Archives, Washington, D.C. The documents in this section are dated from 1912 to 1969.

25. Lieberman introduces the theory of "institutional logic" in *Shifting*.

Chapter 2

1. Tocqueville, *Democracy in Action*, 509.
2. From a 1920 *Survey* article, cited in Ewen, *Immigrant Women*, 186.
3. Smith, "Beyond Tocqueville," 550.
4. McDonagh, "Welfare Rights State," 269.
5. Gutman, *Democracy*, 157–58.
6. King, *Separate and Unequal*, 13.
7. Ibid., 21.
8. McDonagh, "Welfare Rights State," 240.
9. Giddings, *When and Where*, 26.
10. Ibid., 27.
11. McDonagh, "Welfare Rights State," 241.
12. Brundage, *Under Sentence*, 4.
13. Raper, *Tragedy*, 42.
14. B. Baker, "North Carolina Lynching Ballads," 231.
15. Ibid., 222–23.
16. Moore, *Mothers' Pensions*, 40.
17. Johnson and Campbell, *Black Migration*, 79.
18. Ibid., 83.
19. Hartz, *Liberal Tradition*, 8.
20. Key, *Southern Politics*, 407.
21. Ibid., 8.
22. Ibid., 620.
23. Ibid., 627.
24. Smith, "Beyond Tocqueville," 549.
25. Moore, *Mothers' Pensions*, 39.
26. I define central Europe as Poland, Czechoslovakia, Yugoslavia, Hungary, and Austria.
27. I define eastern Europe as the Soviet Union, the Baltic States, Romania, Bulgaria, and European Turkey.
28. I define southern Europe as Spain, Portugal, and Greece. Italy is also a southern European nation but is not included in this statistic.
29. I define northwestern Europe as Great Britain, Ireland, Scandinavia, the Netherlands, Belgium, Luxembourg, Switzerland, and France.

30. U.S. Department of Commerce, Bureau of the Census, *Historical Statistics*, 105–9.

31. Morris, *Immigration*, 18.

32. Ngai, "Architecture," 75.

33. Gordon, *Heroes*, 40.

34. G. Abbott, *Immigrant and the Community*, 235, 283.

35. Ibid., 34.

36. Allen Davis, *Spearheads*, 93.

37. Miller and Miller, *United States Immigration*, 6.

38. Ibid., 19.

39. Cordasco, *Dictionary*, 175.

40. Ibid., 175, 608–9.

41. Miller and Miller, *United States Immigration*, 7.

42. Ngai, "Architecture," 71.

43. Morris, *Immigration*, 55.

44. Ibid., 50.

45. I define the Americas as Canada, Newfoundland, Mexico, and the West Indies.

46. U.S. Department of Commerce, Bureau of the Census, *Historical Statistics*, 105–9.

Chapter 3

1. Beard, *Woman's Work*, 251.

2. Dorr, *What Eight Million Women Want*, 323.

3. Gordon, *Pitied*, 15.

4. Moore, *Mothers' Pensions*, 68–69.

5. Gordon, *Pitied*, 23.

6. Vandepol, "Dependent Children," 225.

7. Trattner, *From Poor Law to Welfare State*, 188.

8. Mangold, *Problems* (1924), 557.

9. Vandepol, "Dependent Children," 230.

10. Lubove, *Struggle*, 95.

11. "Outdoor relief" refers to any assistance that was given to the poor in their own homes.

12. Leff, "Consensus," 397.

13. Gordon, *Pitied*, 72, 78.

14. A complete list of conference invitees can be found in the *Proceedings of the Conference on the Care of Dependent Children*, 20–31; Neubeck and Cazenave, *Welfare Racism*, 43.

15. *Proceedings of the Conference on the Care of Dependent Children*, 36.

16. Ibid., 8.

17. Leff, "Consensus," 411.

18. Sterett, *Public Pensions*, presents an alternative argument. She claims that pensions were not an entitlement and that public money was given for service to other categories of workers in what constituted the first entitlement programs.

19. *Proceedings of the Conference on the Care of Dependent Children*, 9–10.

20. Lubove, *Struggle*, 97.

21. *The Delineator*, August 1912, 85; Skocpol, *Protecting*, 436.

22. *The Delineator*, December 1912, journal cover; Skocpol, *Protecting*, 437–38.

23. *The Delineator*, January 1913, 19.

24. *The Delineator*, April 1913, 263.

25. See, for example, "Pensioning the Widow and the Fatherless," *Good Housekeeping*, September 1913, 282–91, in Bullock, *Selected Articles*, 118–30.

26. "Mothers' Pension Bills," 970–71.

27. "The Mothers' Compensation Law of Colorado," *Survey*, February 15, 1913, 714–16, in Bullock, *Selected Articles*, 16–25.

28. "Widows' Families, Pensioned and Otherwise," *Survey*, June 6, 1914, 270–75, in Bullock, *Selected Articles*, 39–57.

29. "State Pensions to Mothers in Hamilton County, Ohio," *Survey*, December 12, 1914, 289–90, in Bullock, *Selected Articles*, 3–8.

30. "Widows' Families, Pensioned and Otherwise," in Bullock, *Selected Articles*, 54.

31. "Motherhood and Pensions," *Survey*, March 1, 1913, 774–80, in Bullock, *Selected Articles*, 60, 68.

32. *Nashville Tennessean* clipping, Record Group 102, Records of the Children's Bureau, box 240, National Archives.

33. Georgia, Department of Public Welfare, *Georgia's Fight*.

34. Alabama, Child Welfare Department, *Four Years*, 24; Alabama, Department of Public Welfare, *Annual Report* (1937), 27.

35. E. Hall, *Mothers' Assistance*, vii.

36. Kettleborough, "Administration."

37. Leff, "Consensus," 408.

38. For a comprehensive analysis of the role of women's organizations in promoting early social welfare policy in the United States, see Skocpol, *Protecting*.

39. Ibid., 443.

40. Ibid., 543–55.

41. Skocpol and Ritter, "Gender," 77.

42. Skocpol, *Protecting*, 451–52.

43. Gordon, *Pitied*, 42.

44. Ladd-Taylor, *Raising a Baby*, 149–51.

45. Ibid.

46. Tobey, *Children's Bureau*; U.S. Department of Labor, Children's Bureau, *Children's Bureau*.

47. Grace Abbott to Mrs. J. A. Beason, April 25, 1927, Records of the Children's Bureau, Record Group 102, box 418, National Archives.

48. Miscellaneous letters, 1925–28, Records of the Children's Bureau, Record Group 102, box 418, National Archives. These are just a sampling of letters from different agencies and organizations interested in developing mothers' pension legislation or revising existing legislation. There is evidence of communication between the Children's Bureau and different entities seeking advice for almost every state in the nation, including those states that did not adopt legislation until the New Deal era.

49. Bullock, *Selected Articles*, 29.

50. See Bullock, *Selected Articles*, ix–x.

51. Devine, "Pensions," 182–83.

52. At the peak of the veterans' pension program, more than 1 million veterans (more than 90 percent of those eligible) received pensions from the national gov-

ernment. The pensions cost $140 million a year, more than 40 percent of the national government's total revenue. See Hanson, "Conference Panel on Theda Skocpol's *Protecting Soldiers and Mothers*," 121.

53. Moore, *Mothers' Pensions*, 41.

54. Gordon, *Pitied*, 29–30.

55. Stone, "Conference Panel," 115.

56. Leff, "Consensus," 411.

57. Jane Addams represented one exception to this trend. An integral member of this national reform network, she believed that immigrants should preserve their heritage with pride and that everyone would thus benefit.

58. Kelley became a self-proclaimed Marxist after traveling in Europe in the late nineteenth century and did the first English translation of Engels's *The Condition of the Working Class in England in 1844*. She also cofounded the National Child Labor Committee.

59. Gordon, *Pitied*, 86.

60. Neubeck and Cazenave, *Welfare Racism*, 43.

61. See Stone, "Conference Panel," 114–15.

62. Gordon, *Pitied*, 117.

63. Ibid., 87.

64. Breckinridge, *Women*, 24.

65. Gordon, *Pitied*, 118.

66. Ibid., 120–22.

67. Ibid., 123–24.

68. Ibid., 128.

69. Giddings, *When and Where*, 97.

70. Hamilton and Hamilton, *Dual Agenda*, 4–5.

71. Although it is not possible to interpret all claims of race preservation as a call for the preservation of the white race over other races, it is reasonable to suppose that most of these claims arose in response to prevailing nativist concerns.

72. Dorr, *What Eight Million Women Want*, 330.

73. Hale, *What Women Want*, 289.

74. MacLean, *Wage Earning Women*, 28–29.

75. Ibid., 154.

76. Moore, *Mothers' Pensions*, 77.

Chapter 4

1. *Proceedings of the Conference on the Care of Dependent Children*, 9.

2. Supreme Court Justice William O. Douglas in *King v. Smith*, 392 U.S. 309, 1968.

3. U.S. Department of Labor, Children's Bureau, *Laws*, 7. Missouri's 1911 law applied only to Jackson County, in which Kansas City is located.

4. A form of this program, "widows' scholarships," had existed prior to the enactment of the state legislation. The earlier effort was sponsored and run by two women's organizations, the Illinois Consumers' League and the Illinois Federation of Women's Clubs. See Skocpol, *Protecting*, 546.

5. See E. Abbott, "Public Pensions"; Carstens, "Public Pensions."

6. See chapter 6 for an analysis of this relationship.

7. See Davies and Derthick's critique of Lieberman and Quadagno in "Race."

8. Julia Lathrop, chief of the Children's' Bureau, stated in 1914, "the methods and standards prescribed in the different States vary" (U.S. Department of Labor, Children's Bureau, *Laws*, 6).

9. Records of the Children's Bureau, Record Group 102, box 419, National Archives.

10. J. Brown, *Public Relief*, 28.

11. Lundberg, *Public Aid*, 13.

12. J. Brown, *Public Relief*, 28.

13. Moore, *Mothers' Pensions*, 120.

14. G. Abbott, *From Relief to Social Security*, 270.

15. Carstens, "Social Security," 251.

16. Pickney, "Public Pensions," 474.

17. Colorado, Illinois, Idaho, Iowa, Michigan, Minnesota, Missouri, Nebraska, Nevada, New Jersey, Ohio, Oregon, South Dakota, Utah, Washington, and Wisconsin. See U.S. Department of Labor, Children's Bureau, *Laws*, 10.

18. Lundberg, *Public Aid*, 9.

19. Carstens, "Social Security," 251.

20. J. Brown, *Public Relief*, 28; U.S. Department of Labor, Children's Bureau, *Public Aid 1934*.

21. Ada Davis, "Evolution," 579.

22. Kettleborough, "Administration," 557.

23. Lundberg, *Public Aid*, 8–10.

24. Howard, "Sowing," 198.

25. National Resources Planning Board, *Security, Work, and Relief Policies*, 59.

26. Lundberg, *Public Aid*, 4.

27. U.S. Department of Labor, Children's Bureau, *Laws*, 8–9.

28. U.S. Department of Labor, Children's Bureau, *Public Aid 1922*, 4–22. California, Colorado, Delaware, Florida, Hawaii, Minnesota, Nebraska, New Jersey, Oregon, Virginia, and Wisconsin.

29. U.S. Department of Labor, Children's Bureau, *Public Aid 1929*, 4–25. California, Colorado, Delaware, Florida, Idaho, Kentucky, Minnesota, Mississippi, Nebraska, New Jersey, New York, Oregon, Rhode Island, Virginia, and Wisconsin.

30. U.S. Department of Labor, Children's Bureau, *Public Aid 1934*, 2–39. California, Colorado, Delaware, Florida, Idaho, Kentucky, Minnesota, Mississippi, New Jersey, New Mexico, New York, Oregon, Rhode Island, South Dakota, Virginia, and Wisconsin.

31. U.S. Department of Labor, Children's Bureau, *Laws*, 9.

32. U.S. Department of Labor, Children's Bureau, *Public Aid 1922*, 6, 10, 14, 18.

33. U.S. Department of Labor, Children's Bureau, *Public Aid 1934*, 4, 30.

34. U.S. Department of Labor, Children's Bureau, *Public Aid 1922*, 4–22. Kansas, Michigan, Missouri, Nebraska, South Dakota, Virginia, and Wisconsin.

35. U.S. Department of Labor, Children's Bureau, *Public Aid 1929*, 4–25.

36. U.S. Department of Labor, Children's Bureau, *Public Aid 1934*.

37. U.S. Department of Labor, Children's Bureau, *Public Aid 1922*. Arizona, Arkansas, Delaware, Florida, Kansas, Maine, Michigan, Minnesota, Missouri, Nebraska, Ohio, Tennessee, Vermont, Virginia, West Virginia, Wisconsin, and Wyoming.

38. U.S. Department of Labor, Children's Bureau, *Public Aid 1929*. Illinois, New

York, North Carolina, and North Dakota joined the existing states who had done so in 1922.

39. U.S. Department of Labor, Children's Bureau, *Public Aid 1934.*

40. U.S. Department of Labor, Children's Bureau, *Mothers' Aid—1931,* 12.

41. U.S. Department of Labor, Children's Bureau, *Public Aid 1922.* Alaska, Arizona, Arkansas, California, Delaware, Florida, Hawaii, Idaho, Illinois, Iowa, Kansas, Louisiana, Michigan, Minnesota, Missouri, Montana, Nebraska, New York, Ohio, Oklahoma, Oregon, Pennsylvania, South Dakota, Tennessee, Vermont, Virginia, West Virginia, Wisconsin, and Wyoming.

42. U.S. Department of Labor, Children's Bureau, *Public Aid 1929.*

43. U.S. Department of Labor, Children's Bureau, *Public Aid 1934.*

44. Lundberg, *Public Aid,* 4; U.S. Department of Labor, Children's Bureau, *Public Aid 1922,* 6, 14, 18.

45. U.S. Department of Labor, Children's Bureau, *Public Aid 1934,* 6.

46. Moore, *Mothers' Pensions,* 136.

47. Mangold, *Problems* (1936), 460.

48. U.S. Department of Commerce, Bureau of the Census, *Historical Statistics,* 52.

49. U.S. Department of Labor, Children's Bureau, *Public Aid 1922,* 14, 16, 20.

50. Carstens, "Social Security," 459.

51. U.S. Department of Labor, Children's Bureau, *Public Aid 1922,* 4–23. The thirty states and territories funded by the localities alone were Alaska, Arkansas, Colorado, Florida, Hawaii, Idaho, Illinois, Indiana, Iowa, Kansas, Louisiana, Maryland, Michigan, Missouri, Montana, Nebraska, Nevada, New Jersey, New York, North Dakota, Ohio, Oklahoma, Oregon, South Dakota, Tennessee, Texas, Utah, Washington, West Virginia, and Wyoming. The ten states with joint funding were California, Connecticut, Delaware, Maine, Massachusetts, Minnesota, Pennsylvania, Vermont, Virginia, and Wisconsin.

52. Lundberg, *Public Aid,* 14.

53. U.S. Department of Labor, Children's Bureau, *Public Aid 1934,* 2–39. Arizona, California, Connecticut, Delaware, Illinois, Louisiana, Maine, Massachusetts, Missouri, New Hampshire, New Mexico, North Carolina, Pennsylvania, Rhode Island, Vermont, Virginia, and Wisconsin.

54. J. Brown, *Public Relief,* 27–28.

55. California, Delaware, Maine, Massachusetts, North Carolina, Pennsylvania, Rhode Island, Vermont, and Virginia.

56. G. Abbott, *From Relief to Social Security,* 273.

57. U.S. Department of Labor, Children's Bureau, *Public Aid 1922,* 4–23.

58. U.S. Department of Labor, Children's Bureau, *Public Aid 1934,* 2–39.

59. Lundberg, *Public Aid,* 8.

60. U.S. Department of Labor, Children's Bureau, *Mothers' Aid—1931,* 5.

61. Ibid., 17.

62. The dependent variable in the multivariate regression was average monthly grant per family. The independent variables were maximum family grant, percentage state African-American population, percentage state urban population, per capita income, and region. Although the model overall was significant ($p <$ .05, $R^2 = .53$), none of the independent variables were statistically significant.

63. Lundberg, *Public Aid,* 6.

64. U.S. Department of Labor, Children's Bureau, *Public Aid 1922*, 4–23. Arizona, Illinois, Louisiana, Maryland, Minnesota, Missouri, Nebraska, Oregon, Virginia, West Virginia, and Wisconsin.

65. U.S. Department of Labor, Children's Bureau, *Public Aid 1929*, 4–25. Arizona, Connecticut, Illinois, Louisiana, Maryland, Minnesota, Missouri, Nebraska, Oregon, Rhode Island, Virginia, and Wisconsin.

66. U.S. Department of Labor, Children's Bureau, *Public Aid 1934*, 2–39. Arizona, Connecticut, District of Columbia, Illinois, Kentucky, Minnesota, Missouri, Nebraska, New Jersey, New Mexico, North Carolina, Oregon, Puerto Rico, Rhode Island, Virginia, and Wisconsin.

67. Ibid., 2–39. Arkansas, Idaho, Kansas, Montana, Oregon, and Tennessee.

68. Lundberg, *Public Aid*, 7–8.

69. Alaska, Arizona, California, Connecticut, Delaware, the District of Columbia, Florida, Illinois, Indiana, Iowa, Louisiana, Maine, Massachusetts, Minnesota, Mississippi, Missouri (everywhere except St. Louis, which was under fourteen), Montana, Nebraska, Nevada, New Hampshire, New Jersey, New Mexico, New York, Ohio, Puerto Rico, South Dakota, Texas, Utah, Vermont, Virginia, and Wisconsin.

70. Kansas, Kentucky, Maryland, North Carolina, Oklahoma, Oregon, Pennsylvania, Rhode Island, West Virginia, and Wyoming.

71. U.S. Department of Labor, Children's Bureau, *Public Aid 1934*, 2–39.

72. Lundberg, *Public Aid*, 6.

73. Rhode Island required citizenship, three years' residence in the state, and one year's residence in a town for those who did not meet the state settlement requirement.

74. U.S. Department of Labor, Children's Bureau, *Public Aid 1934*, 2–39.

75. Nesbitt, "Family Budget," 361.

76. U.S. Department of Labor, Children's Bureau, *Mothers' Aid—1931*, 1.

77. Lundberg, *Public Aid*, 10.

78. Moore, *Mothers' Pensions*, vii.

79. Bell, *Aid*, 7; U.S. Department of Labor, Children's Bureau, *Public Aid 1934*, 2–39.

80. Moore, *Mothers' Pensions*, 139.

81. Bogue, *Administration*, 29, 68, 129.

82. Lundberg, *Public Aid*, 6.

83. Bogue, *Administration*, 142.

Chapter 5

1. Lundberg, "Progress," 438.

2. Lopata and Brehm, *Widows*, 47

3. Leff, "Consensus," 402.

4. Nelson, "Origins," 145.

5. U.S. Department of Labor, Children's Bureau, *Mothers' Aid—1931*.

6. For the purposes of my analysis, the South includes Alabama, Arkansas, Florida, Georgia, Kentucky, Louisiana, Mississippi, North Carolina, Oklahoma, South Carolina, Tennessee, Texas and Virginia—that is, the eleven Confederate states plus Oklahoma and Kentucky.

7. Florence Hutsinpillar to Earl Chambers, January 28, 1931, Records of the Children's Bureau, Record Group 102, box 419, National Archives.

8. Florence Hutsinpillar to Mrs. Cornish, March 29, 1930, Records of the Children's Bureau, Record Group 102, box 419, National Archives.

9. Florence Hutsinpillar to Mrs. Aley, August 11, 1932, Records of the Children's Bureau, Record Group 102, box 419, National Archives.

10. U.S. Department of Labor, Children's Bureau, *Mothers' Aid—1931*, 11, 25.

11. Carstens, "Public Pensions," 462.

12. Howard, "Sowing," 204.

13. Bogue, *Administration*.

14. Lundberg, *Public Aid to Mothers*, 17.

15. See Davies and Derthick's critique in "Race."

16. U.S. Department of Labor, Children's Bureau, *Mothers' Aid—1931*, 18.

17. U.S. Department of Commerce, Bureau of Census, *Historical Statistics*, Series D, p. 166.

18. U.S. Department of Labor, Children's Bureau, *Mothers' Aid–1931*, 17. Relative to many benefits, however, mothers' pensions were very generous. Even in comparison to AFDC benefits awarded in the 1990s, mothers' pensions were often higher than current levels. The significance of the low mothers' pension benefits relative to other contemporary programs and relative to the contemporary living wage lay in the rhetoric of the program. Mothers' pensions were considered payment for service to the nation. No other noncontributory social welfare program was honored with the same rhetoric, especially not AFDC.

19. J. Brown, *Public Relief*, 28.

20. G. Abbott, "Recent Trends," 198.

21. The smaller N in this test could have contributed to it not being significant. The N was 29, compared with 43 in the other tests.

22. Gordon, *Pitied*, 47.

23. U.S. Department of Labor, Children's Bureau, *Proceedings of Conference on Mothers' Pensions*, 4.

24. Ibid.

25. G. Abbott, *From Relief to Social Security*, 182–83.

26. Ibid., 274.

27. Marcus C. Fagg to Children's Bureau, October 19, 1926, Records of the Children's Bureau, Record Group 102, box 315, National Archives.

28. C. W. Hayhurst to Florence Hutsinpillar, November 25, 1931, and Hutsinpillar to Hayhurst, December 7, 1931, Records of the Children's Bureau, Record Group 102, box 418, National Archives.

29. Mary Milburn to Irene Waalkes, May 17, 1932, Records of the Children's Bureau, Record Group 102., box 419, National Archives.

30. E. Abbott, "Experimental Period," 154.

31. Florence Hutsinpillar to John Joe West, January 10, 1931, Records of the Children's Bureau, Record Group 102, box 419, National Archives.

32. Florence Hutsinpillar to Mrs. Latimer Williams Jr., April 13, 1932, Records of the Children's Bureau, Record Group 102, box 418, National Archives.

33. Lundberg, *Public Aid*, 15.

34. The secretary of the San Antonio Social Welfare Bureau acknowledged in a letter to the Children's Bureau that the mothers' pension bill operated in only two counties. R. C. Hogman to Children's Bureau, April 29, 1930, Records of the Children's Bureau, Record Group 102, box 418, National Archives.

35. Bell, *Aid*, 13; J. Brown, *Public Relief*, 27.

36. G. Abbott, *From Relief to Social Security*, 209.

37. See Lundberg, "Progress," 441; G. Abbott, "Recent Trends," 205–8.

38. Bell, *Aid*, 13.

39. Nesbitt, *Standards*, 32.

40. Ibid., 34.

41. Carstens, "Public Pensions," 461.

42. Nesbitt, *Standards*, 145.

43. U.S. Department of Labor, Children's Bureau, *Laws*, 43.

44. Nelson, "Origins," 140.

45. Gordon, *Heroes*, 50.

46. Moore, *Mothers' Pensions*, 180; E. Abbott and Breckinridge, *Administration*.

47. Nesbitt, *Standards*, 11–13.

48. Ibid., 17.

49. Moore, *Mothers' Pensions*, 181; Nesbitt, *Standards*.

50. Lundberg, *Public Aid*, 24.

51. Nesbitt, *Standards*, 19.

52. Moore, *Mothers' Pensions*, 182.

53. U.S. Department of Labor, Children's Bureau, *Public Aid 1929*, 36.

54. U.S. Department of Labor, Children's Bureau, *Children of Wage-earning Mothers*, 82.

55. Ibid., 30.

56. Bell, *Contemporary*, 21.

57. Mangold, *Problems* (1936), 464.

58. Bell, *Aid*, 9.

59. Myrdal, *American Dilemma*, 360.

60. Bell, *Aid*, 19.

61. Skocpol, "African-Americans," 139.

62. Gordon, *Heroes*, 14–15.

63. Ibid., 15.

64. G. Abbott, "Recent Trends," 208.

65. Ibid., 209.

66. Pumphrey and Pumphrey, "Widows' Pension Movement," 58.

67. Moore, *Mothers' Pensions*, 157; Gordon, *Pitied*, 48.

68. U.S. Department of Labor, Children's Bureau, *Mothers' Aid—1931*, 13.

69. Bell, *Aid*, 9.

70. U.S. Department of Labor, Children's Bureau, *Mothers' Aid—1931*, 13.

71. G. Abbott, *From Relief to Social Security*, 183.

72. Coll, *Safety Net*, 46.

73. Bell, *Aid*, 203; G. Abbott, *Child*, 237.

Chapter 6

1. I am distinguishing here between assistance and insurance programs.

2. Hamilton and Hamilton, *Dual Agenda*, 4–5.

3. Coll, *Safety Net*, 106.

4. Ibid., 46.

5. Gordon, *Pitied*, 256.

6. According to a portion of the committee report, "Old-age pensions are in a real sense measures in behalf of children. They shift the retroactive burdens to

shoulders which can bear them with less human costs, and young parents thus re-
leased can put at the disposal of the new member of society those family resources
he must be permitted to enjoy if he is to become a strong person, unburdensome
to the State. Health measures, which protect his family from sickness and remove
the menacing apprehension of debt, always present in the mind of the breadwinner, are child-welfare measures. Likewise, unemployment compensation is a
measure in behalf of children in that it protects the home. Most important of all,
public-job assurance which can hold the family together over long or repetitive
periods of private unemployment is a measure for children in that it assures them
a childhood rather than the premature strains of the would-be child breadwinner"
(Committee on Economic Security, *Report*, 35). Some claim that the committee
and the president were putting the welfare of children on a basis of equal importance with the welfare of adults. Although the president announced to Congress
that "among our objectives I place the security of the men, women, and children
of the Nation first," the ensuing legislation did nothing to equalize relations
among men, women, and children and, as will be demonstrated, often exacerbated existing inequalities.

7. Vinson later served as chief justice of the Supreme Court during the early
civil rights era.

8. Witte, *Development*, 163–64.

9. Gordon, *Pitied*, 266.

10. Ibid., 268.

11. J. Brown, *Public Relief*, 37.

12. U.S. Department of Labor, Children's Bureau, *Children's Bureau*.

13. Many contemporary social reformers argued that the Children's Bureau
would have ensured that this aid remained focused on the child. Furthermore, by
separating the federal child welfare program from ADC, states and localities had
to establish corresponding separate public welfare programs. The Children's Bureau and the Bureau of Public Assistance required different state plans, developed
different procedures, competed for the same personnel, and were not interested in
coordinating their efforts. However, at the local level, these programs often affected the same families.

14. Social Security Act, Title IV, 406 (a).

15. Howard, "Sowing," 212.

16. Amott, "Black Women," 287–88.

17. Skocpol, "Limits," 303.

18. Hamilton and Hamilton, *Dual Agenda*, 30.

19. Neubeck and Cazenave, *Welfare Racism*, 49.

20. Ibid., 50.

21. Skocpol, "African-Americans," 144.

22. Hamilton and Hamilton, *Dual Agenda*, 14–27.

23. McKinley and Frase, *Launching*, 14.

24. Social Security Act, Title IV, 402 (a).

25. Ibid., 406 (a).

26. Coll, *Safety Net*, 186.

27. Quoted in Neubeck and Cazenave, *Welfare Racism*, 50.

28. G. Abbott, *From Relief to Social Security*, 281.

29. Gordon, *Pitied*, 186.

30. J. Brown, *Public Relief*, 27–28.

31. I have no figures regarding the number for eligible children.

32. Data for other states are not complete and consequently have been omitted from the comparison.

33. J. Brown, *Public Relief*, 32.

34. Bell, *Aid*, 21–22.

35. Lopata and Brehm, *Widows*, 72–73.

36. Hanson, "Federal," 107.

37. Bell, *Aid*, 23.

38. Coll, *Safety Net*, 104.

39. Hanson, "Federal," 111.

40. By the end of 1942, seven states still had not adopted ADC.

41. U.S. Congress, House of Representatives, Committee on Ways and Means, *Social Security Bill*, 24.

42. Bell, *Aid*, 1.

43. J. Brown, *Public*, 371.

44. Bell, *Aid*, 34; Larabee, "Unmarried Parenthood," 447–49; Coll, *Safety Net*, 105.

45. Jane Hoey studied at Columbia University and received a master's degree in political science. On January 7, 1936, she was appointed the director of the Bureau of Public Assistance of the Social Security Board. While at the Board of Child Welfare of New York City, Hoey served as an assistant to Harry Hopkins and helped administer the mothers' pension program. For more details, see Coll, *Safety Net*, 62.

46. Coll, *Safety Net*, 105.

47. Bell, *Aid*, 49.

48. Coll, *Safety Net*, 105.

49. Ibid., 112.

50. Interview, March 10, 1965, 43–44, Social Security Project, Oral History Collection, Columbia University Library, New York.

51. Bell, *Aid*, 182.

52. Coll, *Safety Net*, 116.

53. U.S. Social Security Board, *Third Annual Report*, 100; J. Brown, *Public*, 372.

54. Bell, *Aid*, 51. Alaska, Arizona, Idaho, Indiana, Kansas, Louisiana, Missouri, Montana, Nebraska, New Mexico, North Carolina, North Dakota, Oklahoma, Texas, and Wyoming.

55. Ibid. Connecticut, Illinois, Iowa, Mississippi, and South Dakota.

56. Ibid., 178. Arkansas, Florida, Georgia, Louisiana, Michigan, Mississippi, Tennessee, Texas, and Virginia.

57. The names of the administrators of both ADC and the mothers' pensions were not available for the other states.

58. Bell, *Aid*, 175.

59. Quoted in Neubeck and Cazenave, *Welfare Racism*, 59.

60. Coll, *Safety Net*, 118.

61. Comparative county-level data were not available for all states in one year, so the data used come from 1936–41. For the purposes of this analysis, the South is defined as the eleven states that comprised the Confederacy. County-level population data for Louisiana and Texas were not available, so they were not included in the sample. The figures and correlations presented are based on the entire data set of 814 counties, regardless of the year of the data. The rationale for

this is that it enlarges the data set without much loss in accuracy, as the period covered is relatively short (five years).

62. Coll, *Safety Net*, 119.

63. Howard, "Sowing," 216.

64. Gordon, *Pitied*, 303.

65. Howard, "Sowing," 214.

66. Myrdal, *American Dilemma*, 359.

67. *Aid*, 42.

68. Bell, *Aid*, 34; Larabee, "Unmarried Parenthood," 449.

69. Bell, *Aid*, 35.

70. Myrdal, *American Dilemma*, 359.

71. Bell, *Aid*, 55.

72. Bell, *Aid*, 47.

73. Ibid., 183.

74. Bell, *Aid*, 185.

75. Myrdal, *American Dilemma*, 359–60.

76. Senate Finance Committee Report—S. Rep. no. 165, 87th Cong., 1st sess., 1961.

77. *King v. Smith*, 392 U.S. 309, 1968.

Chapter 7

1. *Report of the Mothers' Pension League.*

2. *Congressional Record*, July 18, 1996, S 8081.

3. Gilens, *Why Americans Hate Welfare*, offers an insightful analysis of public perception about welfare and welfare recipients and how racial stereotypes affected that perception.

4. Lieberman, *Shifting*, 129.

5. Ibid., 162.

6. The remaining 4 percent is for miscellaneous programs. U.S. Bureau of the Census, *Statistical Abstract: 1997*, 313.

7. Gilens, *Why Americans Hate Welfare*, 15–17.

8. Ibid., 18–19.

9. Ibid., 62–63.

10. Fording, "'Laboratories,'" 75–76.

11. This was Gramm's February 24, 1995, announcement of his 1996 presidential bid. The full speech is available at http://www.4president.org/speeches/gramm1996announcement.htm.

12. *New York Times*, February 16, 1995.

13. *Congressional Record*, March 21, 1995, H 3362.

14. Sparks, "Queens," 179.

15. *Congressional Record*, July 18, 1996, S 58080.

16. Ibid., September 7, 1995, S 12758–12759.

17. Ibid., March 21, 1995, H 3365.

18. Soss et al., "Hard Line," 225.

19. See Neubeck and Cazenave, *Welfare Racism*, 117–19.

20. Gilens, "How the Poor Became Black," 117.

21. Avery and Peffley, "Race Matters," 132.

22. Sparks, "Queens," 179.

23. Avery and Peffley, "Race Matters," 145–46.

24. Reagan cited a Chicago "welfare queen" who had supposedly taken $150,000 from the government using eighty aliases, thirty addresses, a dozen Social Security cards, and four fictional dead husbands. Although there were attempts made to identify this welfare queen and her "welfare Cadillac," no such recipient was ever found, raising speculation that the administration had invented this person.

25. Sparks, "Queens," 178.

26. *Congressional Record*, March 23, 1995, H 3706.

27. Ibid., H 3718.

28. Ibid., March 21, 1995, H 3404.

29. Ibid., February 24, 1995, H 2219.

30. Fording, "'Laboratories,'" 86–88.

31. Soss et al., "Hard Line," 226.

32. Piven, "Why Welfare Is Racist," 323.

33. Katznelson and Pietrykowski, "Rebuilding," 305.

34. M. Brown, "Ghettos, Fiscal Federalism, and Welfare Reform," 60.

35. U.S. Commission on Civil Rights, "New Paradigm."

36. Hero, "Racial/Ethnic Diversity," 299.

Bibliography

This bibliography is divided into three sections. General sources appear first, followed by federal government documents and state and local documents.

Abbott, Edith. "The Experimental Period of Widows' Pension Legislation." In *Proceedings of the National Conference of Social Work, Forty-fourth Annual Session, June 6–13, 1917.* Chicago, 1917.

Abbott, Edith. "Public Pensions to Widows with Children." *American Economic Review* 3 (June 1913): 413–18.

Abbott, Grace. *The Child and The State.* Vol. 2, *The Dependent and the Delinquent Child.* Chicago: University of Chicago Press, 1938.

Abbott, Grace. *From Relief to Social Security.* Chicago: University of Chicago Press, 1941.

Abbott, Grace. *The Immigrant and the Community.* New York: Century, 1917.

Abbott, Grace. "Recent Trends in Mothers' Aid." *Social Service Review* 3 (June 1934): 191–210.

Abramovitz, Mimi. *Regulating the Lives of Women: Social Welfare Policy from Colonial Times to the Present.* Boston: South End, 1988.

Altmeyer, Arthur J. *The Formative Years of Social Security.* Madison: University of Wisconsin Press, 1966.

Amenta, Edwin, Elisabeth Clemens, Jefren Olsen, Sunita Parikh, and Theda Skocpol. "The Political Origins of Unemployment Insurance in Five American States." *Studies in American Political Development* 2 (1987): 137–82.

Amott, Teresa L. "Black Women and AFDC." In *Women, the State, and Welfare,* ed. Linda Gordon. Madison: University of Wisconsin Press, 1990.

Avery, James M., and Mark Peffley. "Race Matters: The Impact of News Coverage of Welfare Reform on Public Opinion." In *Race and the Politics of Welfare Reform,* ed. Sanford F. Schram, Joe Soss, and Richard C. Fording. Ann Arbor: University of Michigan Press, 2003.

Baker, Bruce E. "North Carolina Lynching Ballads." In *Under Sentence of Death: Lynching in the South,* ed. W. Fitzhugh Brundage. Chapel Hill: University of North Carolina Press, 1997.

Baker, Helen, comp. *The Development of the Social Security Act: A Selected List of References.* Princeton: Princeton University Industrial Relations Section, 1936.

Bane, Mary Jo. "Politics and Policies of the Feminization of Poverty." In *The Politics of Social Policy in the United States*, ed. Margaret Weir, Ann Shola Orloff, and Theda Skocpol. Princeton: Princeton University Press, 1988.

Beard, Mary Ritter. *Woman's Work in Municipalities.* New York: Appleton, 1915.

Beck, E. M., and Stewart E. Tolnay. "When Race Didn't Matter." In *Under Sentence of Death: Lynching in the South*, ed. W. Fitzhugh Brundage. Chapel Hill: University of North Carolina Press, 1997.

Bell, Winifred. *Aid to Dependent Children.* New York: Columbia University Press, 1965.

Bell, Winifred. *Contemporary Social Welfare.* New York: MacMillan, 1983.

Bensel, Richard. *Yankee Leviathan: The Origins of Central State Authority in America, 1859–1877.* New York: Cambridge University Press, 1990.

Boris, Eileen. *Home to Work: Motherhood and the Politics of Industrial Homework in the United States.* Cambridge: Cambridge University Press, 1994.

Breckinridge, Sophonisba. "Legislative Control of Women's Work." *Journal of Political Economy* 14 (February 1906): 107–9.

Breckinridge, Sophonisba. *Women in the Twentieth Century: A Study of Their Political, Social, and Economic Activities.* New York: McGraw-Hill, 1933.

Bremner, Robert H., ed. *Children and Youth in America: A Documentary History.* Cambridge: Harvard University Press, 1971.

Brown, Josephine Chapin. *Public Relief, 1929–1939.* New York: Octagon, 1971.

Brown, Michael. "Ghettos, Fiscal Federalism, and Welfare Reform." In *Race and the Politics of Welfare Reform*, ed. Sanford F. Schram, Joe Soss, and Richard C. Fording. Ann Arbor: University of Michigan Press, 2003.

Brown, Michael, Martin Carnoy, Elliott Currie, Troy Duster, David Oppenheimer, Marjorie Shultz, and David Wellman. *Whitewashing Race: The Myth of a Color-Blind Society.* Berkeley: University of California Press, 2003.

Brundage, W. Fitzhugh, ed. *Under Sentence of Death: Lynching in the South.* Chapel Hill: University of North Carolina Press, 1997.

Bullock, Edna, ed. *Selected Articles on Mothers' Pensions.* New York: Wilson, 1915.

Bureau of Research in the Social Sciences, State University of Texas. *Texas Children: The Report of the Texas Child Welfare Survey.* Austin: University of Texas, 1938.

Butler, Amos. "Official Outdoor Relief and the State." In *Proceedings of the National Conference of Charities and Corrections.* Chicago: Hildmann Printing, 1915.

Carstens, C. C. "Public Pensions to Widows with Children." *Survey* 29 (January 1913): 459–66.

Carstens, C. C. "Social Security through Aid for Dependent Children in Their Own Homes." *Law and Contemporary Problems* 3 (April 1936): 246–52.

Cates, Jerry R. *Insuring Inequality: Administrative Leadership in Social Security, 1935–54.* Ann Arbor: University of Michigan Press, 1983.

Coll, Blanche. *Safety Net: Welfare and Social Security, 1929–1979.* New Brunswick: Rutgers University Press, 1995.

Cordasco, Francesco, ed. *Dictionary of American Immigration History.* Metuchen, N.J.: Scarecrow, 1990.

Davies, Gareth, and Martha Derthick. "Race and Social Welfare Policy: The Social Security Act of 1935." *Political Science Quarterly* 112 (summer 1997): 217–35.

Davis, Ada J. "The Evolution of the Institution of Mothers' Pensions in the United States." *American Journal of Sociology* 35 (January 1930): 573–87.

Davis, Allen F. *Spearheads for Reform: The Social Settlements and the Progressive Movement, 1890–1914*. New York: Oxford University Press, 1967.

Derthick, Martha. *Policymaking for Social Security*. Washington, D.C.: Brookings Institution Press, 1979.

Devine, Edward T. "Pensions for Mothers." In *Selected Articles on Mothers' Pensions*, ed. Edna Bullock. White Plains, N.Y.: Wilson, 1915.

Dorr, Rheta Childe. *What Eight Million Women Want*. Boston: Small, Maynard, 1918.

Douglas, Paul H. "The Family Allowance System as a Protector of Children." *Annals* 71 (September 1925): 16–24.

Du Bois, W. E. B. *The Philadelphia Negro: A Social Study*. Philadelphia: University of Pennsylvania Press, 1899.

Ellwood, David. *Poor Support: Poverty in the American Family*. New York: Basic Books, 1988.

Epstein, Abraham. *Insecurity: A Challenge to America*. New York: Smith and Haas, 1933.

Ewen, Elizabeth. *Immigrant Women in the Land of Dollars*. New York: Monthly Review Press, 1985.

Fording, Richard C. "'Laboratories of Democracy' or Symbolic Politics? The Racial Origins of Racial Reform." In *Race and the Politics of Welfare Reform*, ed. Sanford F. Schram, Joe Soss, and Richard C. Fording. Ann Arbor: : University of Michigan Press, 2003.

Frankel, Emil. "Child Care Seen through the Eyes of the Child." *Rehabilitation Review* 8 (July–August 1934).

Frazier, E. Franklin. *The Negro in the United States*. Toronto: Macmillan, 1957.

Giddings, Paula. *When and Where I Enter: The Impact of Black Women on Race and Sex in America*. New York: Bantam, 1985.

Gilens, Martin. "How the Poor Became Black: The Racialization of American Poverty in the Mass Media." In *Race and the Politics of Welfare Reform*, ed. Sanford F. Schram, Joe Soss, and Richard C. Fording. Ann Arbor: University of Michigan Press, 2003.

Gilens, Martin. *Why Americans Hate Welfare*. Chicago: University of Chicago Press, 1999.

Glenn, Evelyn Nahano. *Unequal Freedom: How Race and Gender Shaped American Citizenship and Labor*. Cambridge: Harvard University Press, 2002.

Goodwin, Joanne L. *Gender and the Politics of Welfare Reform: Mothers' Pensions in Chicago, 1911–1929*. Chicago: University of Chicago Press, 1997.

Gordon, Linda. *Heroes of Their Own Lives*. New York: Viking, 1988.

Gordon, Linda. *Pitied but Not Entitled: Single Mothers and the History of Welfare, 1890–1935*. New York: Free Press, 1994.

Gordon, Linda, ed. *Women, the State, and Welfare*. Madison: University of Wisconsin Press, 1990.

Grossberg, Michael. *Governing the Hearth: Law and Family in Nineteenth-Century America*. Chapel Hill: University of North Carolina Press, 1985.

Gutman, Amy, ed. *Democracy and the Welfare State*. Princeton: Princeton University Press, 1988.

Halbert, L. A. "The Widows' Allowance Act in Kansas City." In *Selected Articles on Mothers' Pensions*, ed. Edna Bullock, 8–12. White Plains, N.Y.: Wilson, 1915.

Hale, Beatrice Forbes-Robertson. *What Women Want: An Interpretation of the Feminist Movement.* New York: Stokes, 1914.

Hall, Elizabeth L. *Mothers' Assistance in Philadelphia, Actual and Potential Costs: A Study of 1010 Families.* Putnam, Conn.: Patriot, 1933.

Hall, Peter, and Rosemary Taylor. "Political Science and the Three New Institutionalisms." *Political Studies* 44, no. 5 (1996): 936–57.

Hamilton, Dona Cooper, and Charles V. Hamilton. *The Dual Agenda: Race and Social Welfare Policies of Civil Rights Organizations.* New York: Columbia University Press, 1997.

Hanson, Russell L. "Federal Statebuilding during the New Deal: The Transition from Mothers' Aid to Aid to Dependent Children." In *Changes in the State*, ed. Edward Greenberg and Thomas Mayer. London: Sage, 1990.

Hanson, Russell L. "Conference Panel on Theda Skocpol's *Protecting Soldiers and Mothers.*" *Studies in American Political Development* 8 (spring 1994): 119–26.

Hanson, Russell L. "Liberalism and the Course of American Social Welfare Policy." In *The Dynamics of American Politics*, ed. Lawrence Dodd and Calvin Jillson. Boulder, Colo.: Westview, 1994.

Hartz, Louis. *The Liberal Tradition in America.* New York: Harcourt Brace, 1955.

Hathway, Marion. *Public Relief in Washington, 1853–1933.* Washington Emergency Relief Administration, Publication 1. Olympia, Wash.: Emergency Relief Administration, 1934.

Heclo, Hugh. *Modern Social Policies in Britain and Sweden.* New Haven: Yale University Press, 1974.

Hero, Rodney E. "Racial/Ethnic Diversity and States' Public Policies: Social Policies as Context for Welfare Policies." In *Race and the Politics of Welfare Reform*, ed. Sanford F. Schram, Joe Soss, and Richard C. Fording. Ann Arbor: University of Michigan Press, 2003.

Howard, Christopher. "Sowing the Seeds of Welfare: The Transformation of Mothers' Pensions, 1900–1940." *Journal of Policy History* 4, no. 2 (1992): 188–227.

Huntington, Samuel. *American Politics: The Promise of Disharmony.* Cambridge: Belknap Press of Harvard University Press, 1981.

Immergut, Ellen. "The Theoretical Core of the New Institutionalism." *Politics and Society* 26 (March 1998): 5–34.

Johnson, Daniel M., and Rex R. Campbell. *Black Migration in America: A Social Demographic History.* Durham: Duke University Press, 1981.

Jones, Marcus E. *Black Migration in the United States with Emphasis on Selected Central Cities.* Saratoga, Calif.: Century Twenty One, 1980.

Katz, Michael B. *In the Shadow of the Poorhouse.* New York: Basic Books, 1986.

Katznelson, Ira. *Liberalism's Crooked Circle: Letters to Adam Michnik.* Princeton: Princeton University Press, 1996.

Katznelson, Ira, and Bruce Pietrykowski. "Rebuilding the American State: Evidence from the 1940s." *Studies in American Political Development* 5 (fall 1991): 301–39.

Kerber, Linda. "The Republican Mother: Women and the Enlightenment—An American Perspective." *American Quarterly* 28 (summer 1976): 187–205.

Kessler-Harris, Alice. *Out to Work: A History of Wage-Earning Women in the United States.* Oxford: Oxford University Press, 2003.

Kettleborough, Charles. "Administration of Mothers' Pension Laws." *American Political Science Review* 9 (August 1915): 555–58.

Key, V. O. *Southern Politics in State and Nation*. New York: Knopf, 1949.

King, Desmond. *Separate and Unequal: Black Americans and the U.S. Federal Government*. Oxford: Clarendon, 1995.

Koelble, Thomas A. "The New Institutionalism in Political Science and Sociology." *Comparative Politics* 27 (January 1995): 231–43.

Ladd-Taylor, Molly. *Mother-Work: Women, Child Welfare, and the State, 1890–1930*. Urbana: University of Illinois Press, 1994.

Ladd-Taylor, Molly. *Raising a Baby the Government Way: Mothers' Letters to the Children's Bureau, 1915–1932*. New Brunswick: Rutgers University Press, 1986.

Laitin, David D. *Hegemony and Culture: Politics and Religious Change among the Yoruba*. Chicago: University of Chicago Press, 1986.

Larabee, Mary. "Unmarried Parenthood under the Social Security Act." In *Proceedings of the National Conference of Social Work*. New York: Columbia University Press, 1939.

Leff, Mark H. "Consensus for Reform: The Mothers'-Pension Movement in the Progressive Era." *Social Service Review* 47 (September 1973): 397–417.

Lenroot, Katharine F. "Maternal and Child Welfare Provisions of the Social Security Act." *Law and Contemporary Problems* 3 (April 1936): 246–52.

Lieberman, Robert. "Race and the Organization of Welfare Policy." In *Classifying By Race*, ed. Paul Peterson. Princeton: Princeton University Press, 1995.

Lieberman, Robert. "Race, Institutions, and the Administration of Social Policy." *Social Science History* 19 (winter 1995): 511–42.

Lieberman, Robert. *Shifting the Color Line: Race and the American Welfare State*. Cambridge: Harvard University Press, 1998.

Lopata, Helena Znaniecka, and Henry Brehm. *Widows and Dependent Wives: From Social Problem to Federal Program*. New York: Praeger, 1986.

Lubove, Roy. *The Struggle for Social Security, 1900–1935*. Cambridge: Harvard University Press, 1968.

Lundberg, Emma Octavia. "Progress of Mothers' Aid Administration." *Social Service Review* 2 (September 1928): 435–59.

MacLean, Annie Marion. *Wage Earning Women, 1910–1974*. New York: Macmillan, 1910.

Mangold, George. *Problems of Child Welfare*. Rev. ed. New York: Macmillan, 1924.

Mangold, George. *Problems of Child Welfare*. 3d ed. New York: Macmillan, 1936.

March, James G., and Johan P. Olsen. "The New Institutionalism: Organizational Factors in Political Life." *American Political Science Review* 78 (September 1984): 734–49.

March, James G., and Johan P. Olsen. *Rediscovering Institutions: The Organizational Basis of Politics*. New York: Free Press, 1989.

Marx, Anthony W. *Making Race and Nation: A Comparison of the United States, South Africa, and Brazil*. Cambridge: Cambridge University Press, 1998.

McClosky, Herbert, and John Zaller. *The American Ethos: Public Attitudes toward Capitalism and Democracy*. Cambridge: Harvard University Press, 1984.

McDonagh, Eileen. "The 'Welfare Rights State' and the 'Civil Rights State': Policy Paradox and State Building in the Progressive Era." *Studies in American Political Development* 7 (fall 1993): 225–74.

McKinley, Charles, and Robert W. Frase. *Launching Social Security: A Capture-and-Record Account, 1935–1937*. Madison: University of Wisconsin Press, 1970.

Merton, Robert K. *Social Theory and Social Structure*. Glencoe, Ill.: Free Press, 1957.

Michel, Sonya, and Seth Koven. *Mothers of a New World: Maternalist Politics and the Origins of Welfare States*. New York: Routledge, 1993.

Milchrist, Elizabeth Hayward. *State Administration of Child Welfare in Illinois*. Chicago: University of Chicago Press, 1937.

Miller, E. Willard, and Ruby M. Miller. *United States Immigration: A Reference Handbook*. Santa Barbara, Calif.: ABC-CLIO, 1996.

Mink, Gwendolyn. "The Lady and the Tramp: Gender, Race, and the Origins of the American Welfare State." In *Women, the State, and Welfare*, ed. Linda Gordon. Madison: University of Wisconsin Press, 1990.

Mink, Gwendolyn. *Wages of Motherhood: Inequality in the Welfare State, 1917–1942*. Ithaca: Cornell University Press, 1996.

Mink, Gwendolyn. *Welfare's End*. Ithaca: Cornell University Press, 1998.

Moore, Libba Gage. *Mothers' Pensions: The Origins of the Relationship between Women and the Welfare State*. Ann Arbor: University Microfilms International, 1987.

Morris, Milton D. *Immigration: The Beleaguered Bureaucracy*. Washington, D.C.: Brookings Institution, 1985.

"Mothers' Pension Bills." *Hearst's Magazine* 23 (January–June 1913): 970–71.

Myrdal, Gunnar. *An American Dilemma: The Negro Problem and Modern Democracy*. Vol. 1. New York: Harper and Row, 1944.

National Consumers' League. *Report for the Years 1914–1915–1916*. New York, 1917.

Nelson, Barbara J. "The Gender, Race, and Class Origins of Early Welfare Policy and the Welfare State: A Comparison of Workmen's Compensation and Mothers' Aid." In *Women, Politics, and Change*, ed. Louise A. Tilly and Patricia Gurin. New York: Sage, 1990.

Nelson, Barbara J. "The Origins of the Two-Channel Welfare State." In *Women, the State, and Welfare*, ed. Linda Gordon. Madison: University of Wisconsin Press, 1990.

Nesbitt, Florence. "The Family Budget and Its Supervision." In *Proceedings of the National Conference of Social Work, 1918*. Chicago: Hall, 1919.

Neubeck, Kenneth, and Noel Cazenave. *Welfare Racism: Playing the Race Card against America's Poor*. New York: Routledge, 2001.

Ngai, Mae M. "The Architecture of Race in American Immigration Law: A Reexamination of the Immigration Act of 1924." *Journal of American History* 86 (June 1999): 67–92.

O'Brien, Edward J. *Child Welfare Legislation in Maryland, 1634–1936*. Washington, D.C.: Catholic University of America, 1937.

Ofman, Kay Walters. "A Rural View of Mothers' Pensions: The Allegan County, Michigan, Mothers' Pension Program, 1913–1928." *Social Service Review* 70 (March 1996): 98–119.

Omi, Michael, and Howard Winant. *Racial Formation in the United States: From the 1960s to the 1990s*. 2d ed. New York: Routledge, 1994.

Orloff, Ann Shola. "The Political Origins of America's Belated Welfare State." In *The Politics of Social Policy in the United States*, ed. Margaret Weir, Ann Shola Orloff, and Theda Skocpol. Princeton: Princeton University Press, 1988.

Orloff, Ann Shola. *The Politics of Pensions.* Madison: University of Wisconsin, 1993.

Orloff, Ann Shola, and Theda Skocpol. "Why Not Equal Protection? Explaining the Politics of Public Social Spending in Britain, 1900–1911, and the United States, 1880s–1920." *American Sociological Review* 49 (December 1984): 726–50.

Ostrom, Elinor. "New Horizons in Institutional Analysis." *American Political Science Review* 89 (March 1995): 174–78.

Ostrom, Elinor. "Rational Choice Theory and Institutional Analysis: Toward Complementarity." *American Political Science Review* 85 (March 1991): 237–43.

Peterson, Paul E., ed. *Classifying By Race.* Princeton: Princeton University Press, 1995.

Pickney, Merritt W. "Public Pensions to Widows." In *Proceedings of the National Conference of Charities and Correction, Thirty-ninth Annual Session, June 12–19, 1912.* Fort Wayne, Ind.: Fort Wayne Printing, 1912.

Piven, Frances Fox. "Why Welfare Is Racist." In *Race and the Politics of Welfare Reform,* ed. Sanford F. Schram, Joe Soss, and Richard C. Fording. Ann Arbor: University of Michigan Press, 2003.

Piven, Frances Fox, and Richard A. Cloward. *Regulating the Poor: The Functions of Public Welfare.* New York: Vintage, 1971.

Poole, Mary. "The Exclusion of Black Workers from the Social Security Act, 1935." Ph.d. diss., Rutgers University, 2001.

"Public Pensions to Widows." In *Proceedings of the National Conference of Charities and Correction, Thirty-ninth Annual Session, June 12–19, 1912.* Fort Wayne, Ind.: Fort Wayne Printing, 1912.

Pumphrey, Muriel, and Ralph Pumphrey. "The Widows' Pension Movement, 1900–1930: Preventive Child-Saving or Social Control?" In *Social Welfare or Social Control,* ed. Walter Trattner. Knoxville: University of Tennessee Press, 1983.

Quadagno, Jill S. *The Color of Welfare: How Racism Undermined the War on Poverty.* New York: Oxford University Press, 1994.

Quadagno, Jill S. "Welfare Capitalism and the Social Security Act of 1935." *American Sociological Review* 49 (October 1984): 632–47.

Raper, Arthur. *The Tragedy of Lynching.* New York: Dover, 1933.

Recent Progress in Child Welfare Legislation: Papers Read at a Conference Held in Washington, D.C., May 1923. New York: Sage, 1924.

Rogin, Michael Paul. *"Ronald Reagan," the Movie: And Other Episodes in Political Demonology.* Berkeley: University of California Press, 1987.

Ross, Arthur, and Herbert Hill. *Employment, Race, and Poverty.* New York: Harcourt, Brace, and World, 1967.

Rothstein, Robert L. "Epitaph for a Monument to a Failed Protest? A North-South Retrospective." *International Organization* 42 (autumn 1988): 725–48.

Sarvasy, Wendy. "Beyond the Difference versus Equality Policy Debate: Postsuffrage Feminism, Citizenship, and the Quest for a Feminist Welfare State." *Signs* 17 (winter 1992).

Schram, Sanford F., Joe Soss, and Richard C. Fording, eds. *Race and the Politics of Welfare Reform.* Ann Arbor: University of Michigan Press, 2003.

Sewell, William H., Jr. "Ideologies and Social Revolutions: Reflections on the French Case." *Journal of Modern History* 57 (March 1985): 57–85.

Shefter, Martin. *Political Parties and the State: The American Historical Experience.* Princeton: Princeton University Press, 1994.

Sklar, Kathryn Kish. *Florence Kelly and the Nation's Work: The Rise of Woemn's Culture, 1830–1900.* New Haven: Yale University Press, 1995.

Skocpol, Theda. "African-Americans in U.S. Social Policy." In *Classifying by Race*, ed. Paul Peterson. Princeton: Princeton University Press, 1995.

Skocpol, Theda. "Cultural Idioms and Political Ideologies in the Revolutionary Reconstruction of State Power: A Rejoinder to Sewell." *Journal of Modern History* 57 (March 1985): 86–96.

Skocpol, Theda. "The Limits of the New Deal System and the Roots of Contemporary Welfare Dilemmas." In *The Politics of Social Policy in the United States*, ed. Margaret Weir, Ann Shola Orloff, and Theda Skocpol. Princeton: Princeton University Press, 1988.

Skocpol, Theda. "The Origins of Social Policy in the United States: A Polity-Centered Analysis." In *The Dynamics of American Politics*, ed. Lawrence Dodd and Calvin Jillson. Boulder, Colo.: Westview, 1994.

Skocpol, Theda. *Protecting Soldiers and Mothers: The Political Origins of Social Policy in the United States.* Cambridge: Harvard University Press, 1992.

Skocpol, Theda, Marjorie Abend-Wein, Christopher Howard, and Susan Goodrich Lehmann. "Women's Associations and the Enactment of Mothers' Pensions in the United States." *American Political Science Review* 87 (September 1993): 686–701.

Skocpol, Theda, and Gretchen Ritter. "Gender and the Origins of Modern Social Policies in Britain and the United States." *Studies in American Political Development* 5 (spring 1991): 36–91.

Skowronek, Stephen. *Building a New American State.* Cambridge: Cambridge University Press, 1982.

Slingerland, William H. *Child Welfare Work in Pennsylvania: A Co-operative Study of Child-Helping Agencies and Institutions.* New York: Sage, 1914.

Smith, Rogers M. "Beyond Tocqueville, Myrdal, and Hartz: The Multiple Traditions in America." *American Political Science Review* 87 (September 1993): 549–66.

Smith, Rogers M. *Civic Ideals: Conflicting Visions of Citizenship in U.S. History.* New Haven: Yale University Press, 1997.

Smoot, Harry E. *Illinois Manual of Laws Affecting Women and Children.* Chicago: Juvenile Protective Association of Chicago, 1922.

Soss, Joe, Sanford F. Schram, Thomas P. Vartanian, and Erin O'Brien. "The Hard Line and the Color Line: Race, Welfare, and the Roots of Get-Tough Reform." In *Race and the Politics of Welfare Reform*, ed. Sanford F. Schram, Joe Soss, and Richard C. Fording. Ann Arbor: University of Michigan Press, 2003.

Sparks, Holloway. "Queens, Teens, and Model Mothers: Race, Gender, and the Discourse of Welfare Reform." In *Race and the Politics of Welfare Reform*, ed. Sanford F. Schram, Joe Soss, and Richard C. Fording. Ann Arbor: University of Michigan Press, 2003.

Steinmo, Sven H. "American Exceptionalism Reconsidered: Culture or Institutions." In *The Dynamics of American Politics*, ed. Lawrence Dodd and Calvin Jillson. Boulder, Colo.: Westview, 1994.

Sterett, Susan. *Public Pensions: Gender and Civic Service in the States, 1850–1937.* Ithaca: Cornell University Press, 2003.

Stone, Deborah. "Conference Panel on Theda Skocpol's *Protecting Soldiers and Mothers.*" *Studies in American Political Development* 8 (spring 1994): 111–18.

Suggested State Legislation for Social Security. Chicago: American Public Welfare Association, 1935.

Sundquist, James L. *Dynamics of the Party System.* Washington, D.C.: Brookings Institution, 1983.

Swift, Elaine K., and David W. Brady. "Common Ground: History and Theories of American Politics." In *The Dynamics of American Politics*, ed. Lawrence Dodd and Calvin Jillson. Boulder, Colo.: Westview, 1994.

Swift, W. H. *Child Welfare in North Carolina.* New York: National Child Labor Committee, 1918.

Thelen, Kathleen, and Sven Steinmo. "Historical Institutionalism in Comparative Perspective." In *Structuring Politics: Historical Institutionalism in Comparative Analysis*, ed. Sven Steinmo, Kathleen Thelen, and Frank Longstreth. Cambridge: Cambridge University Press, 1992.

Thernstrom, Abigail, and Stephan Thernstrom. *Beyond the Color Line: New Perspectives on Race and Ethnicity in America.* Stanford, Calif.: Hoover Institution Press, Stanford University, 2002.

Thernstrom, Stephan, and Abigail Thernstrom. *America in Black and White: One Nation, Indivisible.* New York: Simon and Schuster, 1997.

Tilly, Charles, ed. *Women, Politics, and Change.* New York: Sage, 1990.

Tobey, James A. *The Children's Bureau: Its History, Activities, and Organization.* Baltimore: Johns Hopkins Press, 1925.

Tocqueville, Alexis de. *Democracy in America.* Boston: Allyn, 1873. Reprint, edited by J. P. Mayer, translated by George Lawrence. New York: Harper and Row, 1969.

Trattner, Walter I. *From Poor Law to Welfare State: A History of Social Welfare in America.* New York: Free Press, 1974.

Trattner, Walter I. *Social Welfare or Social Control?* Knoxville: University of Tennessee Press, 1983.

Vaile, Gertrude. "Principles and Methods of Outdoor Relief." In *Proceedings of the National Conference of Charities and Corrections.* Chicago: Hildmann Printing Co., 1915.

Vandepol, Ann. "Dependent Children, Child Custody, and the Mothers' Pensions: The Transformation of State-Family Relations in the Early Twentieth Century." *Social Problems* 29 (February 1982): 221–35.

Weir, Margaret, Ann Shola Orloff, and Theda Skocpol, eds. *The Politics of Social Policy in the United States.* Princeton: Princeton University Press, 1988.

Witte, Edwin E. *The Development of the Social Security Act.* Madison: University of Wisconsin Press, 1963.

Woman's Christian Temperance Union. *Report of the Thirty-third Annual Meeting, October 5–9, 1906.* Newburgh, N.Y.: Journal Printing House and Book-Bindery, 1906.

Federal Government Documents

Abbott, Edith, and Sophonisba Breckinridge. *The Administration of the Aid-to-Mothers Law in Illinois.* U.S. Department of Labor, Children's Bureau, Legal Series 7, Publication 82. Washington, D.C.: U.S. Government Printing Office, 1921.

Bogue, Mary F. *Administration of Mothers' Aid in Ten Localities.* U.S. Department of Labor, Children's Bureau, Publication 184. Washington, D.C.: U.S. Government Printing Office, 1928.

Committee on Economic Security. *Report to the President.* Washington, D.C.: U.S. Government Printing Office, 1935.

Congressional Quarterly. *Guide to U.S. Elections.* 3d ed. Washington, D.C.: U.S. Government Printing Office, 1994.

Donahue, A. Madorah. *Children of Illegitimate Birth Whose Mothers Have Kept Their Custody.* U.S. Department of Labor, Children's Bureau, Publication 190. Washington, D.C.: U.S. Government Printing Office, 1928.

Lundberg, Emma Octavia. *Public Aid to Mothers with Dependent Children: Extent and Fundamental Principles.* U.S. Department of Labor, Children's Bureau, Publication 162. Washington, D.C.: U.S. Government Printing Office, 1926.

Manning, Caroline. *The Immigrant Woman and Her Job.* U.S. Department of Labor, Women's Bureau, Publication 74. Washington, D.C.: U.S. Government Printing Office, 1930.

National Resources Planning Board. *Security, Work, and Relief Policies.* Washington, D.C.: U.S. Government Printing Office, 1942.

Nesbitt, Florence. *Standards of Public Aid to Children in Their Own Homes.* U.S. Department of Labor, Children's Bureau, Publication 118. Washington, D.C.: U.S. Government Printing Office, 1923.

President's Research Committee on Social Trends. *Recent Social Trends in the United States.* Vol. 2. New York: McGraw-Hill, 1933.

Proceedings of the Conference on the Care of Dependent Children, January 25–26, 1909. Washington, D.C.: U.S. Government Printing Office, 1909.

Rochester, Anna. *Infant Mortality.* U.S. Department of Labor, Children's Bureau, Publication 119. Washington, D.C.: U.S. Government Printing Office, 1923.

Roosevelt, Franklin D. "A Message to the Congress on Social Security." January 17, 1935. Senate Committee on Finance, Economic Security Act Hearings, 74th Cong., 1st sess. Washington, D.C., 1935.

Taylor, Eleanor Brownson. *Children's Progress, 1834–1934.* Washington, D.C.: U.S. Government Printing Office, 1934.

U.S. Commission on Civil Rights. "A New Paradigm for Welfare Reform: The Need for Civil Rights Enforcement." August 2002. http://www.usccr.gov/pubs /prwora/main.htm.

U.S. Congress. House of Representatives. Committee on Interstate and Foreign Commerce. *Public Protection of Maternity and Infancy.* 66th Cong., 3d sess., 1921.

U.S. Congress. House of Representatives. Committee on Interstate and Foreign Commerce. *Public Protection of Maternity and Infancy.* 67th Cong., 1st sess., 1921.

U.S. Congress. House of Representatives. Committee on Ways and Means. *Economic Security Act.* Washington, D.C.: U.S. Government Printing Office, 1935.

U.S. Congress. House of Representatives. Committee on Ways and Means. *The Social Security Bill.* Committee Report 615. 74th Cong., 1st sess., 1935.

U.S. Congress. Senate. *Proceedings of the Conference on Care of Dependent Children.* Document 721. 60th Cong., 2d sess., 1909.

U.S. Congress. Senate. Committee on Finance. *Economic Security Act: Hearings before the Committee on Finance, United States Senate, Seventy-fourth Con-*

gress, First Session, on S. 1130, a Bill to Alleviate the Hazards of Old Age, Unemployment, Illness, and Dependency, to Establish a Social Insurance Board in the Department of Labor, to Raise Revenue, and for Other Purposes. Washington, D.C.: U.S. Government Printing Office, 1935.

U.S. Congress. Senate. *Social Security Amendment.* Committee Report no. 165. 87th Cong., 1st sess., 1961.

U.S. Department of Commerce. Bureau of the Census. *The Fifteenth Census of the United States: 1930. Population, Characteristics of the Population.* Washington, D.C.: U.S. Government Printing Office, 1930.

U.S. Department of Commerce. Bureau of the Census. *Historical Statistics of the United States, Colonial Times to 1970.* Washington, D.C.: U.S. Government Printing Office, 1975.

U.S. Department of Commerce. Bureau of the Census. *The Sixteenth Census of the United States: 1940. Population, Characteristics of the Population.* Washington, D.C.: U.S. Government Printing Office, 1943.

U.S. Department of Commerce. Bureau of the Census. *The Social and Economic Status of the Black Population in the United States: An Historical View, 1790–1978.* Current Population Reports, Special Studies Series P-23, no. 80, Washington, D.C.: U.S. Government Printing Office, 1979.

U.S. Department of Labor. *Regulations of the Department of Labor.* Washington, D.C.: U.S. Government Printing Office, 1915.

U.S. Department of Labor. *Security for Children: Maternal and Child-Welfare Provisions of the Social Security Act.* Washington, D.C.: U.S. Government Printing Office, 1938.

U.S. Department of Labor. Children's Bureau. *The Children's Bureau: Yesterday, Today, and Tomorrow.* Washington, D.C.: U.S. Government Printing Office, 1937.

U.S. Department of Labor. Children's Bureau. *Children of Wage-earning Mothers: A Study of a Selected Group in Chicago.* Publication 102. Washington, D.C.: U.S. Government Printing Office, 1922.

U.S. Department of Labor. Children's Bureau. *Child-Welfare Legislation—1937.* Publication 236. Washington, D.C.: U.S. Government Printing Office, 1938.

U.S. Department of Labor. Children' Bureau. Correspondence. Records of the Children's Bureau, Record Group 102, boxes 418–19. National Archives, Washington, D.C.

U.S. Department of Labor. Children's Bureau. *Grants to States for Maternal and Child Welfare under the Social Security Act.* Bulletin 1. Washington, D.C.: U.S. Government Printing Office, 1935.

U.S. Department of Labor. Children's Bureau. *Laws Relating to "Mothers' Pensions" in the United States, Denmark, and New Zealand.* Publication 7. Washington, D.C.: U.S. Government Printing Office, 1914.

U.S. Department of Labor. Children's Bureau. *Mothers' Aid—1931.* Publication 220. Washington, D.C.: U.S. Government Printing Office, 1933.

U.S. Department of Labor. Children's Bureau. *Proceedings of Conference on Mothers' Pensions, June 28, 1922.* Publication 109. Washington, D.C.: U.S. Government Printing Office, 1922.

U.S. Department of Labor. Children's Bureau. *Proceedings of the Conference on State Child-Welfare Services.* Maternal and Child-Welfare Bulletin 3. Washington, D.C.: U.S. Government Printing Office, 1938.

U.S. Department of Labor. Children's Bureau. *Public Aid to Children in Their Own Homes: A Tabular Summary of State Laws in Effect November 1, 1922.* Washington, D.C.: U.S. Government Printing Office, 1923.

U.S. Department of Labor. Children's Bureau. *Public Aid to Children in Their Own Homes: A Tabular Summary of State Laws in Effect January 1, 1929.* Washington, D.C.: U.S. Government Printing Office, 1929.

U.S. Department of Labor. Children's Bureau. *Public Aid to Children in Their Own Homes: A Tabular Summary of State Laws in Effect January 1, 1934.* Washington, D.C.: U.S. Government Printing Office, 1934.

U.S. Social Security Board. *Characteristics of State Plans for Aid to Dependent Children.* Prepared by Bureau of Public Assistance. Publication 18. Washington, D.C.: U.S. Government Printing Office, 1937.

U.S. Social Security Board. *Third Annual Report.* Washington, D.C.: U.S. Government Printing Office, 1938.

White House Conference on Child Health and Protection. *Dependent and Neglected Children.* Report of the Committee on Socially Handicapped—Dependency and Neglect. New York: Appleton-Century, 1933.

State and Local Documents

Alabama. Child Welfare Department. *Four Years with the State Child Welfare Department, 1923–1927.* Montgomery: Child Welfare Department, 1927.

Alabama. Department of Public Welfare. *Annual Reports.* Wetumpha: Wetumpha Printing, 1935–39.

Arkansas. Department of Public Welfare. *A Bird's Eye View of the Arkansas Department of Public Welfare, 1935–1945.* Little Rock: Department of Public Welfare, 1945.

Arkansas. Department of Public Welfare. *Report of Activities.* Little Rock: Department of Public Welfare, 1936.

California. Department of Public Welfare. *Biennial Report, July 1924–June 1926, with additional Data from July 1922–June 1924.* Sacramento: State Department of Public Welfare, 1926.

California. Department of Social Welfare. *Biennial Reports.* Sacramento: State Printing Office, 1914–16, 1927–38.

Connecticut. *Law, Policies, and Rules of the Department of State Agencies and Institutions in Relation to State Aid to Widows with Dependent Children.* Hartford: State of Connecticut, 1933.

Connecticut. *Report of the Commission of Public Welfare.* Hartford: State of Connecticut, 1917, 1937.

Florida. Welfare Board. *Third Annual Report, July 1, 1939–June 30, 1940.*

Georgia. *Public Welfare: The Human Side of Government: Services Performed by the State Board of Public Welfare.* Atlanta, 1929.

Georgia. Department of Public Welfare. *Annual and Biennial Reports.* Atlanta: Index Printing, 1923–35.

Georgia. Department of Public Welfare. *Georgia's Fight against Dependency and Delinquency: Report to the Legislature of the Work of the Department of Public Welfare during Its First Year Ending March 1, 1921.* Atlanta: Dickerson-Roberts Printing, 1921.

Georgia. Department of Public Welfare. *Official Report*. Atlanta, 1937.

Hodson, William, comp. *A Compilation of the Laws of Minnesota Relating to Children*. St. Paul: Enterprise Printing, 1917.

Illinois. Department of Public Welfare. *Annual Report*. Springfield: Allied Printing, 1932–36.

Illinois. State Archives. Springfield. Roll no. 30-468, Perry County Mothers' Pension Fund, Mothers' Pension Fund Application, 1927–39.

Illinois State Archives. Springfield. Macon County–Miscellaneous, Mothers' Pension Record. Vol. 1, 1919–36, roll no. 30-1874. Vol. 2, 1937–42, roll no. 30-1875.

Louisiana. Department of Public Welfare. *Annual Report*. 1937.

Louisiana. Department of Public Welfare. *Eleventh and Twelfth Annual Reports*, July 1, 1947–June 30, 1949.

Maine. Department of Public Welfare. Ex-Officio State Board of Mothers' Aid. *Biennial Report, Covering the Biennial Period Ending June 30, 1928*.

Maine. Department of Public Welfare. Ex-Officio State Board of Mothers' Aid. *Biennial Report, Covering the Biennial Period Ending June 30, 1930*.

Maine. State Board of Charities and Corrections. Ex-Officio State Board of Mothers' Aid. *Biennial Reports, Covering the Biennial Period Ending June 30, 1918–June 30, 1926*. Waterville, Me.: Sentinel, 1918–26.

Maryland. Board of State Aid and Charities. *Biennial Reports*. 1934–38.

Massachusetts. Department of Public Welfare. *Annual Reports*. 1922–26, 1928–39.

Michigan. Board of Corrections and Charities. *Biennial Reports*. 1915–20.

Michigan. Welfare Commission. *Biennial Reports*. 1921–28.

Michigan. Welfare Department. *Report*. 1936, 1938.

Minnesota. *Proceedings of the First State Conference of Child Welfare Boards with the Board of Control, State Capitol, May 9–10, 1919*. St. Paul, 1919.

Minnesota. State Board of Control. *Biennial Reports*. Stillwater, Minn.: State Prison Printing Department, 1918–38.

Mississippi. *Laws of the State of Mississippi, Passed at a Regular Session of the Mississippi Legislature, January 3, 1928–April 26, 1929*. Jackson: Tucker Printing, 1928.

Mississippi. State Department of Public Welfare. *Biennial Reports*. Jackson, 1939–43.

New York. *Report of the New York State Commission on Relief for Widowed Mothers*. Albany: Lyon, 1914.

New York. Board of Social Welfare. *Annual Reports*. Albany: Lyon, 1922, 1928–40.

New York. Department of Social Welfare. *Annual Reports*. Albany: 1936–39.

North Carolina. Board of Charities and Public Welfare. *Biennial Reports*. 1926–31, 1935–40.

Ohio. *Proceedings of the Ohio State Conference on Dependent Children, in Conjunction with the State Conference of Charities and Correction, Youngstown, Ohio, November 14–16, 1916*.

Ohio. Department of Public Welfare. *Annual Reports*. 1934–37.

Oregon. Child Welfare Commission. *Child Welfare Laws of the State of Oregon*. Salem: State Printing Department, 1922.

Oregon. Child Welfare Commission. *Child Welfare Laws of the State of Oregon*. Salem: State Printing Department, 1926.

Pennsylvania. Commission Appointed to Study and Revise the Statutes of Pennsylvania Relating to Children. *Report to the General Assembly Meeting in 1925.* 2 parts. Harrisburg: State Printing Department, 1925.

Pennsylvania. Department of Public Instruction. *Report to the General Assembly of Pennsylvania of the Mothers' Assistance Fund, 1920.* State Printing Department, 1920.

Pennsylvania. Department of Public Instruction. *Report to the General Assembly of Pennsylvania of the Mothers' Assistance Fund, 1922.* Bulletin 6. State Printing Department, 1923.

Pennsylvania. Department of Welfare. *Biennial Report of the Secretary of Welfare.* Harrisburg: Bureau of Publications, 1924–31, 1935–38.

Pennsylvania. Department of Welfare. *Poor Relief Administration in Pennsylvania.* Bulletin 61. Harrisburg: Department of Welfare, 1934.

Perry County Mothers' Pension Fund Records. Mothers' Pension Fund Application, Microfiche 30-468, Illinois State Archives, Springfield.

Report of the Mothers' Pension League of Allegheny County, 1915–1916. Pittsburgh, 1916.

Rhode Island. *Report of the Rhode Island Children's Law Commission.* Providence: Freeman, 1926.

South Carolina. Department of Public Welfare. *Annual Reports.* 1938–40.

Tennessee. *Child Welfare in Tennessee: An Inquiry by the National Child Labor Committee for the Tennessee Child Welfare Commission.* Nashville: Tennessee Department of Public Instruction, 1920.

Tennessee. Department of Institutions and Public Welfare. *Annual Report for the Period Ending June 30, 1938.* Nashville.

Virginia. Department of Public Welfare. *Annual/Biennial Reports.* Richmond: Division of Purchase and Printing, 1935–40.

Virginia. Department of Public Welfare. *Mothers' Aid Requirements for Reimbursement by State.* Richmond: Division of Purchase and Printing, 1934.

Wisconsin. Board of Control. *The Administration of the Aid to Dependent Children's Law (Mothers' Pension Law) 1921.* Madison: Board of Control, 1922.

Wyoming. Department of Public Welfare. *Biennial Reports.* Cheyenne, 1936–38.

Wyoming. Department of Public Welfare. *Report, 1935–1936.*

Index